*Approaches to Guidance
in Contemporary
Education*

Approaches to Guidance in Contemporary Education

JOSEPH S. ZACCARIA

University of Illinois
Urbana, Illinois

INTERNATIONAL TEXTBOOK COMPANY

Scranton, Pennsylvania

The International Series in

GUIDANCE AND COUNSELING

Consulting Editor

R. WRAY STROWIG

University of Wisconsin

Standard Book Number 7002 2211 1

Preface

As the student in education, guidance, or psychology prepares for his future work in the educational endeavor, he proceeds through a sequence of collegiate and graduate study. Throughout this preparatory process, he studies various types of theories—e.g., theories of philosophy, theories of personality, theories of learning, and general theories of education. The focus upon conceptual approaches to the educative process is then complemented by the acquisition of technical skills appropriate to the particular educational area of specialization the student selects for his future vocation.

The field of education, however, has been the recipient of a great deal of valid criticism for the lack of articulation between theory and conceptual approaches studied in the academic setting and the subsequent application of this theory in terms of practice in the classroom setting, in the counseling interview, and in the administrative offices of the school. Although the primary focus of this book is upon the theory and practice of guidance, the book is relevant for the teacher who works with guidance personnel. It also speaks to various specialists in education, such as the school psychologist, the remedial reading specialist, the school social worker, and the speech therapist. For the school administrator who plans, directs, and controls the process of education, this book describes the alternative strategies of guidance and how they articulate with various approaches to education and the organization of the school system.

Since the major task of the school is to teach students, it follows that the classroom teacher performs the key function in education. The organizational, programmatic, and financial complexities, however, require an administrative function to carry out these noninstructional tasks. Instruction and administration, in turn, must be complemented by the personnel or guidance function whose goal it is to focus upon the total educational, vocational, and/or personal-social development of the student. Thus, the educational process is typically described in terms of these three processes—the instructional function, the administrative function, and the personnel (guidance) function.

Basic textbooks in guidance attempt to give the reader a global survey of guidance. The broad objectives of these books, coupled with limitations of space, necessitate their describing the process of guidance in rather generalized terms. Yet the critical issue facing every guidance worker and his colleagues is the question of what should be the specific nature and scope of the guidance process. One of the objectives of this book is to make the transition from generalized description to the presentation and analysis of assumptions, goals, and techniques associated with the various approaches to the guidance process.

Thus, the basic objective of Part I is to provide the beginning student in guidance and related fields with some of the major orientations to guidance and to demonstrate how each of these orientations can be translated into an operational program in the school setting. Relationships among teachers, administrators, guidance workers, and other specialists are stressed as a means for acquainting the student with alternative orientations to guidance and alternative types of relationships among various school personnel as each tries to help the student. The approaches to guidance are examined in terms of their historical origins and content.

Part II focuses upon broad topics which supersede the various orientations or approaches to guidance described in Part I. Supplementing and complementing Part I, Part II enables the reader to gain a broad perspective on the alternative roles and functions of guidance personnel through the consideration of basic topics such as legal and ethical aspects of guidance, current issues and trends, the impact of automation on the field of guidance, and the nature of the new elementary school guidance and counseling movement. Representative literature and research from various historical periods are provided for all major topics, thereby enabling the reader to understand the evolution of not only the guidance movement in general, but also specific areas within the total field. The extensive bibliographic notations allow the interested reader to delve more deeply into the relevant primary and secondary sources through individual study.

The major theme of the book is that the work of the guidance practitioner should be based at least in part upon a unified and well-articulated theoretical frame of reference. Included in the book, therefore, are descriptions of a number of major systems of thought. The reader is guided toward the exploration of the various strategies of guidance together with an examination of the advantages and limitations of each option. The major concepts underlying the thought and practice of guidance in contemporary education are viewed within the contexts of objectives and means for attaining objectives, balanced by the pervasive trends in the broader educational and sociocultural milieu of which contemporary guidance is a part.

JOSEPH S. ZACCARIA

Urbana, Illinois
February 1969

Acknowledgments

The author gratefully acknowledges the following publishers for their permission to include copyrighted material as noted below.

American Personnel and Guidance Association

A.P.G.A. *Add-A-Division* (1966), pp. 1–5.

A.P.G.A. "Code of Ethics," *Personnel and Guidance Journal*, 40 (1961), 206–9.

Grossman, A., and Howe, R. "Human Economy and Data Processing," *Personnel and Guidance Journal*, 43 (1964), 343–47.

Charles E. Merrill Books, Inc.

Peters, H. J., and Shertzer, B. *Guidance: Program Development and Management* (1963), p. 74.

Harcourt, Brace & World, Inc.

Ohlsen, M. M. *Guidance Services in the Modern School* (1964), pp. 322–23.

Harper & Row, Publishers

Gordon, Ira J. *The Teacher as a Guidance Worker* (1956), exerpts from pp. 3–5.

Mathewson, Robert Hendry. *Guidance Policy and Practice* (1965), pp. 17–18.
———. *Guidance Policy and Practice*, 3d ed. (1962), pp. 193 ("Five Functions of Guidance"). ("Related Operational Phases"), 206 (Diagram: "Model Organization Unit for Guidance at all School Levels"). Copyright © by Robert Hendry Mathewson.

Super, Donald Edwin. *The Psychology of Careers* (1957), p. 169.

Holt, Rinehart & Winston, Inc.

Bloom, B. S., Davis, A., and Hess, R. S. *Compensatory Education for Cultural Deprivation* (1965).

Saylor, J. G., and Alexander, W. M. *Curriculum Planning for Modern Schools*, rev. ed. (1966).

Houghton Mifflin Company

Byrne, R. H. *The School Counselor* (1963), p. 3.

Stewart, L. H. and Warnath, C. F. *The Counselor and Society* (1965), p. 342.

John Wiley & Sons, Inc.
  Vroom, V. H. *Work and Motivation* (1964), pp. 3, 6.

McGraw-Hill Book Company
  Horton, P. B., and Hunt, C. L. *Sociology* (1964), p. 4.
  McKown, H. C. *Home Room Guidance* (1946), pp. 131–46.
  Hoppock, R. *Occupational Information* (1957), pp. 74–75.

The Macmillan Company
  Smith, G. E. *Principles and Practices of the Guidance Program* (1951),
    pp. 5, 24–25.

Prentice-Hall, Inc.
  Hatch, Raymond N., and Stefflre, Buford. *Administration of Guidance
    Services* (1958), pp. 123–25.

Rand McNally & Co.
  Peters, H. J., and Farwell, G. F. *Guidance: A Developmental Approach*
    (1959), p. 276.
  Zeran, F. R., and Riccio, A. G. *Organization and Administration of
    Guidance Services* (1962), excerpts from pp. 2, 35.

Teachers College Press, Columbia University
  Barry, Ruth, and Wolf, Beverly. *Modern Issues in Guidance-Personnel Work*,
    pp. ix, 42–43. © 1957 by Teachers College, Columbia University.

Contents

PART I GUIDANCE WITHIN THE CONTEXT OF CONTEMPORARY EDUCATION . . . 1

1. Some Alternative Bases for Guidance Practice 3
2. The Educative Approach to Guidance 12
3. The Educational-Vocational Approach to Guidance 27
4. The Counseling Approach to Guidance. 41
5. The Problem-Centered/Adjustment Approach to Guidance 61
6. The Services Approach to Guidance 79
7. The Developmental Approach to Guidance 102
8. The Integrative Approach to Guidance. 115
9. An Overview of Contemporary Guidance Theory 131

PART II GUIDANCE WITHIN THE CONTEXT OF CONTEMPORARY SOCIETY . . . 147

10. Elementary School Guidance: Background and Overview. 149
11. Architectural and Financial Aspects of Guidance 171
12. Automation and the Field of Guidance 181
13. Legal Aspects of Guidance. 203
14. Professional and Ethical Aspects of Guidance 216
15. Issues and Problems in the Field of Guidance 230
16. Trends in the Field of Guidance 250
Appendix A A Selected Annotated Bibliography. 262
Appendix B The Evaluation of Guidance Services 265
Appendix C Ethical Standards. 267
Index 275

part I

Guidance Within the Context of Contemporary Education

The guidance movement has grown from a fledgling venture to the point where it is seeking admission to the family of traditionally recognized professions. Although guidance has undergone significant growth and development in its relatively short history of a little over half a century, it has also experienced some trying and difficult periods. Guidance has also received criticism—some valid and some from individuals with vested interests. In short, the field of guidance has emerged from its formative years as a formal endeavor and has become an integral aspect of the educative process.

Part I focuses largely upon seven major approaches to guidance. After an introductory chapter which discusses some stances in regard to alternative foundations or bases for the work of the guidance practitioner, each of the succeeding chapters describes a basic approach to guidance in some detail. While it is evident at the outset that there will be a certain amount of overlapping among the various approaches, each approach has certain unique and identifying underlying assumptions, goals, philosophical position, roles for the guidance worker, organization, etc. The various approaches to guidance are presented in an attempt to allow the reader to make a comparative analysis.

In the last chapter of Part I, the status of contemporary guidance theory is evaluated and a model representing a guidance strategy is presented. The major premise of Part I is that the guidance worker should derive his practice at least in part from theory which in turn should contain both means and ends for the guidance process. Philosophy and the behavioral sciences constitute the relevant source fields for developing both theory and practice.

It is hoped that the reader will evaluate each approach in terms of its relevance for his future work in the educational setting, thereby developing his own point of view and a broader understanding of the major currents that flow through the thought and practice of the field of guidance in contemporary education.

chapter 1

Some Alternative Bases for Guidance Practice

A pathologist after elaborate preparation places a slide under the microscope and adjusts the lens carefully. A Puari war party watch carefully as they place their canoe in the water, for unless it rocks, the raid will not be successful. A man steps from a new station wagon, cuts a forked twig, and carries it around holding it above the ground, while a well-drilling crew stands by, waiting to drill where the twig tells them water will be found. A woman in Peoria, anxious over her teen-age daughter, prays to God for guidance. A physician leafs through the pages of a parasitology textbook as he tries to identify the puzzling skin rash of his latest patient. A senator scans the latest public opinion poll as he wonders how to vote on the farm bill. Each of these persons is seeking guidance. (5, p. 4)

In each of the situations above, a problem is being experienced and a differ-ent approach is being attempted to solve that problem. Thus, each of the people above is proceeding on different premises about the sources of truth and the na-ture of cause-effect relationships. Each of them is seeking guidance from a dif-ferent source. The sources toward which they look for help, in turn, largely de-termine how these individuals face the problem, attack it, and subsequently be-have as a result of the resolution or lack of resolution of the problem.

The guidance worker must also choose. He must choose goals; he must choose a role; he must choose a *modus operandi* in the school setting. Like the people in the quotation above, he can turn to any one of a number of sources as a basis for his practice. The choice of a basis for his work may, indeed, be one of the most critical issues he faces. It will influence his effectiveness in achiev-ing the goals of the guidance program, his relationships with students and staff, and his role as an educator, a practitioner, and a person.

INTUITION OR TRIAL AND ERROR

Intuition has been defined as any flash of insight (true or mistaken) whose source the recipient cannot fully identify or explain. Galen, a Greek physician of the second century, for instance, prepared an elaborate chart of the human body, indicating where it could be pierced without fatal injury. The basis for identifying these nonfatal locations for wounds was intuition. Galen just *knew* which places were more critical than others, and while he and his associates had made some rudimentary studies of human anatomy, Galen relied upon intuition to reveal critical vs. noncritical zones.

Behavior based upon trial and error, on the other hand, utilizes one after another of a series of possible approaches or solutions until the problem at hand is resolved. Much of the incidental and accidental guidance that an individual receives from well-intentioned people—parents, relatives, peers, and friends— is based upon this approach.

Intuition and trial and error have almost never been advocated as adequate bases for guidance. Nor does it appear that intuition or trial and error can be acceptable as the primary basis for any effort to help individuals faced with critical life problems of development, choice, and adjustment. Surely some trial and error may occur, and guidance activities may be based upon intuition, but these bases are clearly inefficient and ineffective as foundations for guidance practice.

COMMON SENSE

It has been noted that when we do not know where our ideas come from or what they are based on, we sometimes call them common sense (5, p. 7). It is usually argued that there is no need for further proof of common-sense practices, for common sense has been tested by experience. But if the guidance worker employs what seems like good common-sense practice, he may be joining others in a collective deception of assuming that these common-sense ideas have *already* been proven.

Guidance practices based upon common sense rest upon an approach which has a respectable front but for which there is no systematic body of supporting evidence. While many common-sense ideas may be correct, these worthwhile common-sense ideas are likely to be mingled with a great number of other ideas that are useless in student guidance.

TRADITION

Practices that rest upon tradition have been said to represent the accumulated wisdom of the ages. Hence, tradition can be one of the most reassuring bases for the work of the guidance counselor. There is comfort and security in doing what has been done for a long period of time. Like common sense, traditional practices often seem to be correct. They must be correct, for they have been done so many times, by so many people, for such a long period of time.

It has been cogently stated, however, that tradition preserves both the accumulated wisdom and the accumulated bunkum of the ages (5, p. 6). For example, though tradition holds that men are intellectually superior to women, data show that neither sex is superior in inherited intellectual abilities. Similarly, tradition notes that the genius is typically delicate, impractical, unstable, and unsuccessful, though empirical studies indicate that the genius is above average in health, emotional adjustment, and income. Phrenology, bloodletting, witchcraft, and astrology are a few of a long list of "traditional" practices found to be inadequate. In like manner, tradition in mathematics, chemistry, physics, medicine, law, etc. has given way to more adequate bases for practices. Thus, the guidance practitioner who selects tradition as a basis for practice may be using many useless and harmful techniques along with some fortuitously beneficial ones.

AUTHORITY

An authority is an accepted source of information or advice, or an expert. The guidance worker can base his practice upon any one of a number of types of authority. Much of the practice of pastoral counseling, for example, is based upon faith in the sacred authority behind religious belief and experience. Prayer, some form of confession, and the Holy Scriptures each have a role in pastoral counseling. The Holy Scriptures are believed to be a product of divine revelation from an ultimate authority—i.e., God. Prayer, on the other hand, can be utilized by the counselor as preparation for counseling, as a vehicle for intercession during counseling, and as a means of closure at the end of the interview.

In pastoral counseling, faith is invested in divine authority as a guide for both counselor and counselee at points of crisis or decision. The entire role of the clergyman as a counselor rests upon his religious faith, his ordination as a clergyman, and the various facets of his "priestly" role, which include some form of confession, absolution, or catharsis. Underlying the entire process of pastoral counseling is an underlying faith in the sacred authority of a supreme being, the scriptures, and the counselor as a mediator between man and God.

Secular humanistic authority, on the other hand, stems not from divine revelation but from human perception. Secular humanistic authority rests upon the belief that certain great men have had remarkable insight into human behavior, the nature of the universe, or some other aspect of "truth." The psychoanalytic movement and psychoanalysis as a form of psychotherapy rests largely upon the perceptions and insights of Freud, who in turn considered himself not a humanitarian but a seeker of truth. Psychoanalytic techniques or practices rest in turn, upon Freud's insights into the organization of the psyche and the dynamics of libidinal energy utilization.

Secular scientific authority rests upon the findings of empirical investigations—broadly speaking, research. Secular empirical authority for guidance would rest upon the findings of scientific research in the source fields of guidance. It is their belief in secular scientific authority that led recent writers in guidance to state, for example (6, p. iv):

> Education for the new variety of guidance and student personnel worker clearly needs broader theoretical foundations than presently exist. Sociology, social psychology, anthropology, economics, political science all have their places in guidance training. Added to these should be the insights which can come only from philosophy and the humanities.

PHILOSOPHY

A number of writers have recently urged that guidance practice should be an outgrowth of an well-formulated and explicit philosophy. A treatise by Beck probably represents the best synoptic study of the philosophically oriented conceptual frameworks for guidance (3). Beck notes the paucity of organized thought in this area, citing the contributions of Cribbin (4), Wrenn (11), Lloyd-Jones (6), Williamson (10), Allport (1), Rogers (9), and Mathewson (8). Beck identifies elements of the following philosophies in contemporary guidance thought: realism, neorealism, theism, idealism, *Daseinanalyse,* determinism, existentialism, positivism, and instrumentalism.

The major concern has been that an inadequate definition of underlying philosophical assumptions may result in inadequate guidelines for guidance practice. Thus, the primary effort has been directed toward aligning the philosophy of guidance with a systematic school of philosophy, presenting the tenets of leading authorities in the field, and stripping away the semantic confusions. Other attempts have been made to establish more adequate linkages between philosophy and practice. Mathewson, for example, has developed a model or paradigm for deriving guidance practice from a philosophy (8):

> A PHILOSOPHY of guidance helps to determine
> POLICY which provides a basis for
> PLANNING which leads to the establishment of
> PROGRAM STRUCTURE or organizational framework for
> PROGRAM ACTIVITIES using various professional
> PROCEDURES requiring trained
> PERSONNEL and adequate
> FACILITIES all bearing upon the
> PROCESS
> OF
> GUIDANCE

The rationale for deriving guidance practice from a philosophy rests on the premise that it is imperative for guidance to have explicit goals and subsequently to keep these goals clearly in mind, utilizing practices consistent with the goals of the program. An adequate philosophical frame of reference would appear to include a formal philosophy of life, an informal philosophy of life, a philosophy of education, and a philosophy of guidance. As noted above, the primary function of a philosophy is to delineate and define goals.

A review of the literature in guidance reveals a wide range of alternative goals for the guidance worker (4). A distinction is necessary, however, between ultimate aims and proximate aims. The ultimate aims of guidance have been variously stated in such categories as the best development of the individual— e.g., "full and balanced," "optimum," "broad-gauged development of the individual physically, intellectually, socially, emotionally, and spiritually," etc. A second major point of emphasis focuses upon self-guidance and maturity. The third category of ultimate aims attempts to maximize students' satisfactions and their social productivity. A fourth category of ultimate aims focuses upon the generalized goal of assisting students to learn to live better lives.

Twelve categories of proximate objectives can be identified with a minimum of overlap among them (4):

1. To develop student initiative, responsibility, self-direction, and self-guidance.
2. To develop in the student the ability to choose his own goals wisely.
3. To know one's self, to know the school, and to be known by the school.
4. To anticipate and prevent crises from arising in the life of the student.
5. To help the student to adjust satisfactorily to school and life.
6. To help the student to recognize, understand, meet and solve his problems.
7. To assist the student in making wise choices, plans, and interpretations at critical points in his life.
8. To help the student acquire insights and techniques necessary to enable him to solve his own future problems.
9. To assist teachers to teach more effectively.
10. To help administrators to administer more efficiently by making a maximum contribution to the total school program.
11. To develop citizens who will participate in and contribute to the democratic way of life.
12. Miscellaneous objectives: assisting in the home, helping the community, building ethic character, fostering human relations and international understanding.

A very recent goal for the guidance worker is that he should be a catalytic agent for change. On the basis of a sociological view of the school as a system, the implication is that the guidance worker is an expert in the broad view of education and that he should be an agent for change in a system of interrelationships which are largely static.

The dilemma of the guidance practitioner is the fact that many, if not all, of the goals above are worthy ones for a program of guidance. He can not, on the other hand, attempt to focus on all of them. Implementation of a guidance program in order to achieve any of the goals presents other difficulties. The key to the realization of the desired goals of guidance is (*a*) clearly defining the goals, (*b*) planning and organizing the program in accordance with its goals, (*c*) allocating specific responsibilities for various procedures and related outcomes, (*d*) coordinating guidance activities, and (*e*) evaluating outcomes in relation to purposes.

THEORY

It has been noted that guidance has grown so quickly and has had so much of a thrust in its formative years that there has been no time for carefully developed unified theory (11). Early practitioners simply had to keep busy working at the job to which they had dedicated themselves. Present-day practitioners, on the other hand, do not have a background in broad theory, because contemporary counselor education programs are rooted in disciplines that are more technique-oriented than theory-oriented.

Although contemporary theoretical approaches to guidance are too fragmentary, too poorly articulated, and too deficient in depth and scope to warrant their being called theories in the strict sense of the term, they can be thought of as embryonic theories. Effort is now being directed toward developing thought in guidance and evolving more well-defined models of the guidance process. Contemporary theories, however, must be called "approaches" or orientations to guidance, rather than "theories of guidance" per se.

UNIFIED THEORY

Although the guidance worker can derive his practice from any one or a combination of the above-mentioned bases, the writer favors the derivation of practice from unified theory to as great a degree as possible. The basic functional dimensions of a conceptual basis for guidance include the objectives (ends) and the vehicles and techniques (means) for achieving these ends. It is on the basis of this rationale that Wrenn discussed the need for ends theories and means theories (11). Obviously, any comprehensive unified theory encompasses both ends and means.

The dichotomies of means-ends and philosophy–behavioral sciences, however, are not so distinct as they appear to be upon initial inspection. A given philosophy, for example, contains certain implicit or explicit views about human development and, conversely, a theory of human development includes elements of ends. The process of guidance can be derived from unified theory—i.e., from both a philosophical basis and from knowledge in the behavioral sciences. Philosophy provides the guidance theoretician and practitioner with objectives (ends) and certain implicit notions about the general means for achieving these ends. Knowledge from the behavioral sciences contributes ideas which in turn relate to means (practices). At the same time, ideas from the behavioral sciences suggest, implicitly at least, certain ends for human development. A major problem is that of amalgamating homologous ends and means, objectives and techniques, or goals and practices. The guidance process can be derived from both philosophy and knowledge in the behavioral sciences (see Figure 1-1).

Theory and theory-building in guidance should synthesize ends and means into a formulation which coherently and meaningfully relates itself to practice. Mathewson's basic model can be revised and augmented to demonstrate how the guidance process can be derived (in part at least) from unified theory. The model is self-explanatory except for the function of evaluation. Evaluation may be carried on utilizing what are deemed as suitable criteria and an appropriate

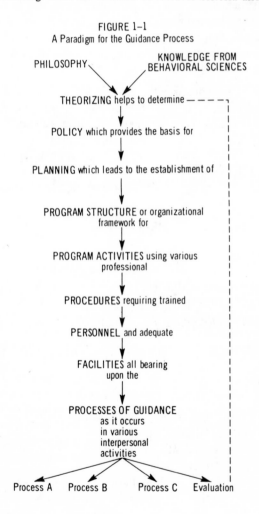

FIGURE 1–1
A Paradigm for the Guidance Process

method of evaluation. Although evaluation is made in terms of the goals and process of guidance, it is conceivable that, as a result of the evaluation, a change would be felt at any point in the total guidance endeavor such as in the theorizing process as indicated by the broken line in the model. Thus, guidance can become dynamic—meaningfully dynamic because of systematic innovations introduced on the basis of careful evaluation and research and implemented on the basis of comprehensive and unified theory.

Barry and Wolf have identified eight basic orientations to guidance (2):

1. The educational-vocational view
2. The services view
3. The counseling view
4. The adjustment view
5. The problem-centered view
6. The educative view
7. The developmental view
8. The integrative view

This classification emphasizes the primary focus of the alternative views of guidance. Although there is some overlapping of focus among these various views, each orientation has certain unique assumptions about the individual and accordingly emphasizes different dimensions of guidance thought and practice. Subsequent chapters will describe each of these approaches, summarizing the similarities and differences among them and considering various dimensions of theoretical and operational aspects of each orientation to guidance.

REFERENCES

1. G. W. Allport, *Becoming.* New Haven, Conn.: Yale University Press, 1955.

2. R. Barry, and B. Wolf, *Modern Issues in Guidance-Personnel Work.* New York: Teachers College Press, Columbia University, 1957.

3. C. E. Beck, *Philosophical Foundations of Guidance.* Englewood Cliffs, N.J.: Prentice-Hall, 1963.

4. J. Cribbin, "Critique of the Philosophy of Modern Guidance," *Catholic Educational Review,* 53 (1955), 73-91.

5. P. B. Horton, and C. L. Hunt, *Sociology.* New York: McGraw-Hill, 1964.

6. E. Lloyd-Jones, *Behavioral Science and Guidance.* New York: Teachers College Press, Columbia University, 1963.

7. E. Lloyd-Jones, and M. Smith, *Student Personnel Work As Deeper Teaching.* New York: Harper & Row, 1954.

8. R. H. Mathewson, "Philosophical and Psychological Foundations," *Guidance Policy and Practice,* rev. ed. New York: Harper & Row, 1955.

9. R. C. Rogers, "The Place of the Person in the New-World of the Behavioral Sciences," *Personnel and Guidance Journal,* 39 (1961), 442-51.

10. E. G. Williamson, "Value Orientations in Counseling," *Personnel and Guidance Journal,* 36 (1958), 302-99.

11. C. G. Wrenn, "Philosophical and Psychological Bases of Guidance and Personnel Work," *Personnel Services in Education, Yearbook of the N.S.S.E.,* Part II, 1959.

chapter **2**

The Educative Approach
to Guidance

In this strategy the process of guidance is presumably going on in all classrooms all of the time and is hence being practiced by all teachers even though these may possess different degrees of competence and professional understanding. It is the pervasive influence which counts, according to this strategy, and the process must be kept decentralized. When a serious behavior problem or emotional disturbance arises which cannot be handled by the classroom teacher, a specialist from some central bureau or department may be called in to make a "diagnosis" and recommend "treatment." Thus a diffuse process and structure of guidance for the many may be combined with a highly centralized one for the few. Teachers form the broad base of the structure.... (14, pp. 17-18)

The educative approach to guidance is not a single approach but a group of unique interrelated approaches. Stated in its simplest form, the essence of the educative approach is that the teacher is the guidance worker and the curriculum is the medium for guidance. Thus, the unique characteristic of this guidance orientation is the exclusive, or at least primary, reliance upon the classroom teacher. This approach, once very popular, is much less prevalent today. The educative approach to guidance has its roots in the work of Jesse Davis and William Wheatley in public education at the secondary level and in the faculty-adviser programs in colleges and universities.

The educative approach is a generalist orientation to guidance in that it places the least emphasis of all orientations to guidance upon the role of professional guidance specialists. Gordon, for example, notes that the following five points define guidance (7, pp. 3-5):

1. Guidance is the organization of information by the school about the child and his community for the purpose of helping the child learn to make wise decisions concerning his own future.
2. Guidance is the organization of life experiences within the school situation so that the child is provided with situations in which he feels completely accepted, in which he is enabled to "take stock" of his potentialities, accept his limitations without threat, and develop a realistic picture of himself and the world around him.
3. Guidance is the provision for satisfactory group experiences in which successful

12

leadership and membership roles are learned and in which the group is able to set goals and solve problems dealing with interpersonal relations.

4. Guidance is the provision of opportunities for the child to understand and value his uniqueness and his relatedness to others.
5. Guidance is the provision of the above experiences and opportunities for all children.

The educative orientation to guidance is made up of four subapproaches: (*a*) the classroom teacher as the guidance worker approach, (*b*) the homeroom teacher as the guidance worker approach, (*c*) the supplementary guidance specialist approach, and (*d*) the teacher-counselor approach. Each of these substrategies of guidance represents a variation on the major theme of the educative approach—i.e., that there should be a natural fusion of teaching and guidance. The idea that the teacher should be concerned with the whole child constitutes one of the most cherished themes throughout the history of education. Guidance as a unique service offered by professionally prepared specialists is rejected on the basis that the entire educational endeavor represents a guidance activity.

In the area of secondary education, Gordon states (7, p. 7): "Most guidance work must be done in the classroom, by teachers who possess the guidance viewpoint and incorporate it in their teaching." The same position in higher education is espoused by Boykin as he first states (4, p. 276): "The principal area of student personnel work is teacher-student relationships, not occasional interviews with specialized counselors," and later asserts (4, p. 278), "Good teaching has emotional and moral, as well as intellectual objectives."

The guidance functions of the teacher fall into three general categories. First, the teacher with a guidance point of view creates a unique classroom environment. This environment enhances both his didactic teaching and his guidance function. Secondly, the teacher adapts the curriculum to meet the needs of the students and to foster the guidance goals of the curriculum. Lastly, the teacher functions in the role of guidance worker as a normal part of teaching his students.

There are four fundamental strategies for implementing the educative approach, arranged (from the point of view of professional guidance) along a continuum. The poles of this continuum are listed as "highly generalized guidance role" to "somewhat specialized guidance role." (See Figure 2-1.)

FIGURE 2-1
A Continuum of Substrategies Within the Educative Approach

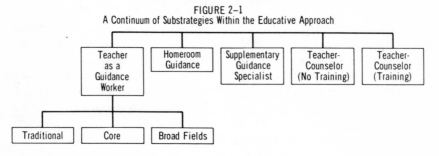

THE CLASSROOM TEACHER AS THE GUIDANCE WORKER

The teacher as the guidance worker is the most fundamental strategy and the one most widely used when guidance is implemented through the educative approach. Since the curriculum is the major vehicle for guidance, the guidance process varies as a function of the structure and focus of the curriculum. Following the general approach described above, the guidance process is implemented somewhat differently as it occurs in the various curricular patterns.

The School Subjects (Traditional) Curriculum

This approach is the familiar one of conveniently and logically organizing the material according to the traditional school subjects based upon the Carnegie unit. A teacher specializes in a subject matter area such as mathematics, science, languages, social studies, business, etc., and typically teaches several subjects within a major area. The process of guidance is implemented by the teacher, the distinguishing characteristic being the implementation of guidance by a large number of teachers. Consequently, any one student receives guidance from as many as six to ten teachers.

The Broad Fields Curriculum

The broad fields curriculum seeks to overcome the weaknesses of the traditional subject matter approach by integrating or fusing traditional subject matter areas into broad fields of academic study. The broad fields approach, like the traditional subject matter approach, focuses upon subjects but brings together into one instructional course a number of related disciplines. Three broad fields areas in secondary education are summarized below:

1. *Social studies*: political science, sociology, history, geography, cultural anthropology, etc.
2. *Biology*: zoology, anatomy, botany, physiology, ecology, bacteriology, etc.
3. *Physical science*: chemistry, geology, astronomy, physics, etc.

The major advantage of the broad fields curriculum over the traditional subject matter curriculum is that the integration of concepts, principles, facts, and other kinds of knowledge from related disciplines provides the teacher with a broader and more adequate point of departure for both teaching and guidance activities. Consideration of broad concepts, such as the nature of man, his culture, his development, his basic problems, etc., constitutes a natural way of beginning to fuse teaching and guidance.

The Core Curriculum

The core curriculum has been described as follows (27, p. 10):

> The secondary school is responsible to help all young people define the major problems of our society and arrive at generalizations and conclusions which will make it possible for the democratic way of living to thrive. To this end, a program of general education, consisting of common learnings required of all students, is an integral part of the secondary program. These common learnings and experiences are cared for in the core class.

The New York City Schools use the term in a somewhat similar manner (3, pp. 4-5):

> First, it means a class which meets two or more periods per day with a teacher who also acts as a guidance counselor for the group. Secondly, it means a class which deals with the problems that are selected by teachers and pupils cooperatively and that cut across traditional subject-manner lines.

The Philadelphia Public Schools use the term similarly, defining "core curriculum" as follows (17, p. 3):

> A total school program within which time is provided for pupils to spend more than one period per day with one teacher. This may be one, two, or three periods plus homeroom time.

Saylor and Alexander describe several approaches to the core curriculum, outlining typical patterns and summarizing the major characteristics of this strategy (22, pp. 310-13). Through the use of the core curriculum, the fragmentation of the students' educational experience is minimized and the guidance function can be carried out by one teacher who spends several periods each day with a block of students. In addition to this, the great flexibility of utilizing school time allows ample time for a wide range of guidance activities that are difficult to carry out by means of traditional schedules and relationships of regular classroom teachers with their students.

THE HOMEROOM TEACHER AS THE GUIDANCE WORKER

Since the homeroom combines a continuing group of students with a teacher who has daily contact with these students, it has been viewed as a natural environment for guidance. The concept of the homeroom as a vehicle for guidance represents an expansion of the earlier purposes of the homeroom. The homeroom was introduced into secondary education during the last quarter of the nineteenth century and was often called a "report room"; handling such matters as attendance and announcements was its most important function. Later, the function of the homeroom was expanded to include administrative and clerical duties, disciplinary duties, and educational counseling. In recent decades the homeroom has been viewed as a place for more and more guidance activities, and it is within this context that homeroom guidance evolved.

Among the many statements of the goals of homeroom guidance is that of McKown (13, Chap. 2):

1. To develop and maintain desirable student-teacher relationships.
2. To provide guidance activities for students.
3. To develop desirable ideals and habits of good citizenship.
4. To expedite the handling of administrative routine educatively.

Ohlsen notes that successful homeroom guidance programs have met most of the following conditions (16, pp. 322-23): (*a*) The school principal had some clear-cut expectations for the homerooms which are consistent with good guidance practices, and he was able to select teachers for this responsibility who were interested in developing good homeroom programs. (*b*) Where the number of qualified teachers who exhibited interest in the homeroom program was insufficient to staff homerooms for the grades in the building, the principal provided a homeroom experience for only the first grade in the building—e.g., the seventh grade in a junior high school. (*c*) Teachers who were selected as homeroom teachers were assigned a proportionately lighter teaching and/or extracurricular activity load. (*d*) In-service education was provided by the guidance personnel, especially when the program was begun. (*e*) Students were asked to state first and second choices for homeroom teachers, and these choices were carefully considered in making assignments. (*f*) A student was always assigned at least one course with his homeroom teacher. At the junior high school level, the schedule was usually arranged so that students spent three consecutive periods—two regular classes and a homeroom period—with the homeroom teacher. Where this was not possible every day, at least once a week a full class period was set aside for a homeroom program. (*g*) Some of the best homeroom teachers were permitted to have two homerooms, one in the forenoon and another in the afternoon. (*h*) Students helped select the discussion topics and conducted the discussions. (*i*) The members of the homeroom brought problems to the attention of their student council representative.

The principles of implementing an adequate program of homeroom guidance have been summarized by McKown as follows (13, pp. 131-46):

1. Each program should have a clear, desirable, and reasonable objective.
2. The material of the program should be appropriate and timely.
3. The program should have both educational and inspirational merit.
4. The homeroom program should emphasize the here and now.
5. In cycle programs previous work should be briefly reviewed.
6. Programs should, in general, represent member and not sponsor activity.
7. Probably all members should participate, formally or informally, in the programs.

8. The homeroom program should not duplicate work that is being, or should be, done elsewhere about the school.
9. The program should reflect all of the various activities of the school.
10. The program should include material from members, sponsor, teachers, and administrators.
11. The program should represent pleasing variety in both materials and methods of presentation.
12. The program should fit the time allotted to it.
13. Parliamentary and business matters should be handled efficiently.
14. Matters of school routine should be reduced to a minimum.
15. There should be little sermonizing by sponsor, officers, or members.
16. A family spirit, free and informal, should prevail.
17. Standards for homeroom programs should be developed and approximated.
18. Appropriate recognition should be given for meritorious work.
19. Suitable programs should be exchanged between rooms and presented in the assembly.
20. Reserve program material should be developed and kept available.
21. The room's program committee should have the responsibility for developing the programs.
22. The program committee should keep a complete file of all program material.

THE SUPPLEMENTARY GUIDANCE-SPECIALIST APPROACH

This strategy is organized around the premise that there should be professional guidance specialists in the school but that they should play a relatively minor role in the total guidance program of the school (23). It is maintained that even if there are professional guidance specialists, most of the guidance program must be implemented by the classroom teachers. Professional guidance personnel are therefore relegated to a position of auxiliary, secondary, or supplemental guidance roles.

THE TEACHER-COUNSELOR APPROACH

The teacher-counselor is a faculty member who functions part-time as a regular classroom teacher and the remainder of his time as a guidance worker. Although the general rationale for the teacher-counselor strategy is similar to that of the teacher as a guidance worker, the teacher-counselor approach emphasizes several important new dimensions to the individual's role and function. First, the teacher-counselor approach stresses a duality of role—i.e., teacher *and* counselor rather than a fusion of teaching and guidance. The faculty member usually is given a lighter than normal teaching load and functions as a regular guidance specialist in his role as a guidance worker. Secondly, there is often an emphasis upon some professional training in guidance. This position holds that the dual roles of teacher and guidance worker reinforce each other.

Although the teacher-counselor approach typically stresses that the faculty member functions as a teacher and a guidance worker in the complete sense of the term, Ramstadt suggests that the teacher-counselor should play a more limited role (20). He feels that because of the usual limitations of professional background in guidance, the teacher-counselor should be responsible for certain guidance functions—e.g., orientation, maintenance of cumulative records, registration, parent converences, etc.—but that the teacher-counselor should not counsel. Counseling is to be performed by a full-time guidance specialist called the head counselor.

Thus, the continuum of thought within the educative approach to guidance is now complete. Described above have been the variations on the major theme that guidance should be closely related to the curriculum of the school and to the process of teaching. Emphases and strategies have varied, but the common factor that typifies this approach is the dependence upon the classroom teacher as the sole or primary guidance functionary.

THE THEORETICAL BASIS

The unity of the child and his experience constitutes a theme underlying the educative approach to guidance. From this basic axiom stem the various substrategies for attempting to unify the total experience of the child. The teacher is utilized as the unifying functionary because he is the only person in the school with psychological training who comes in daily contact with all students. The underlying educational theoretical basis for this approach is the theory of general education.

The total education of the child consists of two overall emphases. Specialized education focuses upon idiographic dimensions of development emphasizing individual potentialities, capacities, and abilities that characterize the student as a unique individual. The term "common learnings" includes the kinds of learnings that all individuals must have, regardless of occupation or place of residence.

The various substrategies of the educative approach to guidance described above represent some of the curricular adaptations for providing a more functional and a more meaningful experience for the student. Through the fusion of guidance activities with the regular learning experiences, the educative approach attempts to utilize the curriculum as the medium through which guidance occurs. Guidance is for all students. Guidance is an aspect of general education. The best way of implementing this phase of general education, therefore, is to use the classroom teacher and an adapted curriculum (6).

Developmental psychology, human relations, learning theory, group dynamics theory, and the psychology of individual differences supplement the pervasive theory of general education as the theoretical foundation for the educative approach. The classroom teacher utilizes the principles of each of these areas as part of the enlarged view of what constitutes complete teaching and the scope and depth of the teacher's functioning. For example, Gordon deals extensively with human development concepts and their use for the teacher as a guidance worker (7, Pt. 2). Therein he summarizes the following principles of growth:

1. The body does not grow as a whole and in all directions at once.
2. Structure and experience mutually affect each other.
3. There is a general pattern of growth for the organism.
4. There are characteristic sex differences in rate of growth.
5. The individual's way of going through the growth pattern is unique.

Gordon then discusses the classroom and guidance implications of these principles (7, pp. 47-50) and aspects of the developmental psychology of youth in terms of (*a*) health and physical defects, (*b*) understanding community forces, (*c*) the contribution of peers to self-development, and (*d*) the child's self. Each of his descriptions is followed by implications, a discussion of related practices and/or "how to do it" sections for the classroom teacher.

In general, the theory of the educative approach views guidance as a part of good teaching. This point of view is expressed by Macomber when he states (12, p. 282): "Guidance . . . now synonymous with the teaching process itself . . . is a part of the whole educative process and difficult to separate from the whole except for purposes of discussion."

PHILOSOPHY AND GOALS

When education and guidance are considered to be synonymous, guidance permeates the entire curriculum. In the one substrategy which holds that the guidance specialist is necessary but the teacher still is the major guidance worker, the general philosophy of the educative approach must undergo some strain. In effect, this latter stance believes that while most guidance activities lie within a philosophically and pedagogically expanded conception of teaching, there are some functions which can best be performed by the guidance specialist.

The teacher-counselor substrategy results in a similar dilemma. The duality of the teacher's role stresses his functioning as a guidance specialist for a portion of the students he teaches. The fusion of teaching and guidance in this substrategy seems, indeed, dubious.

The goals of the educative approach to guidance stem from education rather than from guidance per se. Because of the relative emphasis upon the fusion of guidance with education, goal statements for guidance cannot be considered apart from the general goals of education. The sources for the goals of education are the society, the students (interests, needs, etc.), or a combination of the two. Various formulations of goals of general education have come from educational philosophers such as Rousseau, Herbart, Spencer, Pestalozzi, and Dewey, but goal statements from educational committees and from professional groups have been more directly influential upon education and the educative approach to guidance.

The Commission on the Reorganization of Secondary Education proposed the following Seven Cardinal Principles as the basic objectives of secondary education (5, pp. 10-11):

1. Health
2. Command of fundamental processes
3. Worthy home membership
4. Vocation
5. Citizenship
6. Worthy use of leisure time
7. Ethical character

The fusion of teaching and guidance is quite evident from this statement. Guidance becomes indistinguishable from the whole process of education, and the goals of guidance articulate or fuse with the other aspects of the educative process.

UNDERLYING ASSUMPTIONS

Supported by a cluster of correlative assumptions, one major assumption underlies the educative approach to guidance—i.e., that guidance is a classroom function. Because of this suppositon virtually all of the theory and practice of the educative approach runs contrary to the mainstream of guidance thought, which is based on the premise that guidance practices in the main should be performed by trained guidance personnel working in conjunction with classroom teachers. This fundamental tenet is unique to the educative approach and distinguishes it from every other approach to guidance.

The assumptions related to the major assumption of the educative approach are:

1. Since the teacher sees the student each day, he is in the best position for understanding and helping the student.
2. The teacher should be the guidance worker.
3. The entire curriculum can provide a vehicle for guidance activities.
4. Relatively informal advice about educational and occupational plans and about problems of adjustment to school should suffice as an overall framework for guidance.

5. Supplying information should be the major guidance function.
6. The curriculum can and should acknowledge individual differences.
7. All pupils should benefit from guidance.

Barry and Wolf note that the educative orientation to guidance represents an attempt to provide guidance for all students and to supplement the remedial emphasis of some of the other approaches (2, p. 49). They also note that functionally the educative view is often combined with another view—i.e., the problem-centered or counseling approach.

SOME OPERATIONAL ASPECTS

There are two basic patterns for organizing guidance in the educative approach to guidance. (See Figures 2-2 and 2-3.) The multiple executive

FIGURE 2–2
The Multiple Executive Organizational Pattern

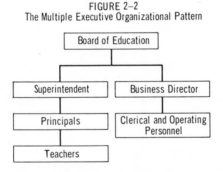

FIGURE 2–3
The Unit Executive Organizational Pattern

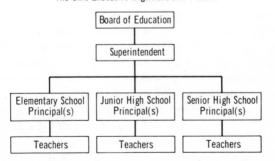

organization has appeal where there are no guidance specialists and where the board of education favors the relegation of instruction to a position of equal importance with the business aspects of operating the school system. Thus, there are two major school executives—the superintendent and a director in charge of clerical and operating personnel. Each of these administrators defines the policies for the operation of his area of concern. The multiple executive organization has significantly decreased in popularity in recent years.

The most prevalent pattern of formal organization for the educative approach to guidance is the unit executive organization shown in Figure 2-3. The superintendent of schools is selected by the board of education and is responsible for the operation of all aspects of the educational system. There is a line relationship from superintendent to principals to teachers. A variation of this pattern is shown in Figure 2-4, in which there are both teachers and teacher-counselors.

FIGURE 2-4
A Formal Organization for a Teacher-Counselor Approach to Guidance

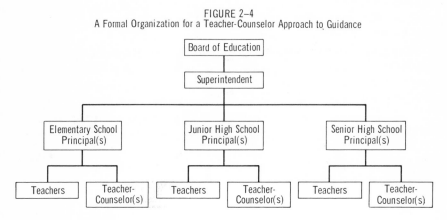

Providing a Guidance Climate

The centrality of a proper classroom climate is emphasized by Watson, who notes (26, p. 254): "The first task of the teacher is to provide a general classroom atmosphere of cooperation, friendliness, and joy of living." This general classroom climate sets the whole tone for the teacher's expanded functioning and provides a point of departure for his interaction with students. Strang describes some dimensions of this good mental hygiene climate in the classroom (24).

The general atmosphere of the school is often one in which academic performance is emphasized and the process by which general mental health is developed becomes de-emphasized. The emphasis upon accomplishment results in a correlative focus upon subject matter marks, promotion, a finished product, or a flawless assembly program. Strang feels that, although a good product is to be desired, the school should not neglect the process by which personality is developed. She underlines the importance of acceptance, noting that when a group accepts an individual and expects the best of him, his conduct and achievement improve.

Adapting the Curriculum for Guidance

When guidance becomes an integral aspect of teaching, the teaching itself can be adapted to include a guidance point of view along with the consideration of the regular subject matter. For example, units about occupations related to a given academic course can be utilized as vehicles for vocational guidance. A variety of techniques can be used, including lectures by the teacher, lecture-discussions, speakers, student reports, discussions, visitations to industries, etc.

Likewise, units about personal problems can be incorporated in many regular academic courses, such as senior problems, hygiene courses, health courses, problems of democratic living, and home economics. In biology and health courses, such topics as smoking, the effects of alcohol on the body, and physiological aspects of sex represent some natural topics for guidance-oriented emphasis via a variety of techniques. English compositions could be written on such topics as "Ways of Handling the Problems of Adolescence," "What I Hope To Be Like Ten Years from Now," "My Future Vocation," etc.

Strang suggests that report cards can reflect a guidance point of view by representing, in addition to the achievement of subject matter, other aspects of growth, such as estimates of personality, cooperativeness, purpose, influence, social sensitivity, emotional maturity, and persistence. Similarly, discipline can be based upon (*a*) an understanding of the student, (*b*) an understanding of the conditions which give rise to socially disapproved behavior, (*c*) mutual respect and affection on the part of student and teacher, and (*d*) counseling which emphasizes student insight rather than an administrative approach to discipline. The system of reporting marks should have the following characteristics (adapted from 24, p. 60):

1. Marks should be accurate.
2. Marks should measure the main objectives set up by the school.
3. Marks should show the student where he can improve.
4. Marks should interpret the student's achievement in relation to his own ability to achieve, as well as in relation to standards for college entrance or the requirements for different vocational fields.
5. Marks should show progress and give the student a sense of growth.
6. Marks should minimize competition.
7. Marks should include the student's appraisal of himself.

There has been a traditional dichotomy in education between the curriculum (subjects) and the extracurriculum (student activities). The educative approach stresses that this traditional distinction is unacceptable because of the fallacious implication with respect to the relative place and worth of subjects and student activities. Student activities are considered as extraclass activities, cocurricular activities, or simply curricular activities. The curriculum then includes all of the learning experiences. Some typical objectives of student activities include developing the following: a sense of worth and of being of service, a feeling of belonging, increased self-confidence, which arises out of successful activity, willingness to share responsibility for group enterprises, special interests and abilities, social skills, and standards for the use of leisure time (24, pp. 209–10).

If the leader has clearly in mind the possible values of the group activities which he sponsors, he will be more likely to realize them. From experiences in his group the members may gain many personal values: a sense of worth and of being of service, a feeling of "belonging," increased self-confidence that arises out of successful activity, willingness to share responsibility for group enterprises, improved scholarship (if participation in extraclass activities is not excessive), development of special interests and abilities, social skills, and standards for the use of leisure time. In addition to these personal values, the group activity may make a contribution to school and community life.

Functioning as a Guidance Worker

As noted above, the expanded role of the teacher in the educative approach also includes his functioning in a guidance capacity. The emphasis, however, is in general not upon a dual role but rather a fusion of teaching and guidance within the frame of reference of expanded teaching. In this role, the teacher performs as a guidance specialist except that the guidance activities take place within the context of an expanded teaching relationship (11). The pervasive theme of the educative approach is that the teacher can adequately function as a guidance worker with little, if any, specialized training beyond that training which constitutes an adequate preparation for teaching. In a series of journal articles (1, 10, 18, 19, 25, 26), handbooks (8, 9), and formal textbooks (7, 13, 24) is suggested virtually the entire range of guidance and guidance-related activities as the possible domain of a "complete" teacher.

SUMMARY AND CONCLUSION

Until the advent of the formal guidance movement, the educative approach was the only approach to guidance. Although the concept of the "complete" teacher has continued to be a popular one, the educative approach has been less enthusiastically supported in recent years. Virtually all theorists and practitioners would assert that the classroom teacher should provide the class with a good mental health climate, adapt the curriculum to meet both the intellectual and other needs of students, and provide them with guidance. But much of contemporary thought recognizes levels of competency for providing guidance help for students. The complexities of growing up in modern society, most people feel, require that professionally trained guidance personnel play a much more central role than typically envisioned by the educative approach.

For some school systems with limited financial resources, the educative approach to guidance may represent the only feasible orientation. At a theoretical level the educative approach stresses a unified educational experience for the pupil. The educative orientation is characterized by a holistic approach to teaching, too. Operationally, however, the educative approach typically results in incidental and accidental guidance. Certainly this point of view in regard to the guidance process is not an adequate one to meet the needs of youth in today's world.

Although it is noble to envision the classroom teacher's having a guidance point of view and providing pupils with adequate kinds of helping relationships, the educative approach simply does not meet the needs of youth. Although the educative approach stresses a diffuse teacher-based guidance, most other strategies of guidance emphasize the utilization of guidance specialists and more balanced team approaches.

REFERENCES

1. D. S. Arbuckle, "The Teacher as a Counselor," *High School Journal*, 40 (1957), 285-86.

2. R. Barry and B. Wolf, *Modern Issues in Guidance-Personnel Work*. New York: Teachers College Press, Columbia University, 1957.

3. Board of Education of the City of New York, *Suggestions to Teachers of Experimental Core Classes*. Curriculum Bulletin, 1950-1951 Series, No. 2. New York: The Board, 1951.

4. L. L. Boykin, "The Role of the Teacher in the Student Personnel Program," *Association of American Colleges Bulletin*, 34 (1962), 276-78.

5. Commission on the Reorganization of Secondary Education, *Cardinal Principles of Secondary Education*. Bureau of Education, Bulletin 1918, No. 35. Washington, D.C.: U.S. Government Printing Office, 1918.

6. Educational Policies Commission, *The Purposes of Education in a Democracy*. Washington, D.C.: National Education Association, 1938.

7. I. J. Gordon, *The Teacher as a Guidance Worker*. New York: Harper & Row, 1956.

8. S. A. Hamrin, *Chats with Teachers about Counseling*. Bloomington, Ill.: McKnight & McKnight, 1950.

9. S. A. Hamrin, *Guidance Talks to Teachers*. Bloomington, Ill.: McKnight & McKnight, 1947.

10. E. A. Koile, "Faculty Counseling in Colleges and Universities," *Teachers College Record*, 55 (1954), 384-89.

11. J. W. Loughary, "Some Considerations Regarding Full-time Counselor Versus Teacher-Counselor Assignment," *Educational Administration and Supervision*, 45 (1959), 199-205.

12. F. Macomber, *Guiding Child Development in the Elementary School*. New York: American Book Co., 1941.

13. H. C. McKown, *Home Room Guidance*. New York: McGraw-Hill, 1946.

14. R. H. Mathewson, *Guidance Policy and Practice*, 2d ed. New York: Harper & Row, 1955.

15. A. G. Nelson, "The College Teacher as a Counselor," *Educational Forum*, 19 (1955), 169-77.

16. M. Ohlsen, *Guidance Services in the Modern School*. New York: Harcourt, Brace & World, 1964.

17. Philadelphia Public Schools, *Core Curriculum in Philadelphia.* Mimeographed. Philadelphia: The Schools, 1949.

18. H. C. Pry, "The Home-room Teacher's Responsibility for Curricular Guidance," *National Association of Secondary School Principals Bulletin,* 43 (1959), 19-25.

19. M. V. Pullen, "Classroom Guidance," *Instructor,* 74 (1964), 38-39.

20. R. W. Ramstadt, "The Teacher as a Guidance Worker," *Journal of Education,* 139 (1957), 1-12.

21. J. Resnick, "The Teacher-Counselor's Role," *Education,* 80 (1959), 206-9.

22. J. G. Saylor, and Alexander, W. M. *Curriculum Planning for Better Teaching and Learning.* New York: Rinehart and Co., 1956.

23. J. A. Smith, "A Continuous Program of Classroom Guidance," *High School Journal,* 40 (1957), 296-304.

24. R. Strang, *The Role of the Teacher in Personnel Work.* New York: Teachers College Press, Columbia University, 1953.

25. H. Stroup, "The College Teacher as a Counselor," *School and Society,* 85 (1957), 120-22.

26. G. Watson, "The Role of the Teacher," in P. Witty and C. S. Skinner, eds., *Mental Hygiene in Modern Education.* New York: Farrar and Rinehart, 1939

27. E. A. Wicas, "The Teacher as a Counselor," *Journal of Education,* 139 (1957), 1-12.

chapter 3

The Educational-Vocational Approach to Guidance

The relationship between man and his work has long attracted the attention of philosophers, scientists, and novelists. The interest of psychologists in this problem dates back to the early part of the twentieth century and is reflected in the emergence and development of such fields of specialization as industrial psychology and vocational guidance. . . . "Work" is a particularly ambiguous term. It is used in physics to refer to the transference of energy by a process involving the motion of an object as a result of the application of a force; in experimental psychology and in physiology to refer to muscle activity; and in everyday language to refer to things as different as artistic productions and unpleasant tasks. (39, pp. 3–6)

The educational-vocational orientation to guidance dates back to the inception of the formal guidance movement. Better known simply as "vocational guidance," the educational-vocational approach has continued to flourish as a result of theoretical advances and innovations in techniques. Brewer suggests that four conditions led to the rise of the vocational guidance movement (3): (*a*) the increasing division of labor, (*b*) the growth of science, (*c*) the extension of vocational education, and (*d*) the growth of technology. As with any historical phenomenon, however, there were also many background influences and tangential forces operating. Numerous histories of this movement are readily available (23, 25, 27). Although the National Vocational Guidance Association has continued to be the primary professional moving force behind the educational-vocational approach, a long line of outstanding names and books have also provided a continuing impetus behind the movement (10, 18, 19, 21, 24, 29, 31, 32).

The basic tenets of the educational-vocational approach parallel many of the most cherished and enduring beliefs in our American culture. For example, the American heritage envisions the good and righteous man as one who labors diligently and prospers as a result of his labor. The pragmatic mode of thought in education also reinforces an emphasis upon those aspects of education that help the individual in terms of basic skills to be used in the world of work and in everyday life. Thus, the educational system is seen from a utilitarian point of view which stresses preparing the student for his future role as a functional citizen and a productive worker. Within this general rationale, guidance becomes largely vocational guidance. Educational guidance also becomes important because of the integral relationship between vocational decisions and the need to implement these decisions through educational choices.

Educational-vocational guidance represents a unique focus—a special frame of reference in which educational guidance and vocational guidance are fused into a synthetic formulation with one main emphasis: helping the student to choose an occupation and to make appropriate educational decisions in line with this choice. Brewer has pointed out the educational dimension of the educational-vocational approach to guidance (4, p. 14):

> Educational guidance may be defined as a conscious effort to assist in the intellectual growth of an individual. . . . Anything that has to do with instruction or with learning may come under the term educational guidance.

In a later book Brewer defines the content of this aspect of guidance as follows (2, p. 114):

> How to study; using the common tools of learning; adjusting school life to other activities; regularly attending school; learning to speak, interview, compose in writing, take examinations, and use libraries; and making the important educational decisions at each of the many forks in the road.

Two traditional definitions of the vocational guidance aspects of the educational-vocational approach to guidance are presented below:

> Vocational guidance is the giving of information, experience and advice in regard to choosing an occupation, preparing for it, entering it, and progressing in it. (3, p. 24)

> Vocational guidance is the process of assisting the individual to choose an occupation, prepare for it, enter upon and progress in it. It is concerned primarily with helping individuals make decisions and choices involved in planning a future and building a career—decisions and choices necessary in effecting satisfactory vocational adjustment. (9, p. 774)

The major difference between these definitions is not immediately evident. While the first definition emphasizes doing something *to* the individual, the second definition places its emphasis upon helping the individual to do something for himself. The kind of thinking reflected in the latter definition has become increasingly popular in vocational guidance.

THEORETICAL BASIS

Two streams of thought provide the theoretical basis for the educational-vocational approach to guidance. First, there is a body of basic theory from developmental psychology, vocational psychology, and psychometry. This basic theory is concerned with the nature and measurement of vocational choice and development. Some rather significant advances in this field have provided guidance with fundamental conceptual schemes from which the practice of vocational guidance can be derived. The second body of theory, not nearly so well developed as the basic theory, consists of principles of vocational guidance. These principles are intended primarily to provide guidelines for translating basic theory into practice. To date, vocational guidance has not been systematically derived from either of these bodies of theory. Rather, much of vocational guidance has evolved from the unique problems of the school system and from the informal application of what superficially seems to be good practice.

Trait and Factor Theory

Parsons' book *Choosing A Vocation* (28), coupled with trait and factor theory in psychology, constitutes one of the two major strands of basic theory underlying vocational guidance. Essentially, trait and factor theory holds that an individual is "keyed" to one or, at most, a few "correct" occupations. Although the individual tends to gravitate toward one of these "correct" occupations, this natural process is inefficient. The individual typically makes some wrong decisions and bad choices; sometimes he never finds that correct occupation. An understanding of the correct occupation into which the individual should go can be learned—through the guidance process. Once an occupational choice is decided upon, the goal should remain constant over a period of time, and all subsidiary educational and vocational decisions should be consistent with the goal.

It was this line of thought that served as the basis for Parsons' original approach to vocational guidance. Parsons' strategy consisted of three major steps. First, the individual should be analyzed by questionnaires and interviews in order to ascertain his abilities, interests, and general background. Second, occupations should be studied through the use of, for example, occupational information. Third, through a process of "true reasoning" or counseling the individual is matched with the appropriate job.

It is clear that Parsons' original formulation becomes, in effect, that of the entire vocational guidance movement. The NVGA has listed as the practices defining educational and vocational guidance (*a*) the study of the individual, (*b*) the study of occupations, and (*c*) counseling (9). Thus, the traditional goal of vocational guidance has been to assist the individual to choose, prepare for, enter upon, and progress in an occupation. This fundamental stance is evident from Parsons through much of the contemporary literature and research of vocational guidance. The basic strategy consists of matching the right person with the right job. Advances in the field of psychometrics served to provide the practitioner with more adequate techniques and instruments for studying the individual, but have not substantively altered basic theory or practice.

Life Pattern Theory

In recent decades there has been some increasing dissatisfaction with the foregoing approach. Katz reviews the nature of trait and factor theory, summarizes research, and quotes numerous writers' evaluations of the theory as a basis for vocational guidance (20, Chap. 2). The major shortcoming of trait and factor theory is its essentially static nature, for it makes no provision for change or development in the individual. Super, for example, notes (37, p. 169):

> That this approach has proved fruitful is clear. That its contributions are of permanent significance seems likely, for the assumption that individuals differ in abilities and interests, and that these differences have vocational implications not only makes good theoretical sense but is borne out by a mass of research. But it is suggested that concern with the development and use of the techniques needed to implement this approach to vocational guidance has led both to a failure to develop a supporting theory and a failure to explore other theories and approaches which would supplement this approach.

TABLE 3-1
A Summary of the Stages of Vocational Development

1. Growth stage (birth to 14 years):	A period of general physical and mental growth.
a Prevocational substage (birth to 3):	No interest or concern with vocations or vocational choice.
b. Fantasy substage (4–10):	Fantasy is basis of vocational thinking.
c. Interest substage (11–12):	Vocational thought is based on the individual's likes and dislikes.
d. Capacity substage (13–14):	Ability becomes the basis for vocational thought.
2. Exploration stage (15 to 24 years):	General exploration of work.
a. Tentative substage (15–17):	Needs, interests, capacities, values, and opportunities become bases for tentative occupational decisions.
b. Transition substage (18–21):	Reality increasingly becomes a basis for vocational thought and action.
c. Trial substage (22–24):	First trial job is entered after the individual has made an initial vocational commitment.
3. Establishment stage (25 to 44 yrs):	The individual seeks to enter a permanent occupation.
a. Trial (25–30);	A period of some occupational changes due to unsatisfactory choices.
b. Stabilization (31–44):	A period of stable work in a given occupational field.
4. Maintenance stage (45 to 65 years):	Continuation in one's chosen occupation.
5. Decline stage (65 years to death):	
a. Deceleration (65–70):	A period of declining vocational activity.
b. Retirement (71 on):	A cessation of vocational activity.

The major line of thought throughout life pattern theory stems from developmental psychology. Indeed, this approach to occupational choice theory has been termed the developmental approach (36). Vocational theorists such as Ginzberg (14), Super (36, 37) Tiedeman and O'Hara (38), and Holland (16), have developed unique but overlapping theories of vocational development based upon the earlier work of Buehler (7), Erikson, (11, 12), Havighurst (15), and others. A summary of the stages of vocational development according to Super's theory (36) is presented in Table 3-1.

According to life pattern theory, vocational development is a process in which a vocational self-concept is developed, implemented, and maintained in the world of work. Vocational development involves synthesis and/or compromise and typically proceeds according to certain general stages such as those suggested by Super. The individual is successful to the extent that he masters a series of general developmental tasks (15) and certain specific vocational developmental tasks (37). Success and satisfaction depend to a great extent upon the degree to which the person can develop and implement his self-concept and can experience a certain style of life. A unique career pattern emerges from a series of work experiences. Thus, the primary focus is not upon occupational choice but upon vocational development, which is seen as a lifelong series of occupations resulting in a career.

SOME OTHER THEORIES OF VOCATIONAL DEVELOPMENT

There are several other theories that can be found in the literature, but they do not seem to have had as profound an influence on guidance as those described above. These theories are generally not well developed. Except for Roe's theory, they seem not to have generated much further research. Most of these theories are hypothetical constructs rather than theories in the true sense of the term. They are presented in summary form below to illustrate the wide range of thought regarding the complex process of occupational choice and development.

Sociological Theories

Sociologists such as Caplow (8) and Miller and Form (26) describe occupational choice from a sociological perspective, emphasizing economic, cultural, and other social factors that influence the individual's process of decision-making Miller and Form, for example, conclude that chance or accident often plays the deciding part in determining an individual's life work. Such factors as the accident of birth determine an individual's race, family background, nationality, and place of residence, and to a certain extent chance factors also influence the individual's educational and cultural opportunities.

Psychoanalytic Theory

Although much of Freud's writing can be related in a very gross manner to vocational choice and adjustment, Freud has not written systematically or extensively about the place of work in an individual's psychic development. That Freud was aware of the importance of work as a meaningful activity in the life of the individual is apparent from his oft-quoted response to a question asked, during one of his lectures, about the requirements for a psychologically healthy life, Freud's famous reply was *Arbeiten und lieben*—"to work and to love."

The psychoanalysts generally feel that the normal person does not need any help in selecting an occupation, because he usually senses the correct course of action. It is when the individual is given advice that he usually runs into difficulty. Occupational choice is seen by the psychoanalysts as specific or general sublimation of instinctual wishes such as these:

Occupational Choice	Instinctual Wishes
Surgeon or butcher	Sadomasochism
Photographer	Voyeurism
Teacher	Domination
Actor	Exhibitionism

Brill (5) sees a bad occupational choice and poor vocational adjustment as resulting from having chosen work for which the individual is emotionally unfit. A lack of self-understanding or an inability to leave a poorly chosen vocation are cited as the major determinants of vocational maladjustment.

Needs Theories

Anne Roe (33, 34, 35) has proposed a theory of vocational choice based on needs and general orientations to satisfying needs, determined largely by early childhood experiences in the home. The climate of the home life—e.g., rejection, neglect, overprotection, overindulgence, etc.—and the interaction patterns between the child and the parents result in the individual's becoming oriented toward ideas, people, or things, and thus toward certain clusters of jobs. The basic needs described by Maslow may be summarized as follows (22):

1. Physiological needs
2. Safety needs
3. Need to belong and to be loved
4. Need for importance, respect, self-esteem, independence
5. Need for information
6. Need for understanding
7. Need for beauty
8. Need for self-actualization

No other factor in an individual's life can satisfy as many needs as an occupation. Occupations are classified into eight broad groups: service, business contact, organization, technology, outdoor, science, general culture, and arts and entertainment. Within each of these groups there are six levels:

Level 1. Professional and managerial workers with independent responsibility

Level 2. Professional and managerial workers with some responsibility but not as much independence of action as workers in Level 1

Level 3. Semiprofessional workers and owners of small businesses

Level 4. Skilled workers

Level 5. Semiskilled workers

Level 6. Unskilled workers

The occupational level toward which the individual moves is influenced by his "need intensity" within the limits set by his socioeconomic background and intelligence.

Hoppock proposes a somewhat different theory of occupational choice. This theory is also based upon needs and is summarized by the following ten postulates (17, pp. 74-75):

1. Occupations are chosen to meet needs.
2. The occupation that we choose is the one that we believe will best meet the needs that most concern us.
3. Needs may be intellectually perceived, or they may be only vaguely felt as attractions which draw us in certain directions. In either case, they may influence choices.
4. Occupational choice begins when we first become aware that an occupation can help to meet our needs.
5. Occupational choice improves as we become better able to anticipate how well a prospective occupation will meet our needs. Our capacity thus to anticipate demands upon our knowledge of ourselves, our knowledge of occupations, and our ability to think clearly.
6. Information about ourselves affects occupational choice by helping us to recognize what we want, and by helping us to anticipate whether or not we will be successful in collecting what the contemplated occupation offers to us.
7. Information about occupations affects occupational choice by helping us to discover the occupations that may meet our needs, and by helping us to anticipate how well satisfied we may hope to be in one occupation as compared with another.
8. Job satisfaction depends upon the extent to which the job that we hold meets the needs that we feel it should meet. The degree of satisfaction is determined by the ratio between what we have and what we want.
9. Satisfaction can result from a job which meets our needs today, or from a job which promises to meet them in the future.
10. Occupational choice is always subject to change when we believe that a change will better meet our needs.

VOCATIONAL GUIDANCE THEORY

Paralleling the two main streams of basic occupational theory in psychology has been another body of theory—i.e., theories underlying vocational guidance as an applied endeavor for helping students. As noted earlier, this body of thought is not theory in the strict sense of the term, but rather principles of guidance—in this case, vocational guidance.

The principles of vocational guidance as summarized by Albertson in the introduction to Parsons' book are (28, pp. i–ix):

1. It is better to choose a vocation than merely to hunt a job.
2. No one should choose a vocation without careful self-analysis, thorough, honest, and under guidance.
3. The youth should have a large survey of the field of vocations, and not simply drop into the convenient or accidental position.
4. Expert advice, or the advice of men who have made a careful study of men and vocations and of the conditions of success, must be better and safer for a young man than the absence of it.
5. The putting down on paper of a self-analysis is of supreme importance.

Following is a statement of principles and practices of the National Vocational Guidance Association (30).

1. Individual differences must be recognized, understood, and given individual attention.
2. The program should provide all pupils with an opportunity for self-inventory, self-direction, self-development, and self realization.
3. Provision should be made to enable teachers and all staff members to develop a better understanding of pupil behavior needs and problems.
4. The complexity of modern occupational life makes it necessary that accurate, comprehensive, and continuous information about occupations and about schools for further training be given to pupils.
5. The individual should receive assistance in inventorying his assets and limitations and the opportunities available, but freedom of choice is his inherent right and is as necessary for his development as equality of educational opportunity.
6. Continuous vocational and educational guidance should be offered the individual because of the changing economic status, changes occurring in occupations, and changes in the developing personality and interests of the individual.
7. Students should not decide upon a vocation too early or too hurriedly but only after the study of occupations and try-out experiences. Provision should be made for continuous reconsideration of plans.
8. In our American democracy, the ideal for which we strive is to give every individual freedom of choice in developing his potentialities, in determining his vocation, and in deciding how he wishes to spend his life. But with freedom of choice there is responsibility both on the part of society to provide facilities so that the individual can have the facts to assist him in making wise decisions and on the part of the individual to make use of these facilities in developing his potentialities to the utmost. Comparison of ability with achievement should be made each year to assist each individual to work up to the level of his ability.

PHILOSOPHY AND GOALS

The basic theory underlying vocational development is quite well defined. Contexts and limits are clear. Distinct theories are discernible. Research centers in universities and other settings are validating contemporary theories and elaborating further upon current thought (1, Chap. 12). Only in the most global sense, however, is there any agreement concerning the optimal philosophical point of departure for implementing a program of vocational guidance. Most theoreticians and practitioners alike will agree that an individual's future occupation will play a significant role in his total development. There is general agreement that society expects the school to provide students with help in the area of occupational choice (6). Furthermore, this kind of service is generally believed to be within the province of education and/or guidance. In summary, there appears to be general agreement about the following points:

1. An individual's occupational choice is one of the most important decisions he makes in his lifetime.
2. Guidance as an aspect of the educational process should help the individual with this vocational choice.
3. The individual is viewed as a potential worker.
4. Vocational guidance attempts to assist the student to make wise occupational choices.
5. Since educational choices are corollary to occupational choices, a focus upon educational aspects of occupational choice becomes necessary.
6. The personal-social aspects of the individual are important primarily as they relate to his vocational development.

The fact that virtually all guidance theoreticians and practitioners believe that vocational guidance is necessary and important may be the very reason for the perplexing state of affairs. Vocational guidance occurs in *every* approach to guidance, but there is no agreement in the field with respect to: (*a*) who should be responsible for it, (*b*) when it should occur, (*c*) how it should be implemented, or (*d*) the general context in which it should occur.

Statements of Goals

Numerous types of goals for vocational guidance are evident from a review of the literature. The classical goal of the educational-vocational approach is derived from the National Vocational Guidance Association statement (30) cited on page 34. It focuses upon helping the student to choose an occupation, prepare for it, enter it, and be successful in it. The second type of goal, derived from occupational choice theory, stresses assisting the student to make sound decisions by helping him to know and accept himself and to use this knowledge of himself. The goal of vocational adjustment emphasizes helping the individuals to become and remain a constructive, well-adjusted, happy, mentally healthy person in his occupational and extra-occupational life.

Many contemporary theoreticians envision the goal of the educational-vocational approach as helping the individual to maintain an adequate level of development. The recent impact of existentialism on the field of guidance has led to another type of goal—i.e., helping the individual to attain and maintain self-realization and to have a fulfilling life through a unique process of "becoming." Lastly, some educators see no distinction between the goals of vocational guidance and the goals of general education and therefore fuse the vocational goals with the statements of goals of general education.

Herein lies the dilemma of the educational-vocational approach. Vocational guidance is included as an aspect of every approach to guidance, but the goals vary in emphasis, in the context in which they are used, and with respect to the operational dimension of guidance. Vocational guidance has been described within the philosophical, psychological, and ideational frameworks of choice, adjustment, development, self-actualization, becoming, learning, etc.

The theoretical basis of the educational-vocational approach is quite clear. Trait and factor theory and career pattern theory constitute the basic theoretical underpinnings. Certain general principles of vocational guidance provide the counselor with a general rationale and some guidelines for action. Two major shortcomings, however, appear as the educational-vocational approach has been implemented through what is more commonly known as vocational guidance. First, it is quite clear that while many guidance programs have tended to function within the general framework of the educational-vocational approach, these programs have not systematically derived their practices from any of the above-mentioned general bodies of theory. Second, there has not been any substantial agreement of what a program of vocational guidance should strive for, how such a program should be organized, and how such a program should be implemented.

SOME OPERATIONAL ASPECTS

It follows from what has been stated above that there is no single educational-vocational approach to guidance. Neither is there a cluster of related approaches, as in the case of some other orientations to guidance. Rather, it appears that the term educational-vocational approach represents an aspect of all approaches to guidance. It constitutes a mode of thought, a dimension of the generic term "guidance." Because of the widespread acceptance of educational and vocational matters as primary concerns of guidance, it is only natural that these focuses should be a part of virtually all approaches to guidance. Thus, it is not surprising, in terms of the organizational and operational aspects of guidance, to find that there is no consensus in regard to how a program of vocational guidance should be implemented. Successful programs of vocational guidance have utilized many approaches including occupations courses, group guidance, individual and group counseling, the homeroom, developmental methods, and team methods.

Although there is no typical program exemplifying the educational-vocational approach, a plan described by Forrester (13, Chap. 1) may be summarized as an example. The formal organizational chart of the school system is shown in Figure 3-1. This program represents a large school system's attempt to provide a

FIGURE 3–1
An Organizational Chart for an Educational–Vocational Guidance Program

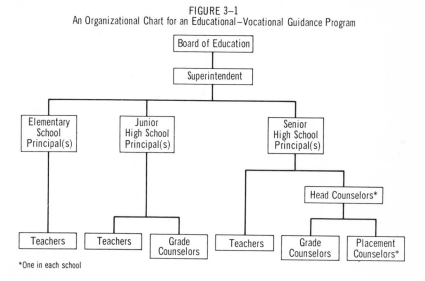

*One in each school

program of guidance within the educational-vocational rationale. Vocational guidance is carried on by three types of counselors: a head counselor for each school, a full-time placement counselor in each of the secondary schools, and grade counselors.

The head counselor is in charge of the entire guidance program and performs the following functions:

1. Participation in city-wide guidance functions—e.g., radio programs, cooperating with community agencies, etc.
2. In-service training of staff members.
3. Administration and scoring of psychological tests.
4. Institutional research, drop-out studies, academic achievement reports, administrative reports.
5. Arranging for college days, career conferences, visitations.
6. Referral of students to grade counselors.
7. Public relations.
8. General coordination and administration of guidance personnel.

The grade counselors carry on a broad range of vocational guidance functions in occupational information, testing, counseling, maintaining the cumulative record, etc. The placement counselor provides a placement service to help students obtain part-time and summer work. He helps drop-outs find permanent full-time work and cooperates with the local State Employment Service and with county vocational schools.

SUMMARY

The broad area of vocational guidance is an aspect of every approach to the guidance process. When the vocational guidance theme becomes the dominant focus of the guidance program, however, the program is utilizing the educational-vocational approach. Trait and factor theory and career pattern theory have emerged as the major theoretical bases for contemporary guidance, supplemented by principles of vocational guidance. Vocational development can be viewed in many ways, depending upon one's selection of personality theory and theory of vocational choice and vocational development.

The vocational theme has had a long tradition, dating back to the inception of the guidance movement. As guidance workers have attempted to help youth find their place in the world of work, it has become evident that vocational concerns are continuing and pervasive ones. The centrality of work in an individual's life precludes his being happy and successful without his having coped with this aspect of growing and maturing.

Contemporary guidance theory and practice have undergone significant development. Vocational guidance has begun to earn a legitimate place in the elementary school setting in addition to its traditional role in the junior high school and the senior high school. More and more, on the other hand, vocational development has come to be viewed in a balanced perspective along with other aspects of the individual's personal-social development. The most important theoretical advance has been the research and theory building relating to the vocational self-concept, while the most significant innovation in practice has been the utilization of developmental procedures for anticipating and preventing vocational crises in the life of the student.

REFERENCES

1. H. Borow, *Man in a World at Work*. Boston: Houghton Mifflin Co., 1964.

2. J. M. Brewer, *Education as Guidance*. New York: The Macmillan Co., 1932.

3. J. M. Brewer, *History of Vocational Guidance*. New York: Harper & Row, 1942.

4. J. M. Brewer, *The Vocational Guidance Movement*. New York: The Macmillan Co., 1928.

5. A. A. Brill, *Fundamental Conceptions of Psychoanalysis*. New York: Harcourt, Brace & World, 1921.

6. W. B. Brookover, *A Sociology of Education*. New York: American Book Co., 1955.

7. C. Buehler, *Der Manschliche Lebenslauf als Psychologiches Problem*. Leipzig: Hirzel, 1933.

8. T. Caplow, *The Sociology of Work*. Minneapolis: University of Minnesota Press, 1954.

9. Committee of the National Vocational Guidance Association, "The Principles and Practices of Educational and Vocational Guidance," *Occupations: The Vocational Guidance Magazine*, 15 (1937), 772-78.

10. J. V. Cribbin, "A Critique of the Philosophy of Modern Guidance," *The Catholic Educational Review*, 53 (1955), 72-91.

11. E. H. Erikson, *Childhood and Society*. New York: W. W. Norton & Company, 1950.

12. E. H. Erikson, "Growth and Crises of the Healthy Personality," *Psychological Issues*, 1 (1959), 50-100.

13. G. Forrester, *Methods of Vocational Guidance*. Boston: D. C. Heath and Co., 1951.

14. E. Ginzberg, *et al*, *Occupational Choice*. New York: Columbia University Press, 1951.

15. R. J. Havighurst, *Human Development and Education*. New York: Longmans, Green and Co., 1953.

16. J. L. Holland, "A Theory of Vocational Choice," *Journal of Counseling Psychology*, 6 (1959), 35-45.

17. R. Hoppock, *Occupational Information*. New York: McGraw-Hill, 1957.

18. A. J. Jones, *Principles of Guidance*, 1st ed. New York: McGraw-Hill, 1930.

19. A. J. Jones, *Principles of Guidance*, 2d ed. New York: McGraw-Hill, 1934.

20. M. Katz, *Decisions and Values: A Rationale for Secondary School Guidance*. New York: College Entrance Examination Board, 1963.

21. L. V. Koos and G. N. Kefauver, *Guidance in Secondary Schools*. New York: The Macmillan Co., 1932.

22. A. H. Maslow, *Motivation and Personality*. New York: Harper & Row, 1954.

23. R. H. Mathewson, *Guidance Policy and Practice,* 3d ed. New York: Harper & Row, 1962.

24. G. E. Meyers, *Principles and Techniques of Vocational Guidance*. New York: McGraw-Hill, 1941.

25. C. H. Miller, *Foundations of Guidance*. New York: Harper & Row, 1961.

26. D. C. Miller and W. H. Form, *Industrial Sociology*. New York: Harper & Row, 1951.

27. W. Norris, "Highlights in the History of the National Vocational Guidance Association," *Personnel and Guidance Journal*, 33 (1954), 205-8.

28. F. Parsons, *Choosing a Vocation*. Boston: Houghton Mifflin Co., 1909.

29. D. G. Paterson, *et al., Student Guidance Techniques*. New York: McGraw-Hill, 1933.

30. *Principles and Practices of Educational and Vocational Guidance*. Washington, D.C.: National Vocational Guidance Association, 1937.

31. *Principles and Practices of Vocational Guidance*. Washington, D.C.: National Vocational Guidance Association, 1924.

32. W. N. Proctor, *Educational and Vocational Guidance*. Boston: Houghton Mifflin Co., 1925.

33. A. Roe, "Early Determinants of Vocational Choice," *Journal of Counseling Psychology*, 4 (1957), 212-17.

34. A. Roe, *The Psychology of Occupations*. New York: John Wiley & Sons, 1956.

35. A. Roe and M. Siegelman, *The Origin of Interests*, Washington, D.C.: American Personnel and Guidance Association, 1964.

36. D. E. Super, *The Psychology of Careers*. New York: Harper & Row, 1957.

37. D. E. Super, *et al., Career Development: Self-Concept Theory*. New York: College Entrance Examination Board, 1963.

38. D. V. Tiedeman and R. P. O'Hara, *Career Development: Choice and Adjustment*. New York: College Entrance Examination Board, 1963.

39. V. H. Vroom, *Work and Motivation*. New York: John Wiley & Sons, 1964.

chapter 4

The Counseling Approach
to Guidance

A young boy is intensely occupied in fitting and hammering together old pieces of wood, embellished with cans and string. "What are you making?" asks an observer. A pause, some frowning looks at the contraption, a scratch or two at the neck, then, "Well, I guess it'll be a rocket ship, or maybe a dragon trap. I'm not sure yet." The observer passes on with a smile, contented with so natural a confession of work without plan. He feels no need to challenge the lad about assembling materials and tools, employing techniques, and developing his energies without knowing beforehand what ultimately he wants to attain, for this is childhood.

To be engrossed in an activity without any conscious goal for the activity is a freedom gladly accorded to children, but not to counselors. (7, p. 3)

The counseling approach to guidance is an outgrowth of the many significant advances in counseling, psychology, and psychiatry immediately preceding and during World War II. During the postwar period, the counseling orientation to guidance has grown considerably. Although counseling plays an important role in virtually every approach to guidance, counseling becomes, in the counseling orientation, almost synonymous with guidance. A number of counseling orientations have been developed (19, 50), and many conceptual approaches to counseling have been utilized in the school setting. On the whole, however, the most prevalent counseling orientations in schools have continued to be the clinical or directive approach (55), the client-centered or nondirective approach (6, 38, 40), and the eclectic approach (18, 54).

The counseling approach stands at an extreme end of the generalist-specialist continuum, for this orientation is the most specialized of all approaches to guidance. It grew out of a fundamental reaction against the generalist view, which holds that the guidance worker should view all aspects of the student's development and that the guidance process should be multiphasic. In contrast, the counseling view holds that the generalist orientation tends to be ill-defined, too diffuse, and in general too nebulous.

Proponents of the counseling view argue first that the generalists have not adequately worked out recognizable methods for implementing their goals and have not really proven the value of their contribution to the educational endeavor. The second major criticism against the generalist view is that it is not professional. The specialist argument is based on the premise that there are no specialized techniques for the generalist and that the acquisition of specialized skills is a major dimension of professional status. Since the generalist has little or no specialized training, the specialist feels that the generalist strategy is unprofessional and thus unacceptable.

The counseling approach focuses upon individuals who need more intensive help with their psychological problems than teachers can give them, but not upon those seriously disturbed individuals who require deep therapy. Counseling focuses upon the psychological problems of students but attempts to help only a limited number of them, depending upon the goals of the counselor and the goals of the school. The primary focus tends to be remedial and therapeutic rather than educative and developmental.

Definitions of counseling vary according to the theoretical orientation of the definer. Williamson defines counseling as a personalized and individualized process designed to help a person learn subject matter, citizenship traits, social and personal values, and all other habits, skills, attitudes, and beliefs (55, pp. 2-3). For Rogers, counseling "consists of a definitely structured permissive relationship which allows the client to gain an understanding of himself to a degree which enables him to take positive steps in light of his new orientation" (39, p. 18). Warters defines eclectic counseling as "that counseling that is based upon different methods, upon concepts and techniques selected from different schools of thought" (54, p. 170).

Byrne distinguishes between lay counseling and professional counseling. The former is viewed as a service of verbal assistance by one person who wishes to help another person in a puzzled or troubled state by influencing his behavior so as to relieve the puzzled or troubled state. In his discussion of the work of school counselor, Byrne evolves a definition of professional counseling (7, p.61):

> Counseling is (1) a service of assistance by a person professionally prepared to counsel (2) in which the intention is to influence the behavior of another person who seeks help in matters of plans and decisions, and in matters of satisfying interpersonal relationships, (3) by inducing growth or change in that person (4) through a unique relationship and verbal practices that are based on scientifically discovered knowledge of human behavior in general, and on the nature of behavior change through counseling in particular.

Thus, the counseling approach to guidance is characterized by the centrality of counseling in the overall guidance strategy, with prevailing therapeutic and psychological overtones. Guidance personnel are called counselors, and many of the traditional guidance activities are carried on by teachers and other personnel. The counseling interview and related procedures constitute the primary focus of the entire guidance program.

THE THEORETICAL BASIS

Broadly speaking, counseling is based upon the theoretical foundations of personality theory, and almost every theory of personality has a correlative form of psychotherapy or counseling associated with it. The counseling approach is based upon the fundamental belief that the personal problems of the individual impair his functioning and that counseling constitutes the means for getting at the cause of difficulties (symptoms) exhibited in the school setting— e.g., underachievement, vocational indecision, discipline problems. Thus, the counseling approach is chiefly psychological. Because the counseling approach is remedial and therapeutic, focusing upon only a limited number of the students, the counselor tends to function separately from administrators, teachers, and other staff members who are primarily educational in their orientation.

Underlying Assumptions

Two fundamental categories of assumptions underlie the counseling approach. The most critical assumption is that counseling constitutes the most fruitful *modus operandi* for the guidance worker and that counseling alone is a sufficient focus for the guidance program. Although the counseling approach nods in passing to related personnel such as the speech therapist, the social worker, the remedial reading specialist, and the psychometrist, these other personnel are clearly auxiliary and relatively unimportant in the overall strategy.

The second group of assumptions relate to the counseling strategy and to the psychological system which is the foundational support for counseling techniques per se. Rogers, for example, has noted some hypotheses regarding the facilitation of personal growth, the characteristics of a helping relationship, and a set of propositions or presuppositions underlying client-centered counseling (38, 40). Client-centered counseling, in turn, rests heavily upon phenomenology and self-concept theory, which are based upon additional assumptions. Each of the other approaches to counseling has its own cluster of underlying assumptions related to the counseling process and a related theory of personality.

Rationale

Although many theories of counseling have been widely utilized in clinical settings, the emphasis on the intellect in educational settings makes the work of the counselor difficult because of his psychological rather than educational orientation. Traditionally the school counselor has been more involved in testing and the information service, devoting relatively little time to counseling per se. The primary job of the counselor, however, is to counsel. He must build a program, and he must have the time to counsel. The major portion of his day should be spent in a direct counseling relationship with students. For purposes of illustration, client-centered counseling in the secondary school will be described in this and subsequent sections.

Client-centered counseling is a dynamic and evolving approach. The worth and dignity of the individual dictate that his psychological needs as well as the traditionally viewed needs should be met by the school. Counseling methods are not merely the execution of techniques but the implementation of a philosophy and certain attitudes. Thus, client-centered counseling is based upon (*a*) total acceptance of the counselee as a person, (*b*) permissiveness, (*c*) sensitive listening, (*d*) empathic understanding, and (*e*) a fundamental belief in the desire of the individual to become psychologically better integrated and self-actualized.

Philosophy and Goals

As in other approaches to guidance, there is no single philosophy of education within which the counseling orientation to guidance must fit. A guidance program based upon this approach can function within any educational system which assumes a responsibility for assisting students as they cope with their psychological problems and delegates to the counseling program the primary responsibility in this area. The only philosophical requisites of a school system utilizing a counseling approach to guidance are as follows (adapted in part from 27, p. 148):

1. The belief that human life, happiness, and well-being are to be valued.
2. The assertion that man is the master of his own destiny, with the right to control it in his own interests in his own way.
3. The determination that the dignity and worth of each person shall be respected at all times and under all conditions.
4. The assumption of the right of individual freedom; the recognition of the right of each person to think his own thoughts and to speak his own mind.
5. The belief that the school should help the student with his psychological problems as well as his educational and vocational problems.

The goals of counseling vary as a function of the philosophy and counseling approach of the counselor and the educational system of which he is a part. The goals of counseling have been stated in many ways, with a multitude of differential emphases, such as these:

1. To help the individual toward better mental health.
2. To assist the individual toward better psychological integration.
3. To encourage spontaneity, independence, self-actualization, etc.
4. To help the individual to know and accept himself, and to apply this knowledge of himself in making wise educational and occupational choices.
5. To help the individual to maintain an adequate level of development.

COUNSELING THEORY

The direct theoretical basis for the client-centered counseling approach to guidance consists of three relatively distinct bodies of theory and research within the broad realm of counseling. These include (*a*) theories and research in psychotherapy, (*b*) theories and research in client-centered counseling, and (*c*) attempts to isolate elements common to all approaches to counseling and psychotherapy.

Theory and Research in Psychotherapy

Although the distinction between counseling and psychotherapy has not always been clear, there has been a marked trend in recent years to differentiate between them. In general, psychotherapy attempts to bring about a major personality change or reorganization. Counseling, on the other hand, does not drastically alter personality dynamics but helps the individual utilize his resources for coping with life and its problems. In general, school counselors have viewed psychotherapeutic theory and practice as a backdrop for their own work. A general familiarity with the psychoanalysis of Freud is often complemented by a survey of the neopsychoanalytic schools of thought of Horney, Sullivan, and Fromm. Other approaches to psychotherapy, such as Adlerian therapy, hypnotherapy, Gestalt therapy, conditioned reflex therapy, psychobiological therapy, Rankian therapy, learning theory therapy, and existential therapy, each in turn have helped to add perspective and dimension to the work of the counselor.

Very often the impact of psychotherapy has been transmitted via the survey of secondary sources (5, 16, 19, 27, 32) as formal course requirements in professional preparation programs, and in routine professional development. Thus, the major contribution of psychotherapeutic theory has been to provide the counselor with an increasing sensitivity to the scope and depth of the helping relationship, coupled with a more adequate perception of the dynamics of the counseling process.

Theory and Research in Client-Centered Counseling

As noted above, the directive, client-centered, and eclectic approaches to counseling have been the most widely utilized strategies of counseling in the school setting. Since a subsequent section of this chapter will describe a client-centered approach in the secondary school, the theory and research in this area is summarized below.

In the 1940's a man, a book, and a theory dramatically appeared on the American psychotherapeutic scene, The man—Carl R. Rogers; the book—*Counseling and Psychotherapy* (39); the theory—the nondirective approach to counseling and psychotherapy. Although the antecedent thinking about this new approach can be traced back several decades, it wasn't until the 1940's that the actual crystallization and presentation of the theory took place. Despite the fact that a voluminous amount of literature and research is now available, the very terms "nondirective" and "client-centered" immediately evoke numerous stereotypes, a flood of questions, and a host of misconceptions.

Theoretical Studies. The early writings about nondirective therapy emphasized techniques rather than theory (34) and described very little beyond the rudimentary constructs of assumptions, premises, and goals. Scarcely a decade after Rogers' first book, however, much had been done to remedy this state of affairs. Rogers himself presented rather detailed descriptions of the theoretical basis of nondirective psychotherapy (41, 44, 45). In Rogers' later major writing (38, 40) the few basic hypotheses had remained essentially intact but had been developed, with additional theory, into a rather complete and well-articulated set of nineteen propositions. These propositions have been buttressed by a schematic representation or model of the total personality (38, pp. 524-32) and general theoretical discussions of counseling (35, 47, 48, 49).

Client-centered therapy has been compared with Adlerian therapy (11) and with the theory and practices of orthodox Freudian psychoanalysis (51, 52). A cross-relationship study has been made of the therapies of Freud, Rank, Taft, Allan, and Rogers (36). Several other writers have described the theoretical foundations of client-centered therapy (5, 16), as has Rogers himself (43). More recently the conditions necessary for therapeutic personality change have been described (37):

1. Two persons are in psychological contact.
2. The first, whom we shall term the client, is in a state of incongruence, being vulnerable or anxious.
3. The second person, whom we shall term the therapist, is congruent or integrated in the relationship.
4. The therapist experiences unconditional positive regard for the client.
5. The therapist experiences an empathic understanding of the client's internal frame of reference and endeavors to communicate this experience to the client.
6. The communication to the client of the therapist's empathic understanding and unconditional positive regard is to a minimal degree achieved.

Although synopsis tends to produce distortion, it appears that client-centered therapy is based upon a synthesis of phenomenology, holistic and organismic theory, interpersonal theory, and the self theories of others together with significant contributions in self theory by Rogers himself. Although many examples of eclecticism are guilty of utilizing a "smorgasbord" approach (8), Rogers and his followers have developed one of the few eclectic formulations which are unified, coherent, and well articulated. The three principal ingredients of his psychological theory are (*a*) the total organism (*b*) the phenomenal field, and (*c*) the self. Rogers' total theory is available to readers in Rogers' own treatise (38), in summary form (16), and in incomplete form in any monograph, text, or journal article espousing the client-centered approach (5, 23, 34).

The misconception concerning the alleged absence of adequate theory (philosophical and psychological) is thus due to incomplete study of available literature. For many individuals, the misconception probably has arisen from the reading of only the early writings of Rogers. Although there are some gaps in the theory of client-centered therapy, there is an adequate theoretical basis for practice. One of the most significant aspects of the client-centered approach has been the voluminous amount of research it has stimulated. Just as this research has netted changes in past theory and practice, so is it probable that client-centered therapy will continue to develop and evolve as a result of research yet to be completed.

The Process of Therapy. In Rogers' first book the nature of the process and the steps or phases of client-centered therapy are clearly outlined (39, pp. 131-237). There is also an abundance of concise descriptions of client-centered therapy in the related literature (5, pp. 193-219; 30, pp. 95-120; 32). The description of the client-centered approach together with illustrative cases is best exemplified by Rogers' own later writing (38). Although there are several variations on the typical pattern, the usual steps in the process are as follows (5, pp. 94-105):

Stage 1. Awareness of need for help
Stage 2. Development of the relationship and overcoming resistance
Stage 3. Expression of feelings and clarification of problem(s)
Stage 4 and 5. Deeper exploration of feelings
Stage 6. The working-through process
Stage 7. Development of insight
Stage 8. Experience outside psychotherapy

Other writers have described the process of client-centered therapy in terms of special aspects such as general client responses (2), client defensiveness (14), maturity of client responses (20), client perceptions (21), and grammatical tense of client statements (46). The total process and its specific aspects are predictable and typically follow one of several patterns.

Counselor Role. When an individual observes, reads about, or listens to recordings of any kind of psychotherapy the natural locus of attention is the counselor. The observer expects some type of analysis, diagnosis, and prognosis. But in client-centered therapy these are not to be found. The counselor seems to be a rather warm and friendly person. He listens. He uncritically accepts the counselee and everything he says. He does not diagnose, he does not exhort, he does not moralize, and he does not ask many questions. There is the tendency to conclude that the apparent lack of overt activity by the counselor means that he is playing a weak and passive role in the therapeutic relationship. But when one understands the nature of the relationship from the internal frame of reference—i.e., as it is experienced by the counselor and the counselee—the perspective changes. Much of the activity and communication may be nonverbal. Attempting to empathize with the counselee, reflecting feeling, really listening to the client, and attempting to assume the internal frame of reference, are passive only in terms of overt behavior. In a sense, this is the most active kind of relationship. Developing and maintaining such a therapeutic relationship requires great energy, attention, and skill.

Even in the gross sense, the client-centered counselor is not passive. If he so chooses, he can subtly control the direction and speed of progress in the interview by his type of response and by the wording and inflection of his statements. Various types of responses possess varying amounts of lead for the interview (5).

Earlier descriptions and discussions of nondirective counseling and psychotherapy had a tendency to overstress technique. A psychotherapy, however, is not based on methods, approaches, or techniques. It is predicated upon a view of man. It stems from a philosophy. It is an implementation of an attitude. Rogers has stated that the effective counselor holds a coherent and developing set of attitudes deeply imbedded in his personal organization and implemented by techniques and methods consistent with it (38, p. 19). A practitioner who slavishly, rigidly, and mechanically bases his counseling on techniques or a "method" is doomed.

Two research studies highlight the priority of personal philosophy or orientation over techniques. In an investigation of counseling "style," it was found that personal characteristics—e.g., general background, experience, attitudes—have significantly more influence upon the course and outcomes of the counseling interview than does the theoretical orientation of the counselor (57). Similarly, two groups of counselors, (a) experienced and expert and (b) inexperienced and inexpert, of three schools of thought were studied in the counseling situation. The therapeutic relationships created by experts of any given school of thought resembled relationships created by experts of other schools more closely than they did the relationships created by nonexperts of the same school of thought (11).

Thus, therapy is not primarily the result of techniques or even a formal theoretical orientation. The therapeutic situation results from the interaction of two individuals, and looming large as a variable determining the nature of that relationship is the counselor himself—his attitudes and values, his background, his personal philosophy, and his basic view of the nature of man. While the therapeutic relationship is overtly built by specific actions and techniques, the primary determinant of the counselor's *modus operandi* lies in the fundamental aspects of his personal organization. In this same vein, it has been said that the counselor himself is the technique (56).

The primary elements of the client-centered interview are warmth, acceptance, and the recognition of the dignity and worth of the individual. Via the technique of reflection of feeling the counselor attempts to communicate to the client that he is being accepted and understood. But there is a difference between "acceptance" and "agreement." Agreement, support, reassurance, sympathy, etc., are in general avoided because of their side effects of fostering dependency upon the counselor. The client-centered counselor or psychotherapist does not "agree"; he "accepts" and "reflects."

Through the use of various techniques, the counselor attempts to develop and maintain a certain type of relationship—a unique climate—a situation within which the counselee can undergo a special kind of growth and experience, a distinctive type of attitudinal learning and personal reorganization. These outcomes do not stem from agreeing with actions and attitudes of clients. They occur when the client experiences a warm, acceptant, nonthreatening counselor who can build a relationship within which the client can become "that self which one truly is" (40, Chap. 8). Client-centered therapy is based upon the proposition that the individual has an innate striving to become a certain type of person— i.e., what others have termed the ego-ideal or the idealized self. Furthermore, it is hypothesized that given the proper conditions in the therapeutic relationship the individual can work through the problem, achieve insight, propose initial tentative plans, carry the plans through, and thereby resolve his problem or conflict. Thus, the client-centered psychotherapist or counselor is not assuming a hypocritical role wherein he accepts the client regardless of his position or stance. Rather, he is a friendly, accepting, uncritical, empathetic, unauthoritarian participant in a unique relationship which is largely nurtured and maintained by his sensitivity and skill.

Client-centered therapy has always emphasized the need for the structuring of the roles of counselor and client, behavioral limits, goals, etc. With the passage of time, however, the emphasis has shifted from the formal setting of limits. Client-centered therapy holds that verbal structuring, or describing the relationship intellectually, may distort the client's experiencing of the relationship. The emphasis, therefore, is not on this formal or verbal defining of limits but on the implicit element in the counseling relationship with respect to the roles of counselor and client.

Structure and limits can be defined largely at the nonverbal level. Rogers points out the value of limits to the therapist and client (33, pp. 90-113). Limits provide a framework and define roles. Without these elements it would be most difficult to build a stable relationship. Rogers identifies limits of time, responsibility, aggression, affection, and dangerous activities. Other writers have added role limits and procedural or process limits (5, pp. 185-89). The timing of structuring and dangers inherent in it have also been described (38, pp. 184-85, 189). Client-centered therapy has limits, and the limits are quite definitive. The establishment of these limits, however, is usually interwoven within the natural process of the therapeutic relationship rather than constituting a separate phase or stage during the course of the psychotherapy.

Individual counseling with a client-centered approach has been shown to be effective for a wide range of problems: mental deficiency, physical handicaps, personality problems (24); maladjustment (38, p. 185); situational problems (30); parent counseling (28); juvenile delinquency (12); allergies (20); marriage counseling, and parent-child problems (5, Chap. 5).

Client-centered group-centered psychotherapy has applied the basic tenets of individual therapy to a variety of problem situations: marriage problems, educational and vocational problems, psychological problems (5, p. 318), neuroses and psychoses (38), and situational problems and conflicts (39, pp. 315-16).

Nondirective play therapy has been shown to be effective in treating cases of psychosomatic allergies, mental deficiency, physical handicaps, personality problems, race conflicts, and reading problems (24). Normal children with situational problems have also been helped (28).

Not only is client-centered therapy applicable to a wide range of problems but the research indicates that it is effective as measured and evaluated by numerous criteria: counselee evaluation (26); standardized tests such as the Rorschach (15, 31), Bell Adjustment Inventory, Kent-Rosanoff Test, Bernreuter Test, TAT, Hildreth Feeling Attitude Scale, Discomfort-Relief Quotient, and achievement tests (38, pp. 176-85); judges' ratings (38, p. 185); analysis of client statements during interviews (38, p. 181); numerous objective criteria (17, 38, p. 181); and galvanic skin response (38, p. 185, 53). Although the above studies are in many respects crude and some of the criteria are somewhat questionable, the bulk of the evidence seems to indicate that client-centered therapy can be a powerful tool when utilized by trained personnel.

A number of thoughtful educators have been impelled to utilize the central tenet of the client-centered approach in aspects of education other than guidance and counseling (38). If one can rely upon the innate capacity of the counselee to deal constructively with his problems when given the proper therapeutic climate, and if significant learning takes place during such conditions in counseling, then applying the same approach to the learning situation in the classroom becomes an intriguing prospect. A definitive description of the goals of student-centered education and tentative hypotheses (38, pp. 387-91) have been developed describing how the student-centered teacher creates an acceptant climate, develops individual and group purposes, and facilitates a special kind of learning through unique techniques (38, Chap. 9). Descriptions and evaluations of the student-centered or nondirective method of teaching are available in literature (9, 10, 13).

Attempts to Isolate Common Elements Among Various Counseling Approaches

Some studies have tried to identify the essential constituents of the counseling process which transcend the idiosyncratic practices of individual approaches. Fiedler's classic study, for example, identified the following characteristics of the "ideal therapeutic relationship" (11):

1. An empathic relationship.
2. Therapist and patient relate well.
3. Therapist sticks closely to patient's problem.
4. The patient feels free to say what he likes.
5. An atmosphere of mutual trust and confidence exists.
6. Rapport is excellent.
7. The patient assumes an active role.
8. The therapist leaves the patient free to make his own choice.
9. The therapist accepts all feelings which the patient has as completely normal and understandable.
10. A tolerant atmosphere exists.
11. Patient feels most of the time he is really understood.
12. Therapist is really able to understand the patient.
13. The therapist really tries to understand the patient's feelings.

Similarly, all approaches to counseling agree on the following as the primary dimensions of counseling: (*a*) acceptance of the counselee, (*b*) respect for the individual, (*c*) a permissive atmosphere in the counseling interview, and (*d*) a learning occurrence during the interview (4, p. 33). Warters describes some principles of counseling frequently violated by school counselors even though these principles seem to transcend theoretical alliances (54, p. 171): (*a*) counseling does not involve compulsion on the part of the counselor, because the student possesses, among other rights, the right of decision, (*b*) success in counseling is based largely upon the quality of the counseling relationship, (*c*) time is required for counseling to achieve its productive possibilities because counseling is a process and not an act.

SOME OPERATIONAL ASPECTS

A typical formal structure for a guidance program based upon a counseling approach is shown in Figure 4-1. The guidance worker—i.e., the counselor—functions within the general school setting but is under the supervision of the Director of Psychological Services rather than the principal of the school. The organizational relationship is a reflection of the emphasis upon the guidance worker as a psychological counselor rather than the typical educationally oriented guidance counselor.

The counselor must create and maintain an image—not a false one, but one which represents what he really is: a counselor of students. Thus, one of the primary and continuing operational goals of the counselor is the establishment and maintenance of a professional identity as a counselor. As such, he makes a continual effort to remain, in effect, apart from the mainstream of routine educational decisions and activities so that he will not become identified as another member of the faculty and staff of the school in the minds of the stu-

FIGURE 4–1
An Organizational Chart for a Counseling Approach to Guidance

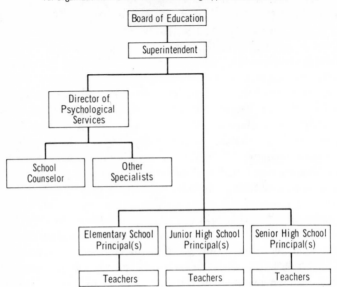

dents who will be coming to him for help with their personal problems. The integral dimensions of the counseling relationship are acceptance, warmth, permissiveness, understanding, and unconditional positive regard. As the counselor functions within the educational setting, therefore, he tries to create an identity as a nonauthority figure.

The counseling approach to guidance emphasizes that in order to develop and maintain this professional identity and in order to be maximally effective as a counselor, there are certain activities in the school which are beyond the scope of his role and function (4, pp. 72-73):

1. He doesn't perform any administrative duties.
   a. Reports—academic, failure, honor rolls, policies, etc.
   b. Orientation—physical plans, curriculum.
   c. Interviewing—failing students.
2. He doesn't instruct, supervise, or proctor.
3. He doesn't discipline students.
4. He doesn't perform routine clerical tasks which prevent him from devoting full time to professional activities.
5. He doesn't schedule classes or arrange academic programs.
6. He doesn't check attendance or function as a truant officer.

The counseling orientation encompasses a broad range of alternative conceptual approaches and, while the focuses and emphases may vary from program to program, the one pervading theme is the necessity for creating and maintaining a therapeutic rather than an educational role for the counselor. Within this general framework there is room for locally conceived roles.

Role and Functions of the Counselor

Although the counselor may at times act as a consultant with administrators and faculty, his major role is that of a counselor of students. He functions largely in the counseling office rather than in the total school community. Whereas the typical guidance worker attempts to function throughout the school in conjunction with the rest of the staff, the counseling approach to guidance is defined as "Guidance through supplementary services." There is one major service—counseling.

Since the counselor is essentially apart from the mainstream of routine academic affairs in the school, it is imperative that he develop an environmental awareness of this role and an understanding of his function with the staff and student population of the school. The counselor's role and function, in turn, are a translation of his personal and professional philosophy into the operational aspects of his daily work, for, as Rogers has noted (38), counseling is not so much the application of methods and techniques as it is the implementation of a philosophy and a basic attitude.

The major functions of the counselor are:

1. Carrying on professional counseling.
2. Motivating students to seek counseling.
3. Conducting research on counseling effectiveness.
4. Placement and grouping of students.
5. In-service education programs for teachers.
6. Consultation with faculty and parents.

Major Dimensions of the Guidance Program

There are three major dimensions to the guidance program: counseling, the information service, and testing. Counseling, the first dimension, is the core of the guidance program. The counseling program includes orientation to counseling for students, teachers, and parents by means of role-playing, audio-visual approaches (movies, slides, etc.), descriptive brochures to students and parents, and a concerted effort to develop and maintain a counseling clientele. Since faculty awareness of the counseling is important, effort is also directed toward orienting them toward the goals and general aspects of the program. After an awareness on the part of the faculty has been developed, the next major goal is for the faculty to accept the program. In-service education of faculty members is also carried on when faculty awareness, acceptance, and interest in the counseling program have been aroused to a level sufficient to enable the in-service training to be effective.

The counseling program includes parent conferences and individual and group counseling. Some students come to counseling by referral; a few come as a result of routine counselor-initiated sessions; but the bulk of counseling sessions ideally begin as a result of self-referrals by students. Educational, vocational, and personal counseling are the three major focuses.

The second major dimension to the guidance program is the information service. Although the core of counselor's work is counseling, the noncounseling information service is another part of his function in the school. It is essential that the student have many kinds of information in order for him to grow, to adjust, and to make the significant decisions in his life. Some of the most important kinds of information the student must have relate to course offerings, post–high school education, scholarships, loans, the effect of supply and demand upon the labor market, and the requirements of the occupations for which he is suited.

Because of the unique role of the guidance worker as a "counselor," the dissemination of information is handled quite differently than it is in the more traditional orientations to guidance. Typically, the guidance worker maintains an occupational file, college catalogues, scholarship information, etc. in or near his office and utilizes this information as an integral part of his work. Thus, the typical guidance counselor has often been stereotyped as a dispenser of information.

In the counseling approach to guidance, a "Career Information Center" is established in the school library. The orientation program encourages students to use the educational, vocational, and personal-social information available there. The information is disseminated by the school librarian, thereby eliminating the image of the counselor as a dispenser of information and emphasizing his role as a psychologically oriented counselor. Although the information is made available through the library, the counselor utilizes the information as a vehicle for counseling. Information becomes meaningful only as it is placed into the context of the student and his reactions to the information.

As a result of the client-centered approach to counseling, the educational, vocational, and personal-social information is considered in the counseling interview in light of the attitudes, values, and self-concept of the student. Students first read and study the information obtained from the Career Information Center in the library; then the implications of that information are considered in the counseling interview.

The third dimension of the guidance program is testing. As it would be expected, the client-centered approach does not emphasize testing. The basic testing program of the school system is coordinated and administered by the Director of Psychological Services, who in turn works with teachers for administering some of the tests. The counseling interview is the core of the guidance program. When a counselee seeks testing in the counseling interview, the counselor and the counselee consider the counselee's attitude toward testing. If testing does occur, the responsibility for the choice of testing lies with the counselee.

The selection of the kind of test to be taken is the responsibility of the counselee, and the choice of the specific test is the professional responsibility of the counselor.

Whenever possible the client-centered counselor attempts to build a non-psychometric image by having someone on the staff called a Director of Research and Measurement, Coordinator of Testing, or Director of Evaluation who organizes testing schedules, orders materials, administers tests, arranges for tests to be scored, conducts research, conducts inservice testing program, interprets test results, etc. Group interpretation of testing results can be utilized as one means of preserving the counselor's image with the students when he must handle the testing program in his school without the assistance of a psychometrist. In schools where there is more than one counselor, the test administration and possibly the test interpretation can be carried on by the counselor who does not counsel the particular student seeking testing.

Relationships with Students

As noted above, the guidance worker is primarily a counselor of students, and he attempts to maintain this kind of relationship with them to as great an extent as possible. His major activities with students include, orientation, counseling, and referral. Orientation will vary from setting to setting, including such activities as role-playing demonstrations, orientation meetings, movies, small group discussions, student handbooks, mimeographed pamphlets explaining counseling, and PTA talks. As a professional person, the counselor is aware of his strengths and his limitations. He refers those students who need a type of help which is beyond his capacity to other individuals or agencies, such as the psychologist, a consulting psychiatrist, or welfare and other social agencies.

Relationships with Teachers

Faculty acceptance and cooperation are both necessary for the adequate implementation of the counseling program. In an ongoing program, each new faculty member is oriented to the nature and function of the counseling program. An integral part of the initiation of counseling is a general orientation for all teachers concerning the role and function of the counselor and the kind of help he can give students and teachers. Although counselors differ with respect to their willingness to serve as consultants to teachers, the guiding principle for the consultant function is that the counselor helps the teacher in a nonauthoritarian and nonadministrative manner and that at no time does he perform any function that will detract from his primary role as a counselor of students.

The counselor first develops a staff awareness of his availability as a resource consultant. After building a working and helping relationship with teachers, he begins his consultant function by (*a*) accepting and understanding teachers as persons, (*b*) understanding the tensions and stress to which they are subjected,

(c) realizing that teaching is an emotionally enervating task, and (d) helping to develop a mutual trust and respect (4, pp. 160-61). These fundamental attitudes and behaviors provide the foundation for the consultative function per se, which includes acting in the capacity of a testing consultant, a curriculum consultant, or in an actual counseling relationship with teachers.

Relationships with Administrators

The counselor can make his availability known to administrators and then develop a working relationship with them. His major contribution to the administrative function is an orientational one. He can assist policy-making committees by providing a psychological perspective to their deliberations and decisions. Especially in regard to promotion, marking, and reporting grades, the counselor can provide the counseling point of view as an additional dimension to the administrative process. Through fundamental skills of sensitive listening, acceptance, and understanding, the counselor can provide an appropriate psychological backdrop for the administrative policy-making decisions.

Relationships with Parents

Counseling parents in relation to student problems, helping them to better understand adolescent behavior, and orienting and interpreting the counseling program to them constitute three major counseling relationships with parents. Unique family dynamics often lie at the root of student problems. In the permissive, accepting, and understanding climate which the counselor creates, parents are offered an opportunity to explore their own feelings as they relate with their children. Their relationship with their children can be better understood when the counselor and parent(s) jointly explore family dynamics as they relate to the student's growth and adjustment.

SUMMARY

Although counseling is important in every approach to guidance, counseling comes very close to being synonymous with guidance in the counseling approach. The major tenet of this strategy of guidance is the importance and centrality of the guidance worker's creating a certain image in the school and then maintaining that image throughout all phases of his work. Directive, client-centered, and eclectic theoretical orientations to counseling have been the most widely used in school systems to date. The focus of the guidance program is psychological rather than educational. The counselor attempts to help the student with psychological problems, because it is assumed that overt problems are symptoms of some underlying psychological difficulty.

Once these psychological difficulties have been resolved through counseling, the student can function more adequately. Although some students are counseled on a referral basis from teachers, the majority of the counseling is done on a self-referral basis because the counseling approach holds that counseling has more meaning to the student and is more effective as a vehicle for helping him when he enters into a counseling relationship because he wants that type of help. Counseling is the most specialized of all the orientations to guidance.

REFERENCES

1. E. Beier, "The Problem of Anxiety in Client Centered Therapy," *Journal of Consulting Psychology*, 15 (1951), 359-67.

2. D. V. Bergman, "Counseling Method and Client Responses," *Journal of Consulting Psychology*, 15 (1951), 216-24.

3. R. H. Bixler and V. H. Bixler, "Test Interpretation in Vocational Counseling," *Educational and Psychological Measurement*, 6 (1946), 145-56.

4. A. V. Boy and G. J. Pine, *Client-Centered Counseling in the Secondary School*. Boston: Houghton Mifflin Co., 1963.

5. L. M. Brammer and E. L. Shostrum, *Therapeutic Psychology*. Englewood Cliffs, N. J.: Prentice-Hall, 1963.

6. J. H. Butler and J. Seeman, "Client-Centered Therapy and the Field of Guidance," *Education*, 70 (1950), 519-22.

7. R. H. Byrne, *The School Counselor*. Boston: Houghton Mifflin Co., 1963.

8. A. Combs, "Phenomenological Concepts in Non-Directive Therapy," *Journal of Consulting Psychology*, 12 (1948), 197-208.

9. P. E. Eiserer, "The Implications of Non-Directive Counseling for Classroom Teaching," *Growing Points in Educational Research*. Washington, D.C.: American Educational Research Assn., 1949.

10. V. E. Faw, "A Psychotherapeutic Method of Teaching Psychology," *American Psychologist*, 4 (1949), 104-9.

11. F. E. Fiedler, "A Comparison Between Therapeutic Relationships in Psycho-analytic, Non-Directive and Adlerian Therapy," *Journal of Consulting Psychology*, 14 (1950), 436-45.

12. C. Gerstenlauer, "Group Therapy with Institutionalized Male Juvenile Delinquents," *American Psychologist*, 5 (1950), 325.

13. L. Gross, "An Experimental Study of the Validity of the Non-Directive Method of Teaching," *Journal of Psychology*, 26 (1948), 243-348.

14. G. Haigh, "Defensive Behavior in Client Centered Therapy," *Journal of Consulting Psychology*, 13 (1959), 181-89.

15. M. L. Haimowitz, *An Investigation into Some Personality Changes*

Occurring in Individuals Undergoing Client-Centered Therapy. Unpublished Ph.D. Thesis, University of Chicago, 1945.

16. C. S. Hall and G. Lindzey, *Theories of Personality.* New York: John Wiley & Sons, 1957.

17. R. M. Hamlin and G. W. Albee, "Muench's Tests before and after Nondirective Therapy: A Control Group for His Subjects," *Journal of Consulting Psychology*, 12 (1948), 412–16.

18. S. A. Hamrin and D. Paulson, *Counseling Adolescents.* Chicago: Science Research Associates, 1950.

19. R. A. Harper, *Psychoanalysis and Psychotherapy: 36 Systems.* Englewood Cliffs, N. J.: Prentice-Hall, 1959.

20. A. E. Hoffman, "Reported Behavior Changes in Counseling," *Journal of Consulting Psychology*, 13 (1949), 190–95.

21. A. Z. Jonietz, *A Study of Changes in Perception to Psychotherapy.* Unpublished Ph.D. Dissertation, University of Chicago, 1948.

22. W. L. Kirtner and C. S. Desmond, "Success and Failure in Client-Centered Therapy as a Function of Client Personality Variables," *Journal of Consulting Psychology*, 22 (1958), 259–64.

23. A. L. Kodis and S. Lazersfield, "The Group as a Psychotherapeutic Factor in Counseling Work," *Nervous Child*, 4 (1945), 228–36.

24. D. Lebo, "The Present Status of Research on Nondirective Play Therapy," *Journal of Consulting Psychology*, 17 (1953), 177–83.

25. D. Lebo, "A Theoretical Framework for Nondirective Play Therapy: Concepts from Psychoanalysis and Learning Theory," *Journal of Consulting Psychology*, 22 (1958), 275–79.

26. S. Lipkin, "The Client Evaluates Nondirective Therapy," *Journal of Consulting Psychology*, 12 (1948), 137–46.

27. J. F. McGowan and L. D. Schmidt, *Counseling: Readings in Theory and Practice.* New York: Holt, Rinehart & Winston, 1962.

28. C. E. Moustakas and G. Makowsky, "Client-Centered Therapy with Parents," *Journal of Consulting Psychology*, 16 (1952), 338–42.

29. C. E. Moustakas and H. D. Schalock, "An Analysis of Therapist-Child Interaction in Play Therapy," *Child Development*, 26 (1955), 143–57.

30. O. H. Mowrer, *Psychotherapy: Research and Theory.* New York: Ronald Press, 1953.

31. G. A. Muench, *An Evaluation of Nondirective Psychotherapy.* Applied Psychological Monograph No. 13. Stanford University Press, 1947.

32. R. L. Munroe, *Schools of Psychoanalytic Thought.* New York: Holt, Rinehart & Winston, 1955.

33. C. H. Patterson, *Theories of Counseling.* New York: Harper & Row, 1966.

34. E. H. Porter, *An Introduction to Therapeutic Counseling.* Boston: Houghton Mifflin Co., 1950.

35. V. C. Raimy, *The Self Concept as a Factor in Counseling and Personality Organization*. Unpublished Ph.D. Dissertation, Ohio State University, 1938.

36. N. J. Raskin, "The Development of Nondirective Therapy," *Journal of Consulting Psychology*, 12 (1948), 92-110.

37. C. R. Rogers, "The Attitude and Orientation of the Counselor in Client-Centered Therapy," *Journal of Consulting Psychology*, 13 (1949), 82-94.

38. C. R. Rogers, *Client-Centered Therapy*. Boston: Houghton Mifflin Co., 1951.

39. C. R. Rogers, *Counseling and Psychotherapy*. Boston: Houghton Mifflin Co., 1942.

40. C. R. Rogers, *On Becoming a Person*. Boston: Houghton Mifflin Co., 1961.

41. C. R. Rogers, "Perceptual Reorganization in Client-Centered Therapy," in R. E. Blake and G. V. Ramsey, *Perception: An Approach to Personality*. New York: Ronald Press, 1951.

42. C. R. Rogers, "A Process Conception of Psychotherapy," *The American Psychologist*, 13 (1958), 142-49.

43. C. R. Rogers, "Significant Aspects of Client-Centered Therapy," *American Psychologist*, 1 (1946), 415-22.

44. C. R. Rogers, "Some Observations on the Organization of Personality" *American Psychologist*, 2 (1947), 358-68.

45. C. R. Rogers and R. F. Dyamond, *Psychotherapy and Personality Change*. University of Chicago Press, 1954.

46. J. Seeman, "A Study of Nondirective Therapy," *Journal of Consulting Psychology*, 13 (1949), 157-62.

47. E. T. Sheerer, "An Analysis of the Relationship between Acceptance of and Respect for Self and Acceptance of and Respect for Others in Ten Counseling Cases," *Journal of Consulting Psychology*, 13 (1949), 169-75;

48. M. B. Smith, "The Phenomenological Approach in Personality Theory: Some Critical Remarks," *Journal of Abnormal and Social Psychology*, 45 (1950), 516-22.

49. W. U. Snyder, "The Present Status of Psychotherapeutic Counseling," *Psychological Bulletin*, 43 (1947), 338-59.

50. B. Steffire, *Theories of Counseling*. New York: McGraw-Hill, 1965.

51. H. H. Strupp, "An Objective Comparison of Rogerian and Psychoanalytic Techniques," *Journal of Consulting Psychology*, 19 (1955), 1-7.

52. H. H. Strupp, "The Performance of Psychoanalytic and Client Centered Therapists in an Initial Interview," *Journal of Consulting Psychology*, 22 (1958), 265-78.

53. W. N. Thetford, *The Measurement of Physiological Responses to Frustration before and after Nondirective Therapy*. Unpublished Ph.D. Dissertation, University of Chicago, 1949.

54. J. Warters, *High School Personnel Work Today*. New York: McGraw-Hill, 1946.

55. E. G. Williamson, *Counseling Adolescents*. New York: McGraw-Hill, 1950.

56. E. G. Williamson, "The Counselor as a Technique," *Personnel and Guidance Journal*, 41 (1962), 108-11.

57. C. G. Wrenn, "Counselor Orientation: Theoretical and Situational," *Journal of Counseling Psychology*, 7 (1960), 40-45.

chapter 5

The Problem-Centered/Adjustment
Approach to Guidance

Inadequate adjustments have undoubtedly been made as long as mankind has existed. Up to the present century the prevailing attitude toward adjustive difficulties has been a moralistic one. The essence of such an attitude is that the maladjusted person is "bad." The origin of this popular opinion is not hard to find. First, a person with adjustive difficulties is often a nuisance to his family and friends, as well as no comfort to himself. He is hard to get along with. Second, his behavior does not seem reasonable, and most people cannot understand why he acts as he does, often against his own best interests. His conduct is irrational and lacking in common sense . . . . Lecturing, punishment, and even well-meaning advice have proved to be notably ineffective methods for dealing with adjustment problems. A worrier is not cured by being told he should not worry. A "shiftless" person is aided very little by preaching or threats. Such attempts make matters worse by convincing the maladjusted one of his own weakness and worthlessness. He then has an additional social thwarting to bear. (50, pp. 7-8)

Although the problem-centered approach and the life adjustment approach have been described as two separate orientations to gudiance (5, Chap. 3), the basic differences between them are chiefly a matter of emphasis. Thus, for purposes of presentation, these two closely related orientations will be combined into one approach—the problem-centered/adjustment approach. The problem-centered/adjustment approach differs from other orientations to guidance in that while other orientations emphasize providing help of some kind to all students, this view focuses its attention only upon those students who have problems—i.e., those who are maladjusted. The guidance worker helps the student with individual problems as they arise and attempts to alleviate or solve them. Historically, the problem-centered/adjustment view has evolved from two main streams of thought—the mental health movement and life adjustment education.

There are both personal and social dimensions to mental health. Personal mental health refers to the positive psychological characteristics of the individual such as (a) pursuing reasonable and purposeful objectives, (b) making fruitful use of talents and abilities, (c) having a sense of self-respect and self-reliance, (d) knowing that he is liked, loved, and wanted, (e) feeling that he belongs and is respected, (f) learning to accept, respect and love others, (g) distinguishing between feeling and fact, (h) acting realistically and rationally, (i) tolerating tension, (j) postponing gratification when necessary, (k) substituting more socially acceptable gratifications for those which are less socially acceptable, and (l) achieving self-realization in an accepted role (8, 55).

Good mental health from a social perspective, i.e., from society's point of view, includes such qualities as (a) being happy and productive, (b) making a useful contribution to fellow human beings, and (c) contributing to the society (56, p. 825). Jahoda refers to active adjustment to, rather than passive acceptance of or inability to cope with a changing environment (26). The personal and social dimensions of good mental health fuse, for society cannot rise above the level of the individuals of which it is composed.

Life adjustment education, the second major historical body of thought behind the problem-centered/adjustment view of guidance, is closely related to the mental health movement. Life adjustment education has been defined as that education "which better equips all American youth to live democratically with satisfaction to themselves and profit to society as home members, workers, and citizens" (45, p. 1). It was within the context of secondary education as a means of facilitating better adjustment that problem-centered/adjustment guidance evolved.

Because this orientation to guidance helps the student primarily during times of stress, it has often been called "crisis guidance." The focus tends to fall not upon students as *unique individuals*, but rather upon students as members of some *problem group*. The point of reference is an external aspect of society such as the classroom, the educational institution, the community, or the nation. It is the demands of the environment that determine the problems of individuals in the society (e.g., students), and thus many of the problems of adjustment are subject to societal needs and demands. Even current fads (of which there are many in education) may determine who will be categorized as members of a problem group and who will then receive guidance help.

The problem-centered/adjustment approach to guidance is external not only in its primary focus upon the needs and demands of the society, but also in its insistence on helping the individual to fit into the group. The student has problems and/or is maladjusted when he deviates significantly from the group norm. Identification of problem students is typically followed by diagnosis and treatment aimed at helping to solve or alleviate problems.

There is a tendency to perceive these problems from an institutional or societal point of view in that individual maladjustments are bothersome to the smooth functioning of the educational institution and the general society. On the other hand, problems of maladjustment have also been viewed from the personal dimension of improving adjustment or mental health by the removal of personal or institutional obstructions that may stand in the way of ongoing healthy personal development.

Functionally, the problem-centered/adjustment view places its stress on the need for objective data, on the usefulness of sociocomparative data, on the importance of social consequences, on the need for individual guidance at various critical problem-points, and on the use of professional and specialized services at such points. It has been noted that while this strategy of guidance has received less delineation and theoretical support in the guidance literature than any other views, its critical practitioners form perhaps the largest group of guidance workers today (5, p. 48).

THEORETICAL BASIS

The theoretical basis for the problem-centered/adjustment approach to guidance consists of three relatively distinct bodies of theory and research, none which fall within the theoretical boundaries of guidance-personnel work, per se. These are: (*a*) mental hygiene and mental health, (*b*) the psychology of adjustment, and (*c*) the area of developmental psychology dealing with adolescence and adolescent problems.

Mental Health Theory

Lambert describes the general theory and practices of mental health as they relate to the school setting (32). Prevention and remediation are the two focuses of the school's mental health program of which guidance is a part.

One of the keys to good mental health is the ability to cope with stress in a crisis. The essence of helping people within the context of mental health is first to recognize patterns of effective and ineffective coping behavior, second, to identify students that are using poor coping mechanisms, and, lastly, to interact with these students in an effort to influence them to adopt more effective patterns. Direct intervention by working with students and indirect intervention through in-service education for teachers, consultation, and collaboration with other nonguidance school personnel represent the two global approaches for improving mental health in the school setting.

The Psychology of Adjustment

Although there is no generally acceptable definition of good adjustment, a number of writers have described aspects of adjustment. No one formulation is completely adequate. Several formulations must be considered simultaneously if a complete understanding of the concept is to be achieved. In general, adjustment is conceived as a vague state of well-being and happiness (30, p. 7). As the individual reacts with his changing cultural milieu, however, he must constantly seek a balance between internal demands—e.g., needs, motives, and drives—and the fluctuating demands of the environment—e.g., socialization, developmental tasks, and patterning. Thus, another view of adjustment focuses upon a process of adaptive reactions which have certain elements of consistency that lend to stability of behavior (24, 36). A third view of adjustment emphasizes the conformity of individual behavior to societal expectations. Adjustment, therefore, involves compromise between an individual's drive for self-realization and the conforming demands of society, without subordinating the unique aspects of individuality to the point where over-conformity becomes an escape from adjustment.

Kaplan has surveyed various writers' criteria of conformity (1, 27, 51) and has selected the following five criteria which most writers would agree constitute the basic core of adjustment (30, pp. 9-11): (*a*) a unifying outlook on life, (*b*) a realistic self-perception, (*c*) emotional maturity, (*d*) social sensitivity, and (*e*) a dynamic equilibrium. The individual must adjust whenever his needs or drives

TABLE 5-1*
Adjustment to Stress

Reaction	Description
1. Positive coping behavior	Healthy problem-solving
2. Aggressive reactions	
Attack	Direct attempt to overcome a frustration.
Displacement	Directing an emotion toward something other than the frustration producing it.
Projection	Ascribing to others our own unworthy feeling.
Identification	Reacting as if the experiences of another were our own, "feeling as if" we were he.
3. Withdrawal reactions	
Simple withdrawal	Running away from a problem or threat.
Denial of reality	Pretending things are not what they really are.
Fantasy	Daydreaming.
Repression	Refusing to recognize one's true feelings, shutting them out of consciousness.
Regression	Emotionally retreating to an earlier time of life when the frustration did not exist.
4. Compromise reactions	
Compensation	Achieving satisfaction in one area to atone for frustration in another.
Sublimation	Escaping threatening desires by converting them into socially approved ones.
Rationalization	Justifying a preferred course of action on grounds other than the true reason for it.
5. Symptoms of neuroses	Anxiety Guilt feelings
	Phobias Feelings of inadequacy
	Tenseness Egocentricity
	Poor insight Social maladjustment
	Chronic fatigue Chronic unhappiness
	Somatic complaints

*Adapted from 15, 17, 30, 50, 52, 54.

change or when the environmental demands change. At such times he experiences an emotional state with varying degrees of stress and must adjust both to the psychological condition of stress and to the demand made by the environment. Table 5-1 shows some healthy and unhealthy reactions to stress. Symptoms of serious maladjusted behavior include reality distortions (e.g., illusions and hallucinations), mental aberrations (e.g., delusions, obsessions, paranoid ideas), emotional distortions (e.g., depression, phobias, manic-depression), motor reactions (e.g., compulsive acts such as pyromania, kleptomania, homocidal mania), and personality disorganization (e.g. depersonalization, schizophrenia, psychosis).

Some behavioral symptoms of maladjustment, however, are less serious and so widespread that many people exhibit one or more of them from time to time during periods of frustration or stress. These symptoms include: belligerence, excessive moodiness, exaggerated worry, suspiciousness, mistrust, selfishness, dependency, poor emotional control, daydreaming, and hypochondria.

Problems of Adolescence

A great deal of literature and research in developmental psychology is available in the area of the general problems of the adolescent period (3, 18, 20, 21, 22, 25, 28, 29) and the specific expressed problems of adolescence (11, 20, 41). Problems are an outward manifestion, i.e., symptoms, of some kind of maladjustment in the individual's personality. The problems of adolescence can be classified as either *situational* in that they are idiosyncratic to the individual and the particular setting to which he is having adjustment difficulties, or *developmental* and common to many individuals in a given developmental stage of life. Most of the problems requiring the help of a guidance counselor are not situational, but developmental (38, pp. 97-98).

From a psychological point of view, a problem ordinarily indicates a barrier to the satisfaction of a drive or need. These barriers include (*a*) barriers to the satisfaction of needs, (*b*) inadequate social and emotional learning, (*c*) conflicts, (*d*) anxiety, and (*e*) inadequate escapes and defenses from anxiety (14, 16). The needs and drives of the individual have been described from many points of view by various personality theorists and developmental psychologists, and include, for example:

1. One primary motive: hedonism (seeking pleasure).
2. Two types of motives: conscious and unconscious.
3. Multiplicity of motives: instincts.
4. Hierarchy of motives: physiological, safety, belongingness, etc.

Empirical studies of students' problems have found that the most frequent problems of junior high school and senior high school students include weight, posture, complexion, study, self-expression, grades, unpopularity, conversation, friendships, dating, temper, worry, daydreams, regrets, and vocational choice (2, 20, 29, 38, 44). Of educational, vocational, and emotional problems, the emotional problems are usually the most intense (4). Specific problems often overlap the various conventional problem categories, and students more often have several problems rather than a single problem (41). Studies of student problems typically classify them into general categories such as educational, vocational, financial, social-emotional-personal, family and physical. Bordin on the other hand, has classified problems into the following five diagnostic categories in order to help the counselor to understand the significance of the individual's behavior and to serve as a basis for choice of treatment (9):

1. *Dependence*: the individual is passive and has not assumed the initiative in solving his own problems.
2. *Lack of information*: the individual accepts the responsibility for making decisions, takes initiative, but needs some additional information.
3. *Self-conflict*: the individual experiences conflict between several roles, or between a self-concept and his inability to achieve it.
4. *Choice anxiety:* the individual must make a choice between two or more unpleasant alternatives.
5. *No problem*: the individual seeks to have a check-up on his present personal status.

The meaning of the words "problem," "adjustment," and "mental health" vary according to the context in which they are used. There is a *subjective dimension* of a problem which, psychologically speaking, refers to an individual who (*a*) has needs that are blocked, and (*b*) recognizes the situation for what it is. It has been found, for example, that many of the problems of children and adolescents result from their perception of a disturbing environment. The individual therefore may have a problem because of the pressure exerted by the environment—i.e., the general culture or the subculture of which he is a part.

An *objective dimension* of problems, on the other hand, is evident if one choses to use the culture as the point of reference rather than the individual and his perception. Thus, the culture requires certain modes of behavior. The range of accepted behavior varies greatly from culture to culture and also varies in regard to what is considered appropriate behavior within the various aspects of social, vocational, emotional, moral, and ethical behavior. Although mental health theory recognizes the possibility of both an objective and a subjective focus, the problem-centered/adjustment approach to guidance has tended to emphasize the objective dimension and has used some aspect of the society as the point of reference in determining the nature and severity of problems and maladjustment.

Underlying Assumptions

One of the most crucial assumptions of the problem-centered/adjustment approach to guidance is that most students are able to function within the normal or adjusted range of tolerable behavior in the society without any long-term continuing intervention by guidance personnel. It is further assumed that the guidance process should emphasize remediation for those few students who need some assistance with adjustment problems at crisis points in their lives. Thus, only a minority of the student body need guidance and those individuals who do require some assistance need help only in times of crisis and stress.

Another closely related assumption is that most referred problems will be solved if they are properly diagnosed and if appropriate procedures are adopted on the basis of professional recommendations. Problems and maladjustment are detected through observation, testing, and the use of diagnostic devices.

Professional help by a guidance specialist is typically favored over the more general kind of assistance available through teachers. Once the help has been given at various problem-points of adjustment it is assumed that the student can proceed on his own thereafter, at least until another problem is encountered or another maladjustment is sensed by either the student himself or by some member of the school staff.

SOME CONTEXTS FOR GUIDANCE

The problem-centered/adjustment view of guidance typically focuses on one or a cluster of problem groups of students without any pretense of helping with total growth and development of the individual. The guidance program then functions within the context of helping students who have the particular kind of problem(s) which constitute the current focus of the program. As noted above, the emphasis of the program typically changes as the demands and concerns of the society fluctuate. Some contemporary and recent problem areas are briefly discussed below.

The Dropout

Sofokidis and Sullivan summarize the characteristics of dropouts as follows (56, pp. xvii–xix):

> Studies of dropouts have shown a fairly consistent pattern. Most dropouts are "underachievers," have a record of failure in regular school work, and are usually behind grade level in reading ability. Many have been retained in grade at least once in elementary school and, at the time of dropping out, are a year or two behind their age level in class placement. Irregular attendance and frequent tardiness are characteristic of the potential dropout. Many pupils have experienced frequent changes of schools. Most show a marked disinterest in school and are failing in one or more subjects at the time they drop out. Most potential dropouts do not participate in out-of-class activities such as athletics, dramatics, or special interest clubs which make school more interesting for their successful classmates. Their activities are centered outside the school. Many of the male dropouts are car owners who spend their leisure time away from their home, school, and even

the local community. A sizeable proportion of dropouts have been discipline problems at one time or another, although this may not have resulted in suspension from school. Some have an active record of delinquency. Many have had difficulty with community agencies and the law.

Dropouts are usually from low-income groups, generally from trade or labor occupations. The education of parents is usually below the eighth grade level. Many dropouts have unhappy home and family situations. They are unable to compete successfully with their brothers and sisters. Their parents may have a negative or even antagonistic attitude toward the school and frequently attach no importance to high school graduation for their children. Most dropouts have some special characteristics or situations which separate them from their successful classmates, such as: inability to afford the normal expenditures for their age and grade level; marked difference in physique, personality development, dress, social class, and interests. Many have physical or emotional handicaps which retard their school performance or acceptance by their peers.

Usually potential dropouts are purposeless and have no clearly defined goals for achievement. Not knowing what they want, they fail to see the value of school in their individual futures and are willing to settle for short-range satisfactions. More boys than girls are school dropouts. The dropout ratio of Negro youths is double that of the comparable white school-age population. Per cent studies have raised questions as to the long-held beliefs concerning dropouts. For example, the Maryland dropout survey of 1960-61 provided information to help explode these myths:

1. that dropouts are usually delinquents. Actually, the large majority of dropouts, 79 per cent of the group studied, had not been considered serious behavior problems by their counselors or principals and 76 per cent had never been suspended from school.
2. that dropouts are usually homeless, or the product of broken homes. Actually, 91 per cent of the pupils studied lived with their parents (or with parent and step-parent) and 72 per cent were with both parents living together.
3. that lack of intelligence is a dominant cause of school dropout. Actually, approximately half (49.8 per cent) of the dropouts studied had average or above average intelligence.

The above writers also summarize the reasons for dropout (56, pp. xvi–xvii):

Surveys and observations of school officials over the years show that most students say they leave school because they "just aren't interested." This may mean that a student is discouraged over his progress, that he dislikes a certain subject or teacher, or that he sees no value in what he is studying. It may mean that he feels excluded from the social life of the school. Sometimes teenagers drop out to help with the care of the family or to add to the family income. Boys, especially, suppose they will improve their chance as wage earners by starting young. The foregoing observations have been substantiated by findings of the summer 1963 dropout campaign (identified in more detail below). Composite reasons for dropout, according to school officials and individual dropouts in the communities which participated in the 1963 campaign, were predominantly in these areas:

1. Disinterest in school, compounded from such matters as discouragement because of failing grades; other adverse school experience, including rejection by fellow students or the school staff; and dissatisfaction with the school program, particularly because of the absence of specific vocational training desired by the student.

2. Home responsibilities, including a real need to work to help support the family or to stay at home and care for younger brothers and sisters or ailing parents. In a low economic area in one community, for example, a dropout peak was reached in the age group too old to qualify for further welfare assistance.

3. Unfavorable parental attitude, including lack of feeling for the importance of school, general lack of concern for the child, inability to cope with or influence child's behavior, desire for financial assistance from the child or to train child in father's business, and support of child's desire to leave school and be "independent." Parents of most dropouts were dropouts themselves. (However, the Summer 1963 Dropout Campaign indicated that, contrary to popular belief, many parents of potential or actual dropouts are in favor of their children remaining in, or returning to school.)

4. Peer influence, social pressure, sometimes translated by the student into economic pressure—the compulsion to earn money in order to buy cars, to dress as well as classmates, have equivalent spending money, and the like. In some cases, peer influence had resulted in general delinquent behavior and trouble with school authorities.

5. Unhappy home situations coupled with the desire to be independent of parental ties led many youngsters to take jobs, enter the military service, or get married rather than continue to live at home and attend school.

Lichter *et al.* (37) describe the psychological characteristics of intellectually capable dropouts and potential dropouts, problems and their treatment, guides for teachers and counselors, and case illustrations. Counseling and casework are suggested, including a diagnostic evaluation which identifies the problem, provides an understanding of the dynamics involved, and also suggests a treatment method.

The problem-centered/adjustment approach to guidance may focus upon the dropout for any one of a variety of reasons. For example, the dropout creates severe unemployment problems for our society. While approximately one out of every fifty college graduates is unemployed, one out of every ten workers who failed to finish elementary school is unemployed. Among male dropouts, the rate of unemployment is three times higher than among high school graduates, and the unemployment rate of teenage Negro youth is double that of white youth. This group therefore represents a loss of human resources and a general economic liability in terms of unemployment and welfare payments. The problem is further aggravated because:

Less than half of U.S. employers will even consider hiring a high school dropout. Furthermore, the dropout, if hired, is the first fired, is the lowest paid, and has the least chance for advancement. Roughly 18 per cent of our unskilled workers are now unemployed. This is about double the rate for semiskilled workers. Eighty per cent of those now unemployed did not finish high school. (12, p. 165)

The dropout may also be considered a problem because of humanitarian reasons and because of the personal loss to the dropout himself in terms of the full realization of his potential. Although the estimated rates of retention in high school have increased steadily in recent years, approximately one third of the students graduating from elementary school still fail to complete high school. In view of the continuously diminishing place in the world of work for the unskilled, the opportunity for self-development of this group constitutes a major source of concern for education in general and guidance in particular (47, 48).

Retention rates in public and nonpublic high schools from 1950 to 1962 have been shown as follows (59):

Year	Retention per 1,000 Students Previously Entering Grade Five
1950	505
1955	559
1960	621
1962	636

The Culturally Deprived

The culturally deprived or the disadvantaged, as they commonly are called, constitute another group of students upon which problem-centered/adjustment guidance may choose to focus. The roots of cultural deprivation as an educational problem can be traced back to homes which have not transmitted the cultural patterns necessary for the types of learning required by schools and the larger society. Poverty, large family size, broken homes, minimal level of education in parents, discrimination, slum conditions, and recent immigration to the United States represent a few of the many possible factors that contribute to the problem. The culturally deprived do not lack for culture: they have a culture. This culture, however, is so different from the dominant culture in our country that children and adolescents from these kinds of backgrounds are not adequately prepared to learn. They participate minimally in an educational system for which they are neither psychologically nor intellectually ready. Compared below are the general goals of education and the characteristics of the culturally disadvantaged revealed by the general literature and research (13, 46):

General Goals of Education	Research Findings Concerning the Disadvantaged
High level of aspiration	Low level of aspiration
High level of task orientation	Low level of task orientation
Adequate utilization of abstract symbols	Poor utilization of abstract symbols
High ability in language communication	Low ability in language communication
High intellectual stimulation	"Low-keyed" intellectual stimulation
High achievement	Generally underachievement
Good relationships with teachers	Suspicion of teachers
Quick mental style	Slow mental style
Flexible thinking	Inflexible one-track thinking
High reading ability	Limited reading ability
Efficient test-taking skills	Inefficient test-taking skills
Good grasp of school "know-how"	Lack of school "know-how"

A number of special programs have been implemented within a wide range of theoretical frameworks. Counseling and guidance has played an important role in many of these efforts. Some of the most notable educational efforts to combat cultural deprivation include the Higher Horizons Project (33), Project Head Start (7), The Great Cities Grey Areas Project (39), and the Doolittle Project (10). From the standpoint of guidance strategy, the above projects and other attempts have utilized counseling, group guidance, testing, educational and occupational information, case conferences, and parent conferences.

The Handicapped

Traditionally, the definition of handicapped children has included groups with marked visual impairments (blind and partially seeing), hearing impairments (deaf and hard of hearing), motor impairments (polio, cerebral palsy, etc.), intellectual subnormality (educable and trainable mentally handicapped), speech and communication disorders (including aphasia and dyslexia), emotional and social problems, and combinations of these difficulties generally included under the caption "multiple handicaps."

It has been estimated that approximately 10 to 15 per cent of the school population is so afflicted, and requires special educational services. The percentage of handicapped children in a particular geographic area is dependent upon many factors, including the diagnostic criteria and the socioeconomic level of the community (31, 42). The following figures provide a general working estimate of the number of children per thousand who are sufficiently handicapped to warrant special services (31):

	No. per 1,000
Mentally retarded	
Educable	15 to 20
Trainable	2 to 4
Emotionally and socially handicapped	20 to 30
Speech handicapped	20 to 40
Motorically handicapped (crippled)	5 to 10
Visually handicapped	
Blind	2 to 3
Partially seeing	4 to 6
Hearing handicapped	
Deaf	1 to 2
Hard of hearing	5 to 10
Others (learning disabilities, health problems, etc.)	20 to 30
Total out of 1,000	94 to 155 (10% to 15% of school population)

It has also been estimated that only approximately one fourth to one third of these handicapped children are now receiving special services (58).

The primary emphasis in handling the problems of handicapped students has been in making curricular adaptations to fit their special needs, and these curricular changes together with teaching have occurred largely within the context of special education. Counseling and guidance has, in general, played only a minor role in the education of the handicapped. Of all the types of handicapped, the mentally retarded have received the most attention from guidance. Leland and Smith, for example, describe the theory and practice of play therapy with mentally subnormal children (34). Blodgett suggests that parents of handicapped students should be counseled about the acceptance of the disability, attitudes and feelings, and making short and long-term plans (6). Willey and Waite describe counseling of the parents of handicapped students in terms of accepting the disability, learning about the special needs of the student, and planning for his needs (59). Relatively little progress appears to have been made in modifying general guidance practices to meet the needs of handicapped students. Research, prevention, residential care, special education, vocational rehabilitation, social services, parent counseling, diagnostic and clinical services have been utilized. As in the case of the dropout and the culturally deprived, the problem of the handicapped has a humanitarian and an economic dimension. The Committee on Mental Retardation of the U.S. Office of Education, for example, describes the following economic concerns of mental retardation (49, p. 6).

> The cost in human suffering cannot be estimated but it is believed that mental retardation is extremely costly to the nation's economy. Even the relatively small number of the more severely retarded currently confined in institutions cost relatives and communities over $300 million annually. A total of over $280 million in Federal funds has been obligated to go toward special education, welfare, health, rehabilitation and other benefits and services, and over $120 million in income maintenance. State and private expenditures are not included. It is impossible to estimate the indirect hidden costs resulting from the absence of earning capacity and inability to contribute to the nation's economy. There is hope of reducing many of these costs over the next decade by the investments to be made in prevention and alleviation of the condition.

The Gifted

Initially it may appear difficult to see how the gifted can be a problem and therefore require a special focus for problem-centered/adjustment guidance. There are several contexts in which the gifted may be considered a problem group. If one takes a "guidance and manpower" point of view, the gifted constitute a prime source of manpower as a national resource. As early as 1817 Thomas Jefferson proposed a plan for selecting promising boys and providing them with further education at public expense (23). Through the years there have been exhortations from many individuals and interested groups for identifying and developing this "national resource" within a guidance context (40, 53). Not until the National Defense Education Act of 1958, however, was there any nation-wide action taken. The major intention of the total Act is to provide highly trained manpower to meet the nation's needs. Title V of the NDEA Act deals specifically with guidance and specifies that in order to participate in the program—i.e., receive federal funds—a state must submit a plan which sets forth (a) "a program of testing secondary students to identify those with outstanding aptitudes and ability . . ." and (b) "a program of guidance and counseling in its public secondary schools to advise students of courses of study best suited for them and to encourage outstanding students to complete high school, take the courses needed for admission to institutions of higher education, and to enter such institutions . . ." (43). In this context then, the gifted represent a unique problem of identification, education, and guidance.

The gifted are also a problem in that while they face the same general developmental problems as other youth, they often cope with these problems in unique ways (19). The gifted also have unique behavior resulting in situational problems. Some problems of the gifted are (49):

1. Reaction to society's sanctions against divergent behavior.
2. Fear of alienating friends in maintaining creativity.
3. Lack of well-roundedness.
4. Divergence from sex norms.
5. Preference for learning on their own.
6. Undertaking dangerous tasks.
7. Possession of different values.
8. Inability to stop working.
9. Searching for their own uniqueness.
10. Psychological estrangement.
11. Unique problems resulting from repressed creativity.

PHILOSOPHY AND GOALS

The problem-centered/adjustment orientation to guidance does not espouse any particular philosophy of education. Barry and Wolf note that there is a philosophically implicit view of an essentially static and present-oriented society (5). Individuals are required to adjust first to their class group and then to the larger community. Adjustment is determined as "good" or "bad" to the extent that the individual's behavior conforms or deviates from group norms. Any educational program which stresses conformity, normal behavior, and normal achievement can utilize this approach to guidance. Problem-centered/adjustment guidance may be the only approach feasible in an overcrowded and understaffed educational program.

The general goal of guidance is to assist the individual to solve his problems of adjustment so that he will be more satisfied and successful and in order that the society may run more smoothly. The society is important because it constitutes the backdrop for understanding the individual. There is an implicit notion, however, that the society is more important than the individual.

The problem-centered/adjustment approach to guidance has been popular in part because of the flexibility of emphasis on the particular type(s) of problems decided upon by the program, in part because of the economy factor of this approach, and in part because it seems to make sense to many administrators, teachers, and counselors.

Since this approach emphasizes adjustment, conformity, and the amelioration of problems, the problem-centered/adjustment view is philosophically antithetical to views that attempt to promote self-understanding, self-development, and self-actualization. Although the general goal of guidance is to help students solve their problems and become generally more well adjusted, there is a tendency for programs to operate at a functional level on isolated types of problems or maladjustments.

As noted above, identifying problem students and providing help for them represents the basic strategy of the problem-centered/adjustment approach. Students with problems are identified by teachers and administrators through daily interaction and referred to the guidance counselor for help. Some students with problems come to guidance on the basis of self-referral. There are no unique patterns of organizing and implementing guidance except that a diagnostic testing program is often an important phase of guidance, and counseling is typically used as the means for helping the student to solve his problems and bring about more adequate adjustment.

SUMMARY

The problem-centered/adjustment approach to guidance is characterized by a largely remedial focus. Life adjustment education, the psychology of adjustment, and the mental health movement constitute the major streams of thought which have contributed to the theoretical basis for this approach. Although the focus may be on problems or adjustment and although some authors have distinguished between problem-centered guidance and adjustment guidance, it would appear that problem-centeredness and adjustment-centeredness more accurately represent subapproaches within the broader framework of a general remedial orientation to the guidance process.

The dropout, the gifted, the culturally deprived, the handicapped, and the college bound represent a few of the more common focuses for the problem-centered/adjustment approach with its emphasis upon conformity and normal behavior. The guidance worker is, in effect, either a therapeutic agent (problem-centered) or a socialization agent (adjustment). The paradox is that while this approach to guidance historically has been the most commonly employed one, it also has received the most criticism. For many school systems with limited staff and limited facilities, however, this approach combines the availability of professional guidance help with the pragmatic realities of limited resources for the guidance program.

All guidance programs focus on problems. All approaches to guidance are concerned with the student's adjustment. All types of guidance activities have a remedial component. The major shortcoming of the problem-centered/adjustment approach, however, is its lack of emphasis on prevention of problems and its lack of emphasis on fostering positive growth.

REFERENCES

1. G. W. Allport, "Personality: Normal and Abnormal," *Personality and Social Encounter.* Boston: Beacon Press, 1960.

2. G. W. Allport and J. M. Gillespie, *Youth's Outlook for the Future.* New York: Random House, 1955.

3. D. P. Ausubel, *Theory and Problems of Child Development.* New York: Grune and Stratton, 1958.

4. H. W. Bailey *et al.*, "Counseling and the Use of Tests in the Student Personnel Bureau of the University of Illinois," *Educational and Psychological Measurement,* 6 (1946), 37-60.

5. R. Barry and B. Wolf, *Modern Issues in Guidance-Personnel Work.* New York: Teachers College Press, Columbia University, 1957.

6. H. E. Blodgett, "Helping Parents in the Community Setting," *The Thirty-Third Spring Conference of the Woods Schools.* Minneapolis: May 2-3, 1958.

7. B. S. Bloom *et al.*, *Compensatory Education for Cultural Deprivation.* New York: Holt, Rinehart & Winston, 1965.

8. P. Blos, "Aspects of Mental Health in Teaching and Learning," *Mental Hygiene,* 37 (1953), 555-69.

9. E. S. Bordin, "Diagnosis in Counseling and Psychotherapy," *Educational and Psychological Measurement,* 6 (1946), 169-84.

10. A. Y. Boswell, "Some Special Projects of the Chicago Board of Education," in U.S. Office of Education, *Programs for the Educationally Disadvantaged.* Washington, D.C.: U.S. Government Printing Office, 1963.

11. J. R. Brough, "The Junior High Schooler: His Concerns and Sources of Help," *The School Counselor,* 13 (1965), 71-76.

12. W. Buckingham, "The Impending Educational Revolution," in L. H. Evans and G. E. Arnstein, eds. *Automation and the Challenge to Education.* Washington, D.C.: National Education Association, 1962.

13. J. B. Conant, *Slums and Suburbs.* New York: McGraw-Hill, 1961.

14. J. G. Darley and C. T. Williams, "Clinical Records of Individual Student Problems," in A. H. Brayfield, ed., *Readings in Modern Methods of Counseling.* New York: Appleton-Century-Crofts, 1950.

15. K. D'Evelyn, *Meeting Children's Emotional Needs.* Englewood Cliffs, N.J.: Prentice-Hall, 1957.

16. J. Dollard and N. E. Miller, *Personality and Psychotherapy*. New York: McGraw-Hill, 1950.

17. E. Z. Friedenberg, *The Vanishing Adolescent*. Boston: Beacon Press, 1959.

18. F. L. Goodenough and L. E. Tyler, *Developmental Psychology*. New York: Appleton-Century-Crofts, 1959.

19. J. C. Gowan and G. D. Demos, *The Education and Guidance of the Ablest*. Springfield, Ill.: Charles C. Thomas, 1964.

20. J. K. Hagburg, *Geographic Location and Perceived Problem Areas of North Dakota High School Students*. Unpublished Master's Degree Project, University of North Dakota, 1965.

21. R. J. Havighurst, *Human Development and Education*. New York: Longmans, Green and Co., 1953.

22. R. J. Havighurst, "Research on the Developmental Task Concept," *School Review,* 64 (1956), 215-23.

23. R. J. Honeywell, *The Educational Work of Thomas Jefferson*. Cambridge: Harvard University Press, 1931.

24. J. McV. Hunt, "Experience and the Development of Motivation: Some Interpretations, *Child Development,* 31 (1960), 489-504.

25. E. B. Hurlock, *Developmental Psychology*. New York: McGraw-Hill, 1959.

26. M. Jahoda, *Current Concepts of Positive Mental Health*. New York: Basic Books, 1958.

27. M. Jahoda, "Toward a Social Psychology of Mental Health," in A. M. Rose, ed. *Mental Health and Mental Disorder*. New York: W. W. Norton & Company, 1955.

28. A. T. Jersild, *The Psychology of Adolescence*. New York: The Macmillan Co., 1957.

29. E. W. Johnson, *How to Live through Junior High School*. New York: J. B. Lippincott Co., 1959.

30. L. Kaplan, *Foundations of Human Behavior*. New York: Harper & Row, 1965.

31. S. Kirk, "Educating the Handicapped," *White House Conference on Education*. Washington, D.C.: U.S. Government Printing Office, 1965.

32. N. M. Lambert, *The Protection and Promotion of Mental Health in School*. Bethesda, Md.: National Institutes of Mental Health, U.S. Dept. of Health, Education, and Welfare, 1965.

33. J. Landers, "The Higher Horizons Program in New York City," in U.S. Office of Education, *Programs for the Educationally Disadvantaged*. Washington, D.C.: U.S. Government Printing Office, 1963.

34. H. Leland and D. E. Smith, *Play Therapy with Mentally Subnormal Children*. New York: Grune and Stratton, 1965.

35. E. C. Lindeman, *Mental Hygiene and the Moral Crisis of our Time*. New York: Hogg Foundation, 1952.

36. E. Lindemann, "Mental Health—Fundamental to a Dynamic Epidemiology of Health," in I. Gladston, ed. *The Epidemiology of Health*. New York Academy of Medicine, 1953.

37. S. O. Lichter *et al.*, *The Drop-outs*. Glencoe, N. Y.: Free Press of Glencoe, 1962.

38. F. McKinney, *Counseling for Personal Adjustment*. Boston: Houghton Mifflin Co., 1958.

39. C. Marburgher, "Working Toward More Effective Education: A Report on the Detroit Great Cities Project—after One Year," in U.S. Office of Education, *Programs for the Educationally Disadvantaged*. Washington, D.C.: U.S. Government Printing Office, 1963.

40. C. H. Miller, *Foundations of Guidance*. New York: Harper & Row, 1961.

41. R. C. Mooney, "Surveying High School Students' Problems by Means of a Problem Check List," *Educational Research Bulletin*, 21 (1942), 57-69.

42. Office of Education, *Biennial Survey of Education in the United States*. Washington, D.C.: U.S. Dept. of Health, Education, and Welfare, 1962.

43. Public Law 85-864, 85th Cong. H.R. 13, 247, September 2, 1958.

44. H. H. Remmers and C. G. Hackett, *Let's Listen to Youth*. Chicago: Science Research Associates, 1950.

45. *Report of the National Conference on Life Adjustment Education*. Chicago, Oct. 16-18, 1950. Washington, D. C.: U.S. Office of Education (mimeo.), 1950.

46. F. Riessman, *The Culturally Deprived Child*. New York: Harper & Row, 1962.

47. D. Schreiber, ed., *Guidance and the School Dropout*. Washington, D.C.: National Education Association, 1964.

48. D. Schreiber, ed., *The School Dropout*. Washington, D. C.: National Education Association, 1964.

49. The Secretary's Committee on Mental Retardation, *An Introduction to Mental Retardation: Problems, Plans and Programs*. Washington, D. C.: U.S. Government Printing Office, 1965.

50. L. F. Shaffer and E. J. Shoben, *The Psychology of Adjustment*. Boston: Houghton Mifflin Co., 1956.

51. M. B. Smith, "Mental Health Reconsidered: A Special Case of the Problems and Values in Psychology," *The American Psychologist*, 16 (1961), 299-306.

52. T. F. Staton, *Dynamics of Adolescent Adjustment*. New York: The Macmillan Co., 1964.

53. E. Steele, "The Role of the High School Counselor in the Guidance of the Gifted." Unpublished Class Paper (Gowan), UCLA, 1942.

54. G. S. Stevenson, *Mental Health Planning for Social Action*. New York: McGraw-Hill, 1956.

55. R. Strang, "Mental Health," in C. W. Harris, ed., *Encyclopedia of Educational Research*. New York: The Macmillan Co., 1960.

56. J. H. Sofokidis and E. Sullivan, *A New Look at School Dropouts*. Washington, D.C.: Dept. of Health, Education, and Welfare, 1965.

57. E. P. Torrance, *Guiding Creative Talent*. Englewood Cliffs, N.J.: Prentice-Hall, 1962.

58. U.S. Dept. of Health, Education, and Welfare, *Biennial Survey of Education in the United States*. Washington, D.C.: U.S. Office of Education, 1962.

59. R. D. Willey and K. B. Waite, *The Mentally Retarded Child*. Springfield, Ill.: Charles C. Thomas, 1964.

60. S. L. Wolfbein, *Employment and Unemployment in the United States*. Chicago: Science Research Associates, 1964.

chapter **6**

The Services Approach
to Guidance

Since guidance is concerned with meeting pupil needs, it can be structured properly only as a service. The administrative framework, then, is a group of professionally appropriate functions based on local needs. These functions offer a concrete means of translating the guidance point of view into actual processes which assist pupils. (6, p. 2)

The day is long past when an "incidental" organization made up of "educational generalists" could be depended upon for the preparation of all young people for a life in a rapidly changing world. Today's education requires a streamlined organization for maximum service with a minimum of duplication, and it also requires the utilization of an effective staff in roles of the greatest competence for each. (15, p. 118)

The services approach began as student personnel work in the college setting and has only recently begun to be popular as an orientation to guidance in secondary education. As experts in testing, in mental hygiene, and in vocational guidance came into prominence during the early 1920's, they were added to the personnel staffs of colleges. Within a few years the pattern of student personnel work was emerging in the form of a series of specialists, each offering a unique service. These specialists functioned within a single department, typically called the personnel bureau. Later, a series of reports in 1926 (17), 1932 (5), and 1937 (2) attempted to describe the goals and the scope of these services within the context of student personnel work. The wide distribution and general acceptance of the recommendations of these reports resulted in the adoption of the services approach to student personnel work. This general organization and implementation has continued virtually unchanged to the present time.

The general strategy of the services approach remained the same when the services concept was transplanted from colleges to the secondary school setting. Each of the services emphasizes a unique nonintellective dimension of the individual's development. In conjunction with the instructional function of the school, the series of services stresses the student as a whole, with each of the services contributing to one aspect of his growth and adjustment. The services are based upon the needs of the student.

It was an increasing dissatisfaction with the prevailing notion that the guidance worker should be a generalist—i.e., counselor, part-time teacher, clerical worker, *quasi* administrator, and a plethora of other roles and duties—that led to the services orientation to guidance. This new thinking insisted that the complexities of growth and development required a series of specialists to give the student the kind of help he really needed. Cumulatively this series of highly specialized services provides assistance to the individual in response to his own unique needs. There are two major subapproaches within the general service orientation to guidance—*the guidance services approach* and the *pupil personnel services approach.*

THE CONCEPT OF GUIDANCE SERVICES

The concept of guidance services has become the dominant one as the services approach has emerged in secondary education (19). The distinguishing characteristic of a program organized around the concept of guidance services is that virtually the entire range of services is carried out by one person—the guidance specialist. Although various guidance theoreticians have developed unique formulations of these guidance services, there is substantial consensus that guidance should include: (*a*) the information service, (*b*) the appraisal service, (*c*) the counseling service, (*d*) the orientation service, and (*e*) the research and evaluation service.

The Information Service

One of the fundamental tenets of guidance is that planning, thinking, and looking ahead are crucial prerequisities for a satisfactory and successful life. Information becomes a part of guidance whether the practitioner views his work as assisting the student to make better choices, helping him to become better adjusted, facilitating optimum development, or aiding the student in the process of "becoming." The method of using information varies from orientation to orientation, but information is part of virtually every guidance program. In the services approach to guidance, information is organized and utilized as a distinct guidance service—i.e., the information service.

Information provided by this service can be divided into three categories: 1) educational information, 2) occupational information, and 3) personal-social information. Summarized below are some examples of the various types of information within each of the three major categories:

1. Educational information
   a. Catalogues from colleges, universities, junior colleges, community colleges, technical schools, etc.
   b. Directories of various types of post-high school institutions of learning.

    c. Books containing scholarship and loan information
    d. Films and filmstrips
    e. Books, booklets, and pamphlets about studying and study skills
    f. Wall charts
2. Occupational information
    a. Occupational abstracts, briefs, guides, monographs, and pamphlets
    b. Occupational dictionaries
    c. Occupational file
    d. Military career information manuals
    e. Films and filmstrips
    f. Wall charts
3. Personal-social information
    a. Workbooks and reading guides
    b. Booklets for increasing self-understanding
    c. Personal hygiene material
    d. Films
    e. Miscellaneous reading materials
    f. Wall charts

Zeran and Riccio summarize the general goals of the information service as follows (31, p. 35):

1. To develop a broad and realistic view of life's opportunities and problems at all levels of training.
2. To create an awareness of the need and an active desire for accurate and valid occupational, educational, and personal-social information.
3. To provide an understanding of the wide scope of educational, occupational, and social activities in terms of broad categories of related activities.
4. To assist in the mastery of the techniques of obtaining and interpreting information for progressive self-directiveness.
5. To promote attitudes and habits which will assist in the making of choices and adjustments productive of personal satisfaction and effectiveness.
6. To provide assistance in narrowing choices progressively to specific activities which are approximate to aptitudes, abilities, and interests manifested and to the proximity of definite decisions.

Factors such as physical facilities, financial resources, the educational philosophy of the school, and the psychological orientation of the guidance worker determine whether the information service will play a central or a peripheral role in the total guidance program. Similarly, there are various people who might play a role in disseminating the information—e.g., the guidance worker, the school librarian, clerical personnel, teachers, and student helpers. The guidance practitioner's office, the waiting area for the guidance department, the school library, classrooms, and specially designed areas in the school have been suggested as possible places where the information can be kept, depending upon who assumes the responsibility for disseminating it. Since the information service is usually considered an important aspect of formal guidance, the services approach often emphasizes the storing of the information somewhere in the guidance office area. The other places listed above are suggested as secondary locations.

Information can play a vital role in the counseling interview in conjunction with the counseling service. Norris (22) describes numerous ways in which information can be utilized in the elementary school classroom, and Hoppock (18) discusses the use of information in secondary school classrooms. Stone (28), Cuony and Hoppock (9, 10), and Lowenstein and Hoppock (20) describe the formal guidance course—e.g., occupations—as another medium for disseminating occupational information, and Sinick and Hoppock (25) describe some additional programs, demonstrating the effectiveness of the occupations course. A variety of group guidance activities, such as career days, college nights, work-experience seminars, and discussion groups, constitute some additional media for implementing the information service. Samler notes some limitations of the information service in that (a) the information is based upon a theory which is unsatisfactory and incomplete, (b) the information is incomplete, (c) the information is not psychologically based, and (d) the realities of work, the labor force, and the labor structure are not adequately considered (24, Chap. 18).

The Inventory (Appraisal) Service

As he progresses through school, the student faces problems and must make choices. As the guidance worker seeks to help the student, he must know the essential facts about the individual in order that he may be helped to realize the opportunities that education offers him. This continuing study of the individual has been referred to by various guidance authorities as individual appraisal, the individual inventory, child (pupil) study, and, most commonly, the inventory service. The essence of the inventory service consists of (a) collecting essential data about each pupil, (b) recording and storing the data, and (c) providing for the use of the data by the appropriate school staff. The primary purposes for collecting the data are to provide a record of the student's progress and to help the guidance worker and others to understand him more adequately.

Collecting the Data. The many sources for gathering pertinent and useful data about the individual include: (a) autobiographies, (b) home visits, (c) sociometric devices, (d) case conferences, (e) parent conferences, (f) personality rating scales, (g) anecdotal reports from teachers, and (h) questionnaires.

Although these sources are useful for collecting relevant data about the individual, the two major sources of data are his past academic record and the testing program. Past performance has been shown to be one of the best predictions of future performance, and a complete record of the individual's marks in his various courses is not only invaluable but is a legal requirement for the school.

Storing the Data. Virtually every school system stores pertinent data about the student in a cumulative record. The cumulative record, as the name implies, is the official legal record of the school in regard to the characteristics of the student and his performance in the school. The cumulative record may take any one of a number of forms, such as a file folder, a loose-leaf notebook, a jacket into which sheets of paper containing the data are stored, or a folded accordion-like sheet of cardboard with a printed format for the pertinent information.

There are three major types of forms for the cumulative record: (*a*) the commercial form, (*b*) the state form, and (*c*) the local form. Hatch and Stefflre discuss the advantages and disadvantages of these forms (15, pp. 181-86). The commercial form of the cumulative record contains a standardized format and has the advantage of being easy to obtain and to start. Commercial forms also contain categories of information needed in all guidance situations, and many new staff members are accustomed to similar forms or the same form if they have taught in another district. Also, the per-copy price is lower than the expense of developing a local form. The major disadvantages of the commercial form include a lack of flexibility (since all of the available space on the form is used in order to provide for all major types of pertinent information) and a lack of provision for the unique needs of the local schools or the schools within a state.

A number of states have developed cumulative records on a statewide basis. Since these cumulative record forms are identical from school to school within the state, their advantages and disadvantages are similar to those of the commercial form except that the state form can reflect the unique needs of schools in that state, cumulative record data can be transferred from one school to another within the state, and training in the use of records by state training colleges and universities can be facilitated.

If a school district has a fairly large pupil enrollment, it may be feasible to develop a local form. Use of the development of the form as an in-service technique, maximum staff utility of the cumulative record data, and the opportunity for integrating all forms and information into a single record system constitute some of the advantages of the local form. Per-copy cost, considerable expenditure of time, and the fact that the locally developed form does not lend itself for direct transfer to another school system as effectively as commercial or state forms are some of the limitations of this format.

Dissemination and Use of the Data. More important than either the type of data collected or the form in which they are stored is the manner in which the data are used. The data can either be utilized to facilitate the total program of guidance services or they can be misused, thereby counteracting the potentially beneficial contributions of the inventory service. For example, the cumulative record contains a great deal of useful data for carrying on institutional research or for preparing for parent conferences, case conferences, or counseling. On the other hand, the cumulative record can be misused by a teacher as a threat against the student or by a guidance practitioner as a crutch for avoiding other roles and functions. (Also see Chapter 15 for other ethical considerations.)

The data in the cumulative record can also be used to make a case study of a student. The case-study technique brings together and organizes the pertinent data about a student and provides the school staff with recommendations concerning what they can do to alleviate his problem. A case study is helpful when a student has a problem that cannot be easily understood. Someone, often a counselor, initiates a case study by collecting data about the individual, studying his problem, and recommending some procedures that the school staff might perform in its attempt to help the student. Included in a case study are the following typical categories:

1. Identifying data
2. Home background
3. Health information
4. Educational history
5. Anecdotal remarks
6. Case summary
7. Recommendations

Hahn and MacLean summarize the case study technique as follows (14, p. 99):

> The case study is an old method which has been rediscovered and adapted to the complex business of modern counseling. Strictly speaking, it is not a tool or technique in quite the same sense as are statistics, anecdotal records, or psychological tests. Its major function is to bring together the information collected by the other tools and their techniques in such a manner that these data can be systematically reviewed and analyzed and clinical weightings assigned them. Basically it is an individualized, discriminating, systematically planned method of record keeping and interpretation.

Because of its complexity and the amount of time it requires, teachers do not typically carry out a case study. The counselor, on the other hand, should be trained to carry it out. The case study is not a popular approach for studying and understanding the individual, since it requires that a disproportionate amount of time and effort be directed toward a limited number of problem students. A case study is neither required nor feasible for all students, and thus it is used for the occasional troubled student who cannot be helped without the intensive focus of the case study.

The Counseling Service

Counseling in the services approach to guidance is generally similar to counseling in any other orientation to guidance except that it is organized and implemented as one of a number of distinct services. The emphasis may be on developmental counseling, problem-centered counseling, therapeutic counseling, educational counseling, vocational counseling, etc. The primary focus of the service approach is not so much on any one aspect of the guidance program, such as counseling or testing, but upon a broad and balanced set of services. Thus, unlike many other approaches to guidance, counseling in the services approach is relegated to the position of one of a series of services. A general description of counseling theory and practice is included in Chapter 4.

The Orientation Service

Although orientation has been considered as a major aspect of the counseling service and as part of group guidance, it has been most often considered as one of the major services of the guidance program. The major goals of the orientation service include: (*a*) providing for articulation and continuity from one level of education to another, (*b*) providing the new student with information about school routine, regulations, facilities, and personnel, (*c*) helping the student to become established in the school, and (*d*) helping the student to become established in appropriate curricular and extracurricular activities. Bennett, however, describes orientation from a broader and more adequate conceptual framework (4, p. 179):

> We might say that orientation is a mutual process of *learning* on the part of new students, the faculty, and student body of an institution, whereby each group becomes better acquainted with the others, and each participates in an ongoing process which will help the new students to become an effectively functioning part of the institution and help the institution to become responsive to the needs of a changing student body.

The major procedures for orientation include the following:

1. Letters, handbooks, and other orientation materials sent to parents or students or both.
2. Orientation day—newly entering students come to the school one day early for an orientation program.
3. Visitation—pupils from "feeder schools" come to the new school for tour, talks, etc.
4. Meetings with parents before school or at the beginning of the school year.
5. Visit by guidance counselor—guidance counselor from the high school, for example, visits the junior high school and orients pupils.
6. Big brother and big sister program—an upperclassman is assigned to each entering student to help him with a general orientation to the new setting.
7. Group guidance program—carried on in either the homeroom or assembly by the homeroom teacher and/or the guidance specialist.
8. Talks by upperclassmen—either prior to or at the beginning of the school year.
9. Orientation unit—a special unit in the early part of the year in a regular academic subject.
10. Parent or family conferences—by any of the school staff.

11. Initial counseling interview—counselor meets with each new student early in the year to get acquainted with him.

The Research Service

Although the services approach includes research in the broad context as one of the major guidance services, most of the research efforts focus upon evaluation. Hatch and Stefflre note some of the purposes of evaluation (15, pp. 252-54). For example, evaluation can check on the extent to which the guidance program is meeting its objectives. A program of guidance consists of many practices, each practice in turn allegedly contributing to certain goals. But the guidance practitioner cannot be sure that a given practice is really making the contribution it was intended to make unless guidance practices are evaluated. Evaluation can also provide a basis for curriculum revision or guidance program development.

School personnel often cannot see the end results of their efforts. Without evaluation, the guidance staff cannot know about the progress being made by students and the contribution that guidance is making to their development. Evaluation can give the guidance staff greater psychological security because of a knowledge of the effectiveness of its efforts.

Since the school receives its authority from the community, it has an obligation to report back to the community concerning its strengths, its weaknesses, its progress, etc. Through a sound program of public information and public relations, the school and the community can be informed concerning the progress and accomplishments as well as the needs of the guidance program.

Evaluation is a complex undertaking, fraught with many problems, such as (a) knowing when to evaluate, (b) enlisting the interest and cooperation of teachers and other staff members, (c) devising ways to get action from the faculty and students, (d) interpreting evaluation results to the community. Dressel summarizes the criticisms of evaluative studies under the following categories (13):

1. Lack of clear, acceptable statements of objectives in terms of observable student characteristics and behavior.
2. Failure to relate student personnel objectives to all institutional-educational objectives.
3. The use of immediate and easily available criteria accompanied by failure to validate the immediate criteria against long-term goals.
4. The tendency to regard certain goals as equally desirable for all individuals, thereby ignoring individual differences.
5. Confusion of means with ends or of process with outcomes.
6. Excessive use of subjective reactions.
7. Little or no attention to determining a satisfactory experimental design.

An adequate program of evaluation should have the following characteristics (15, pp. 258-60):

1. Evaluation should be comprehensive and not yield to the temptation to ignore areas where test construction has not supplied completely defensible scientific instruments.
2. Evaluation should be focused on changes in the individual's total behavior.
3. Evaluation should result in organized findings that will furnish the greatest amount of meaning to public, students, and staff.
4. An evaluation program should be continuous; it cannot be "done" and forgotten.
5. Evaluation should be related to local curriculum development.
6. Evaluation should involve the widest possible staff participation.

Although there is a wide range of approaches to evaluation, the essential steps in the process are (29, p. 89): (*a*) stating the objectives of the program, (*b*) defining the objectives in terms of specific activities and services, (*c*) providing facilities and experiences essential to these services, (*d*) appraising the effectiveness of the facilities by means of appropriate objective and subjective methods, (*e*) adapting and adjusting the program in accordance with the appraisal data.

THE CONCEPT OF PUPIL PERSONNEL SERVICES

The concept of pupil personnel services became a functional reality largely because of several shortcomings in programs based upon a guidance services approach. The term "guidance" has increasingly fallen into disrepute because the word "guidance" represents almost the exact antithesis of the work of the practitioner both at the theoretical and operational level. Implicit in the term "guidance" are notations of directing, leading, managing, regulating, steering, controlling, etc. What the work of the practitioner consists of, however, is facilitating, freeing, supporting, reinforcing, assisting, etc. Thus, the guidance specialist does not guide in the usual sense of the term but rather provides a series of services which both stem from student needs and focus upon these needs, The work of the practitioner is client-centered (aside from any Rogerian connotations of the term), and the "clients" in the school setting are called students.

Secondly, even if the term "guidance" were not so unacceptable, a program of guidance services is too limited to serve the whole person and his entire range of unique needs. Thus, a truly complete range of services includes the traditional guidance services plus the following:

1. Pupil accounting and attendance service
2. Health services
3. Special psychological services
4. Special individual and group experiences

Business and industry have industrial personnel workers or personnel managers; colleges have student personnel workers; the use of the term pupil personnel services in public education provides for consistency and clarity of terminology and for ease of communication (7, 27).

Pupil Accounting and Attendance Service

Pupil accounting and attendance date back to the 1800's when the first compulsory school attendance legislation required school districts to identify children of school age in their districts (accounting) and to provide for their coming to school on a regular basis (attendance). Culbertson notes (8, p. 92):

> Although the goals of attendance administration in many countries have shifted from legal enforcement to the broader concept of providing attendance services, its basic tasks have remained unchanged. Aiding in the enforcement of compulsory attendance laws, maintaining an adequate school census and enrollment and attendance records, and studying factors related to and affecting attendance are its major tasks.

The pupil accounting and attendance service emphasizes the need for a trained attendance worker in place of the truant officer or "hooky cop" of earlier decades. Although the primary responsibility for pupil accounting and attendance has remained relatively unchanged, an additional focus emphasizes the attendance worker's functioning in conjunction with other personnel workers within a therapeutic frame of reference. Thus the major focuses of pupil accounting and attendance include: (*a*) developing a school census containing information about the number of youth living in the school district who are of school age, the number who live in areas served by specific buildings in the school district, and the age and grade status of all pupils; (*b*) maintaining an account of the children in the school district who are enrolled in private or parochial schools; (*c*) checking on the status of school-aged children who are not attending any school; (*d*) working with other pupil personnel workers to alleviate the causes of nonattendance in pupils who should be in school.

The pupil personnel point of view is evident in the following statement from a state department of public instruction (12, p. 85):

> The fundamental purpose of the program has shifted with the changing philosophy of education. The way in which provisions of the school laws are worked indicates quite clearly that according to the earlier conception of this particular function, home and school visitors were considered attendance officers. While this particular responsibility is not now ignored, the home and school visitor, acting in the light of special preparation and on the basis of an enlightened philosophy of education, is not only concerned with the fact of nonattendance or irregular attendance, and employment, but is also interested in the educational, psychological, medical, and social problems and needs of children who are attendance problems.

Health Services

The physical health and well-being of the pupil is a prerequisite for his benefiting from the total school program. Primary responsibility for the health of the pupil rests with his parents, but every state has enacted legislation to protect and improve the health of pupils. In some school systems without the pupil personnel services orientation, the health program is performed either by relatively uncoordinated health specialists or by a cooperative arrangement between the board of education and a community agency such as the county board of health. Because of the limitations of this latter type of health service, summarized by Reeder (23, p. 438), the cooperative arrangement appears to be decreasing in prevalence.

The most common pattern for organizing the school health program is to have a physician (often hired on a part-time basis) in charge of the program, in which are found dentists, nurses, dental hygienists, and dieticians, each functioning separately but loosely coordinated by the school system's physician. The services approach does not emphasize any radical change in the usual functioning of the health specialists except that their work be administered and coordinated by the chief administrator of the pupil personnel program (16, 30).

Special Psychological Services

The special psychological services aspect of pupil personnel services focuses upon students who are physically and mentally handicapped or emotionally disturbed. Although psychological services were originally intended to help teachers and administrators with the problems of exceptional children, these services have become much broader in scope and include provisions for all students. Special psychological services are implemented by the school psychologist, the school social worker, the psychometrist, and the consulting psychiatrist. The functions of each of these pupil personnel specialists are summarized as follows.

The School Psychologist. The school psychologist is a psychologist with training and experience in education. He typically uses his knowledge of assessment, learning, and the dynamics of interpersonal relationships to foster the growth and development of all students and to identify and deal with exceptional children. As Cutts states (11, pp. 30-31):

> The school psychologist serves in an advisory capacity to school personnel and performs the following functions:
> 1. Measuring and interpreting the intellectual, social, and emotional development of children.
> 2. Identifying exceptional children and collaborating in the planning of appropriate educational and social placements and programs.
> 3. Developing ways to facilitate the learning and adjustment of children.
> 4. Encouraging and initiating research, and helping to utilize research findings of the solution of school problems.
> 5. Diagnosing educational and personal disabilities, and collaborating in the planning of re-educational programs.

The School Social Worker. The major focuses of school social work include identifying and working with students who have social and emotional problems that interfere with school performance. The social worker attempts to help students make adjustments not only to themselves but also to others and to their social environments. Although the three major methods of social work are (*a*) social case work, (*b*) group work, and (*c*) individual counseling, case work typically emerges as the dominant technique. To help the student, the school social worker may work either with the individual, with his parents, or in cooperation with other staff. Thus, the school social worker often serves as a link between the school and the home.

The School Psychometrist. The psychometrist is an expert in testing, and as such he is responsible for administering and scoring the individual and group standardized tests that are part of the school system's testing program. But since the school psychologist typically has a more adequate background in the testing area, the psychometrist's function can be more economically performed by the school psychologist in all but very large school systems. Thus, the services of a psychometrist cannot usually be justified in small and medium-sized school districts.

The (Consulting) School Psychiatrist. The school psychiatrist has the function of providing a specialized service of helping students with severe problems of maladjustment. Because of the shortage of school psychiatrists and the cost of their services, only the largest school systems employ full-time psychiatrists on their staffs. Although his primary function is to provide therapy for the seriously disturbed, some school systems also utilize the psychiatrist to coordinate the mental and/or medical health program of the school system. The most prevalent pattern of providing a psychiatric service for students is to utilize a practicing private psychiatrist as a referral source. Thus, if there is a psychiatrist in the community, he typically serves as a referral agent, with parental consent being required prior to any treatment. The cost of psychiatric care may be borne by the school system, by the parents, by community agencies, or by a joint arrangement. Many school systems suggest to the parents the possibility that their child needs psychiatric care but leave all arrangements for such help to the parents.

Special Individual and Group Experiences

Special individual and group experiences include the areas of special education, speech correction, remedial reading, and student activities. Each of these areas can have a place within the broad spectrum of pupil personnel services. These services have been referred to as the "twilight zone" services in that they include a pupil personnel dimension along with other emphases. While all of these services can be included without having a pupil personnel service orientation per se, a pupil personnel service approach allows more adequate coordination and articulation than other approaches.

THEORETICAL BASIS

Barry and Wolf note that the services approach stems from faculty psychology (3, pp. 42-43):

> Whereas some guidance-personnel workers might claim that a theory of individual differences underlies and justifies the services approach, this approach seems to stem more directly from faculty psychology than from any later psychological theories. In its simplest terms the faculty psychology that provided a rationale for the classical college curriculum divided the individual into parts: usually intellect, feeling, and will or volition. The growth of intellectualism in the colleges and universities during the nineteenth century caused educators to regard the intellectual factor as preeminent and to ignore the other faculties. Even today, when faculty psychology has been relegated to the past, the services approach seems to fit a faculty psychology pattern even better than one of individual differences. An individual's intellectual faculty is handled through his courses; his feeling or emotional faculty, through personnel services; his will develops as a function of the two other types of activities.

Although there have been elements of the foregoing thinking throughout the literature and research of the services approach, a comprehensive look at the scope and content of the services orientation suggests other pervasive and more significant emphases. It is true, for example, that the various guidance services or pupil personnel services are not primarily instructional—i.e., cognitive—in the usual sense of the term. It is likewise true that there appears to be a cleavage between the instructional function and the personnel or guidance function. But it is also true that teamwork, planning, coordination, articulation, and careful organization represent some fundamental theoretical constructs undergirding the services approach.

Thus, theoretically and functionally it appears as if the services approach stems more importantly from psychological and psychometric developments in the 1920's. There is an emphasis on the whole person, but the method for understanding and helping the whole person utilizes a series of specialists. Each of these specialists focuses upon a different aspect of the individual, and the unity of the approach results from minimal overlapping among the services, careful planning, adequate articulation, and smooth, cooperative functioning among the various specialists. Teamwork represents a major emphasis in contemporary thought in the services orientation. Thus, the basic strategy for understanding and helping the whole person is to view all of the separate aspects in which he differs from others.

Philosophy

The content and scope of the services approach can vary widely. Rather than representing a unique philosophy of education or guidance per se, the services approach represents a philosophy of organizing and implementing the guidance or personnel function in the school. The primary philosophical requirement is a belief in the advantage of utilizing guidance personnel who have been highly trained and who concomitantly provide highly specialized services to students.

Smith emphasizes the organization-centeredness of this approach in order to provide an efficient service for the individual (26, pp. 5, 24-25):

> The guidance process consists of a group of services to individuals to assist them in securing the knowledge and skills needed in making adequate choices, plans, and interpretations essential to satisfactory adjustment in a variety of areas. These services are designed to result in efficiency in areas which require that the individual make adjustments in order that he may be an effective member of society.
>
> . . . .
>
> The school's responsibility for providing adequate guidance services dictates that sound practices be employed in utilizing the available resources in the school and community. Incidental guidance activities are characterized chiefly by lack of relationship one with another since the skilled leadership required to bind them together into an integrated pattern is often absent. Without definitely assigned responsibility for trained leadership, the school's efforts to provide acceptable guidance services will meet with only partial success at best.

A similar rationale is evident in Hatch and Stefflre, who note that a smoothly functioning guidance program will provide services to students in such a manner as to eliminate omissions, reduce overlapping, and provide guidance services at the most appropriate time. They describe the importance of good organization, appropriate supervision, and thorough evaluation, noting that in such a program the prime requirement is careful and thoughtful administration (15, Chap. 4).

Underlying Assumptions

As in the case of other orientations to guidance-personnel work, certain fundamental assumptions underlie the services approach. The first and most critical assumption is that while the teacher is the most important member of the school staff, working continuously and directly with the student, the basic objectives of the teacher cannot be realized without highly trained supplementary assistance from the various pupil personnel specialists. It is assumed that pupil personnel services function separately from the school's instructional program in order that each student may profit more from teaching as a result of his experience with various services offered.

A second major assumption related to the general role and function of the guidance personnal worker and consists of the implicit notion that a well organized group of services offered by specialists will give a more adequate kind of help than other, more generalized approaches. This assumption is similar to the one in medicine which holds that a group of medical specialists functioning within the framework of a medical clinic can function more adequately than the individual medical generalist—i.e., the general practitioner. Related to this idea is the assumption that the best way to help the whole person is through intensive study and help for his component parts.

It is also assumed that various services are essentially facilitative. The guidance-personnel specialists may facilitate directly by providing a service to the student or may be indirectly facilitative by working with teachers, administrators, parents. McDaniel notes the facilitative dimension in guidance services as follows (21, p. 30): "They do not themselves undertake to carry out the objectives of educational programs but rather provide aids to the pupil, the teacher, and the administrator which are intended to facilitate the development of the pupil and the success of the teacher's work with him."

The services approach also assumes that teachers, administrators, and guidance-personnel specialists will both desire to cooperate and be able to cooperate effectively and work together in a team effort. The instructional, administrative, and guidance (personnel) functions are considered to represent unique but related processes whose goals cannot be met without mutual trust and cooperation.

Goals

Statements of the goals of guidance services, although numerous, are not unique to the services approach. Zeran and Riccio, for example, note the following as the goals of guidance services (31, p. 2):

1. Aiding the individual in the identification of his abilities, aptitudes, interests, and attitudes.
2. Assisting the individual to understand, accept, and utilize these traits.
3. Helping the individual recognize his aspirations in light of his traits.
4. Providing the individual with opportunities for learning about areas of occupational and educational endeavors.
5. Aiding the individual in the development of value senses.
6. Helping the individual in obtaining experiences which will assist him in the making of free and wise choices.
7. Assisting the individual in developing his potentials to their optimum so that he may become the individual he is capable of becoming.
8. Aiding the individual in becoming more and more self-directive.

SOME OPERATIONAL ASPECTS

Formal Organization

The oft-quoted statement that the organization of a school system is a reflection of the philosophy of that system becomes even more meaningful in terms of the services approach. The services approach is entirely predicated upon a functional organization of the staff. Figures 6-1 and 6-2 show the most com-

FIGURE 6-1
An Organization of Guidance Services for a Small School System

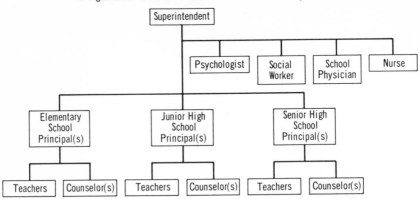

mon basic organizational patterns for programs based upon a guidance services approach.

In small and medium-sized school districts the basic structure in Figure 6-1 is frequently utilized. Because of the small number of counselors in the system, there is no administrator of guidance. The guidance counselors function in a line relationship with the principal. The school physician, the psychologist, the social worker, and the nurse function relatively independently throughout the entire school system.

Figure 6-2 shows an organizational structure for guidance services in a large school district. While the basic pattern is similar to that of Figure 6-1, a guidance administrator is added to coordinate the functioning of the many counselors in the system. The director of guidance services serves in a line relationship with the superintendent of the school system. Guidance counselors, in turn, serve either in a staff relationship with the director of guidance services or else typically function within a dual relationship with the director of guidance services and the principal of the school in which they function.

A variation of the same basic pattern is shown in Figure 6-3, in which an administrator called the Assistant Superintendent for Instructional Services is directly responsible for three divisions—instructional services, special education, and guidance and health services. This organization attempts to rectify the over-centralization of authority in the superintendent by the addition of a second major administrator. Although this pattern can be very functional in a medium-sized school system, in a large system the assistant superintendent probably might not be able to devote enough time and energy to each of the three divisions because of a multiplicity of duties.

Figure 6-4 shows an organization chart for pupil personnel services. This organization clearly separates guidance services administrater by a director of guidance from the other pupil personnel services which are in effect an assortment of functioning relatively independently pupil personnel services. In this

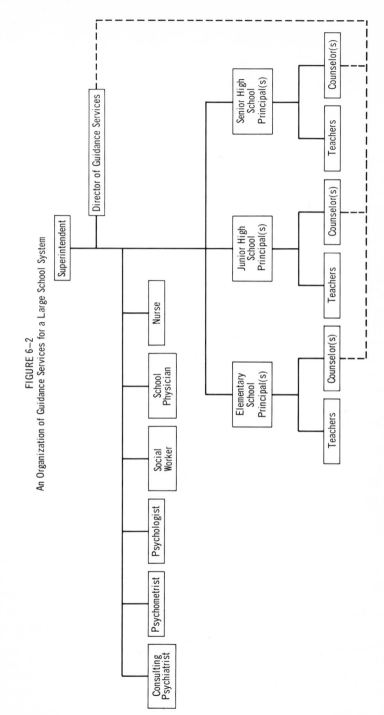

FIGURE 6-2
An Organization of Guidance Services for a Large School System

FIGURE 6-3
An Organization of Guidance Services for a Medium or Large-Sized School System

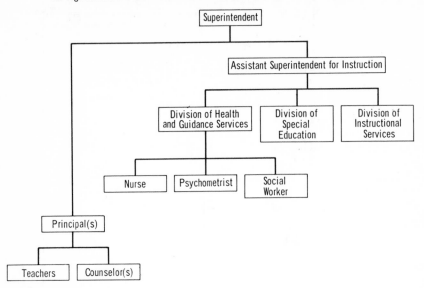

pattern an administrator—the Assistant Superintendent of Pupil Personnel Services—is in charge of four directors and their staffs, which constitute the pupil personnel staff. The guidance counselors have line relationships with the principals of the buildings in which they work.

Organization and Administration

Because of the importance of adequate organization and administration of the various specialists, the literature emphasizes theory and principles of organizing and administering the guidance services or pupil personnel services program. Hatch and Stefflre identify the following key concepts in the organization of the services approach (15, pp. 123-25):

1. An analysis of the guidance requirements of the pupils to be served will be a major guide in organization.
2. A survey of what guidance activities are existent and the staff member responsible will serve as a guide to an appropriate guidance organization.
3. It is far more realistic to plan an organization that is in keeping with staff abilities and alter the structure later with the addition of qualified staff.
4. The organizational plan for the guidance services must be so structured as to allow for total staff participation in the planning phase.
5. The assigned line and service functions of a guidance program must be identified and understood by all members of the staff.
6. The organization of the guidance program is developed in proportion to the staff time and energy available to staff the structure adequately.
7. Responsibility for primary leadership in the guidance program must be assumed

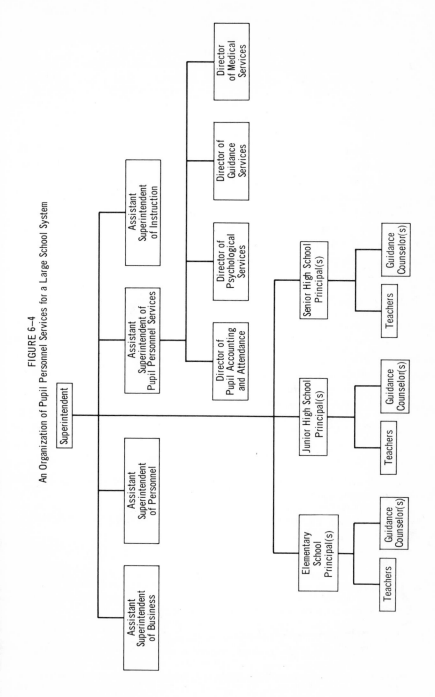

FIGURE 6–4
An Organization of Pupil Personnel Services for a Large School System

by the superintendent or assigned by title to the next level of administration, or the structure will be relatively ineffective.

8. The organization for guidance services provides for vertical supervision from the chief executive officer to every facet of the school district.
9. The organizational framework is the skeleton upon which the guidance program is constructed and permits additions or changes in keeping with an ever-improving program.*

Functional Aspects

Because of the wide range of types of specialists, numbers of personnel, of organization, goals of the program, etc., it is impossible to make many statements that would have general application to all programs of guidance services or pupil personnel services. The three common elements in every ideal program are: (*a*) a well defined set of services, (*b*) a functional organization of staff, and (*c*) a carefully implemented team effort to achieve the goals of the program. One of the most concise summaries of the functional aspects of the services approach has been put forth by the Connecticut State Department of Education (1, pp. 4-6):

School personnel workers, as members of the school staff, are concerned with helping pupils:

to clarify their interests and attitudes,
to understand their personal motives,
to know their abilities, to formulate goals, to try to realize their potentials and to evaluate their goals realistically,
to have a feeling of worth and a sense of belonging,
to feel that someone is concerned with them as individuals—someone whom they can trust and who can help them,
to develop and realize an adequate and acceptable self-concept,
to understand themselves in relation to their environment,
to see ways in which frustrating and tension-creating situations may be handled,
to understand ways in which adjustment may mean change in self or change in the environment,
to orient to new situations and to understand difficult situations,
to understand and accept the need for limitations on their behavior,
to get on well with others,
to develop plans of action based on a careful analysis of themselves and of the factors influencing their situations,
to discover and engage in activities or programs which will contribute to their educational growth and development.

School personnel workers also approach pupil problems:

by respecting the responsibilities of parents for their children, and by recognizing that parental responsibilities are particularly important in the phases of child development listed above,

*Raymond N. Hatch and Bulford Stefflre, *Administration of Guidance Services, Organization, Supervision, Evaluation*, © 1958. Reprinted by permission of Prentice-Hall, Inc., Englewood Cliffs, New Jersey.

by working with the family and other persons or groups important in the child's environment,

by referring pupils to those who can render help not available in the home or school,

by effecting various changes that improve the environment situation.

School personnel workers assist the school staff:

by helping to identify pupils who need special attention and by suggesting ways in which teachers can help them,

by furnishing teachers with more comprehensive knowledge about individual pupils and their backgrounds so teachers can work more effectively,

by identifying and clarifying needs of pupils which can be met through the curriculum,

by engaging in research which will help the school perform its functions,

by helping teachers plan activities for evaluating individual pupil progress and for defining learning weaknesses and strengths,

by working individually with pupils identified by teachers as having learning or adjustment problems,

by cooperating in the planning of a total program of testing and evaluation,

by helping teachers keep up to date on developments in special areas of psychology—especially in the areas of learning and adjustment.

The necessarily long and involved description of alternative patterns for organizing guidance services and pupil personnel services reflects the functional emphasis of the services approach. As an orientation to guidance, the main focus of the services approach is upon organizing, offering, and implementing a set of services carried out by trained specialists.

SUMMARY AND CONCLUSIONS

As the field of counseling and guidance has moved toward increasing both the number of personnel and the degree of specialization, the services approach has continued to grow as an orientation to guidance. For many theoreticians and practitioners alike, the division of the broad guidance process into its component parts represents a necessary and desirable antecedent for providing the student with adequate help. From an emphasis on the organization of helping relationships according to a functional design has emerged two basic patterns for providing assistance to students—guidance services and pupil personnel services.

The services approach emphasizes specialized training for the practitioner and coordination among the various specialists. A major continuing criticism, however, has been that this approach results in an overfragmentization of the student. Proponents of the services concept, on the other hand, argue that a well-planned, smoothly articulated, and effectively implemented program of guidance services or pupil personnel services provides the student with a kind of help vastly superior to the other, more limited or more generalized conceptions of school guidance.

While there are differences within the services approach in terms of types of personnel and organizational patterns, the distinguishing characteristics of the services approach include a well-defined group of services, a functional organization of staff, and a carefully implemented team effort to achieve the goals of the program. The movement toward some type of services concept represents one of the significant trends in contemporary guidance.

REFERENCES

1. Advisory Personnel Committee, *The Team Approach in Pupil Personnel Services.* Connecticut State Department of Education, 1955.

2. American Council on Education, *The Student Personnel Point of View.* American Council on Education Pamphlet, 1937.

3. R. Barry, and B. Wolf, *Modern Issues in Guidance-Personnel Work.* New York: Teachers College Press, Columbia University, 1957.

4. M. E. Bennett, *Guidance and Counseling in Groups,* 2d ed. New York: McGraw-Hill, 1963.

5. R. C. Clothier, "College Personnel Principles and Functions," *Personnel Journal,* 10 (1932), 9-17.

6. H. C. Cottingham, *Guidance in Elementary School, Principles and Practices.* Bloomington, Ill.: McKnight & McKnight, 1956.

7. Council of Chief State School Officers, *Responsibilities of State Departments of Education for Pupil Personnel Services.* Washington, D.C.: Council of Chief State School Officers, 1960.

8. J. Culbertson, "Attendance," *Encyclopedia of Educational Research,* 3d ed. New York: The Macmillan Co., 1960.

9. E. R. Cuony, and R. Hoppock, "Job Course Pays Off," *Personnel and Guidance Journal,* 23 (1954), 389-91.

10. E. R. Cuony, and R. Hoppock, "Job Course Pays Off Again," *Personnel and Guidance Journal,* 37 (1957), 116-17.

11. N. E. Cutts, ed., *School Psychologists at Mid-Century—A Report of the Thayer Conference on the Functions, Qualifications, and Training of School Psychologists.* Washington, D. C.: American Psychological Association, 1955.

12. Department of Public Instruction, *Manual for Child Accounting and Pupil Personnel Work in Pennsylvania.* Harrisburg, Pa.: Department of Public Instruction, 1953.

13. P. L. Dressel, "Personnel Services in High School and College," *Occupations,* 29 (1951), 331-40.

14. M. E. Hahn, and M. S. MacLean *Counseling Psychology,* 2d ed. New York: McGraw-Hill, 1955.

15. R. N. Hatch, and B. Stefflre, *Administration of Guidance Services.* Englewood Cliffs, N.J.: Prentice-Hall, 1958.

16. M. A. Hinrichs, "Health Services Elementary and Secondary," *Encyclopedia of Educational Research,* 3d ed. New York: The Macmillan Co., 1960.

17. L. B. Hopkins, "Personnel Procedures in Education, Observations and Conclusions Resulting from Visits to Fourteen Institutions of Higher Learning," *The Educational Record*, 7; Supplement No. 3 (October 1926).

18. R. Hoppock, *Occupational Information.* New York: McGraw-Hill, 1957.

19, J. A. Humphreys, A. E. Traxler, and R. D. North, *Guidance Services.* Chicago: Science Research Associates, 1960.

20. N. Lowenstein, and R. Hoppock, "High School Occupations Course Helps Students Adjust to College," *Personnel and Guidance Journal*, 34, (1955), 21-23.

21. H. B. McDaniel, *Guidance in the Modern School.* New York: Holt, Rinehart & Winston, 1956.

22. W. Norris, *Occupational Information in the Elementary School.* Chicago: Science Research Associates, 1963.

23. W. G. Reeder, *The Fundamentals of Public School Administration*, 4th ed. New York: The Macmillan Co., 1958.

24. J. Samler, "Occupational Exploration in Counseling: A Proposed Reorientation," Chapter 18, in H. Borow, ed. *Man in a World at Work.* Boston: Houghton Mifflin Co., 1964.

25. D. Sinick, and R. Hoppock, "Research on the Teaching of Occupations," *Personnel and Guidance Journal*, 42 (1964), 504-7.

26. E. G. Smith, *Principles and Practices of the Guidance Program.* New York: The Macmillan Co., 1951.

27. State Committee on Credentials for Pupil Personnel Services, "The Preparation and Training of Pupil Personnel Workers," *Bulletin of the California State Department of Education*, 21, No. 5 (April 1952).

28. C. H. Stone, "Are Vocational Orientation Courses Worth Their Salt," *Educational and Psychological Measurement*, 8 (1948), 161-81.

29. E. Stoops, *Guidance Services: Organization and Administration.* New York: McGraw-Hill, 1959.

30. C. C. Wilson, ed., *School Health Services.* Washington, D.C.: National Education Association, 1953.

31. F. R. Zeran, and A. C. Riccio, *Organization and Administration of Guidance Services.* Chicago: Rand McNally & Co., 1962.

chapter 7

The Developmental Approach
to Guidance

If the guidance point of view emphasizes the positive, developmental, preventative, and therapeutic approaches for releasing the best in the person and in turn this fosters the progressive ability of the individual to obtain self-direction and self-adjustment, the program of guidance services must begin in the first year of school. If guidance practices of the school are conceived of as necessitating a continuous–longitudinal emphasis–rather than a cross sectional approach, we may be on the way toward fostering the self-direction of which we speak as a cardinal principle in guidance practice. (8, p. 276)

It was an interest in the concept of developmental tasks (3, 4), coupled with the increasing influence of developmental psychology, that gave rise to the developmental approach to guidance after World War II. In its broadest sense, developmental guidance represents a change from crisis guidance toward a preventive and positive approach for helping students. The developmental guidance concept arose from an increasing dissatisfaction with adjustment- and problem-centered guidance with their emphases upon dealing primarily with the troubled student and waiting until problems become rather serious before offering assistance. By 1960 it seemed that there was sufficient research evidence to enable the counselor to identify potential problems in individuals through their behavior at an early stage of development, thereby enabling him to deal with potential or incipient problems rather than waiting for the maladjustment to become so acute as to be debilitating. This movement away from adjustment counseling, crisis guidance, and problem-centered guidance toward a preventive approach has continued to be a major and dominant theme of developmental guidance.

Although developmental guidance attempts to identify potential problems in their early stages, to deal with the causes underlying symptoms, and thereby to prevent serious problems in later stages of development, developmental guidance is more than a preventive measure. Behind the application of techniques is the broad and encompassing goal of helping the individual to achieve maximum development in all aspects of his life. Although there is a primary emphasis upon a positive approach for preventing problems and promoting maximum development of the student, these efforts are balanced with remedial efforts, for it is unrealistic to expect to eliminate the need for corrective and curative measures. The developmental approach to guidance attempts to minimize the necessity for them.

It is only through a long-term, relatively continuous effort extending from the elementary school through the high school that a program of developmental guidance can be implemented. Developmental guidance is also cumulative: i.e., each level of guidance builds upon the natural development of the pupil and upon the guidance that has occurred at an earlier developmental stage. Likewise, the developmental approach to guidance focuses attention upon many aspects of the individual's development rather than emphasizing a single aspect, such as educational, vocational, or personal-social development.

It is highly unrealistic to assume that a guidance counselor with the typical counselor-to-student ratio can realize the broad and encompassing goals of the developmental orientation to guidance. Thus, developmental guidance is coordinative rather than specialized, involving the coordinated efforts of the entire school staff. The teacher is primarily responsible for the instructional function of the school, and the guidance counselor focuses upon the integration and general development of the individual. The guidance process is broadly conceived, occurring at the core of the educative process, with the teacher and the counselor operating with other members of the guidance team. Teaching and guidance are two aspects of the total educational enterprise, with considerable overlapping between them.

Since the guidance process includes a number of people besides the guidance counselor, developmental guidance stresses the importance of adequate planning, functional policies, and adequate communication. Each member of the guidance team has a unique role to play, and each role must articulate smoothly with the roles and functions of the other team members. In its focus on many aspects of human development, developmental guidance uses a wide range of guidance practice in the realization of its goals.

A variety of techniques and vehicles are used as developmental guidance focuses upon the understanding that the individual has of himself and his environment and of the relationship between self and environment. Academic achievement and progress, personal-social relations, and education-vocational outlooks have been identified as three pertinent areas for a program of guidance which will have reasonable bounds, attainable objectives, and feasible methods. Individual and group counseling, testing, the cumulative record, statistics, diaries, autobiographies, questionnaires, self-rating charts, speakers, field trips, and the case study have been discussed as some of the techniques within developmental guidance. Developmental guidance has been defined as follows (7, p. 141):

> Guidance is the systematic, professional process of helping the individual through educative and interpretive procedures to gain a better understanding of his own character and potentialities and to relate himself more satisfactorily to social requirements and opportunities in accord with social and moral values.

THE THEORETICAL BASIS

Developmental guidance theory is only in its formative stages. The suggested practices are based upon knowledge about human development in various disciplines, but theoretical discussions to date have focused upon generalized aspects of the guidance process and its underlying conceptual framework. Tyler, for example, notes biological, psychological, and sociological dimensions of this fundamental body of knowledge, but states that this complex field of study ignores disciplinary boundaries (11, Chap. 14). Of course, developmental tasks (3, 4) and psychosocial crises (1, 2) are key concepts in the theoretical fabric of developmental guidance, as are many secondary constructs such as life stages, developmental pattern, socialization, life style, self-actualization, etc. However, now that a rationale for the approach to developmental guidance has been developed, future theory must concentrate more on operational aspects of the process, in order to evolve specific methods for implementing the goals of the program.

Underlying Assumptions

A cluster of related and overlapping assumptions underlie the concept of developmental guidance. These assumptions, both general and specific, are listed below:

1. Students need help in getting information which they might not be able to discover for themselves without paying too high a price in time, money, or effort.
   a. Information about personal characteristics such as potential aptitudes, directions of interest, motivations.
   b. Information about educational opportunities, occupational requirements, available social services.
   c. Information about appropriate ways of behaving in various situations.
2. Students need help in adjusting to social requirements, meeting problems as they arise, overcoming weaknesses, and making plans for the future.
3. It is beneficial both for the individual and for the society when the individual achieves success and satisfaction in education, in his work, and in other aspects of his life.
4. Since there are so many alternative courses of action open to individuals, choice must be made, and planning, taking thought, and looking ahead are beneficial for the individual in this process of choice.
5. The individual has an innate urge to make something of himself, to strive, and to grow.
6. The worth and dignity of the individual are a prime concern of guidance.

7. Although developmental guidance assists individuals toward certain socially desirable goals, the ultimate decision in a situation rests with the individual.
8. The school may unknowingly interfere with the development of the individual, may aggravate existing problems, and may even precipitate additional problems.
9. Guidance can attempt to create conditions in the individual and his environment which will facilitate his maximum development.
10. Literature and research about human development in the various behavioral sciences constitute a basis for theory and practice in education and a developmental approach to guidance.
11. Processes in guidance can be so arranged in terms of timing and sequence that a later phase of development can be understood in the light of a former phase.
12. Many general techniques can be adapted to a developmental orientation to guidance—e.g., counseling and testing.
13. The emphasis in guidance should not be upon dealing with surface traits (symptoms) but upon causes—i.e., guidance should focus on dynamics behind behavior.
14. The student can learn about the factors that underlie behavior and can apply these learnings to others, to his own actions, and to the guiding of his own development.
15. When the individual understands himself and can formulate a plan of life that is best suited for him, he will be more satisfied and make a better contribution to society than he would without such a plan.

Rationale

In its broadest context, education is a formal institution charged with the socialization and general development of the child. The task of education is, therefore, defined in part by society and in part by the educational endeavor itself. As one aspect of education, guidance attempts to implement certain goals of the school through the utilization of specialized principles and techniques of the behavioral sciences.

Since the guidance worker is employed by an educational system to achieve certain fundamentally educational objectives, he is basically an educator utilizing the behavioral sciences as vehicles for theory and practice. The guidance worker is an educational generalist with specialized training in guidance. He focuses upon the total development of the student by an integrative role, acting in conjunction with faculty and other specialists, who in turn focus upon more limited aspects of development.

The goals of guidance represent its aims or purposes and thus are statements of desired attitudinal or behavioral changes in students as a result of the guidance effort.

Philosophy and Goals

There are numerous philosophies of education within which a developmental approach to guidance can operate. The primary philosophical requirements for a school system to incorporate a developmental strategy for guidance are as follows:

1. A belief in the progressive desire and ability of the individual to explore and understand himself.
2. A desire to foster self-evaluation, self-insight, and self-direction in the student.
3. A confidence in guidance and the developmental approach as a means for attaining the goals of guidance and the educational system of which it is a part.
4. A philosophical and financial commitment to the fostering of the total development of the student.

Current formulations of the goals of developmental guidance are rather broad, as reflected by the following excerpts from the goal statements of leading exponents of the developmental approach to guidance. Little and Chapman state that the major purpose of developmental guidance is to "provide for each pupil guidance services which are planned and implemented to help him develop personally, socially, and educationally" (5, p. 257). Similarly, Mathewson notes that the purpose of guidance is "to improve the capability of the individual to understand self and environment and to deal with self-situational relations for greater personal satisfaction and social usefulness in the light of social and moral values" (7, p. 134).

Guidance impinges upon the academic, educational-vocational, personal-social aspects of the individual's life as a service offered by the school. The major emphasis of this service is that guidance is a longitudinal, relatively continuous, coordinated, cumulative effort directed toward assisting the student to gain an understanding of himself and his environment, thereby enabling him to relate more effectively with the environment.

As noted above, the concepts of developmental stages, developmental patterns, and developmental tasks are central to developmental guidance. The most important of these is the developmental tasks concept. In actuality there is not one concept of developmental task, but three unique though related formulations: developmental tasks (3, 4), vocational developmental tasks (9, 10), and psychosocial crises (1, 2). One would not expect that a sociologist interested in education, a vocational psychologist attempting to describe development, and a psychoanalyst focusing upon human development within the framework of cultural anthropology would evolve identical formulations as each considers human development from his own vantage point. But if a theoretical content analysis is performed on the writing of these three men and their colleagues, a cluster of common elements can be identified in their literature and research.

Some Fundamental Similarities

Below is a list of general statements about human development and the role of developmental tasks in this development. These statements constitute some dimensions of a gross orientation to the developmental task concept and provide a point of departure for understanding the fundamental similarity among the three developmental task formulations. Havighurst, Super, and Erikson appear to be in agreement with respect to each of the following statements (12, p. 373):

1. Individual growth and development is continuous.
2. Individual growth can be divided into periods or life stages for descriptive purposes.
3. Individuals in each life stage can be characterized by certain general characteristics which they have in common.
4. Most individuals in a given culture pass through similar developmental stages.
5. The society makes certain demands upon individuals.
6. These demands are relatively uniform for all members of the society.
7. The demands differ from stage to stage as the individual goes through the developmental process.
8. Developmental crises occur when the individual perceives the demand to alter his present behavior and master new learnings.
9. In meeting and mastering developmental crises, the individual moves from one developmental stage of maturity to another developmental stage of maturity.
10. The task appears in its purest form at one stage.
11. Preparation for meeting the developmental crises or developmental tasks occurs in the life stage prior to the stage in which it must be mastered.
12. The developmental task or crisis may arise again during a later phase in somewhat different form.
13. The crisis or task must be mastered before the individual can successfully move on to a subsequent developmental stage.
14. Meeting the crisis successfully by learning the required task leads to societal approval, happiness, and success with later crises and their correlative tasks.
15. Failing in meeting a task or crisis leads to disapproval by society.

Only a relatively limited number of implications for guidance can be drawn if a single developmental task concept is used. For any developmental stage, however, a synthetic formulation can be evolved by ordering and hybridizing the three formulations. Thus, it is possible to arrange the three developmental task concepts into a hierarchical arrangement. Although bringing the three developmental task formulations together requires some theoretical "forcing," the resultant hybrid formulation could conceivably have significantly more implications for the theory and practice of developmental guidance than any one developmental task concept singly. The synthetic formulation of the three developmental task formulations relating to adolescence is shown below (12, p. 373):

GENERAL DEVELOPMENTAL TASK: Developing a sense of identity
    Basic Developmental Tasks
        1. Achieving new and more mature relations with agemates of both sexes.

    2. Achieving a masculine or feminine social role.
    3. Accepting one's physique and using the body effectively.
    4. Achieving emotional independence of parents and other adults.
    5. Achieving assurance of economic independence.
    6. Preparing for marriage and family life.
    7. Selecting and preparing for an occupation.
Sub-Vocational Developmental Tasks
    1. Crystallizing a vocational preference.
    2. Specifying a vocational preference.
    3. Implementing a vocational preference.

A Perspective

The study of human development reveals some general principles. While they apply to large segments of the population, they are by no means universal. The concepts related to these principles have sometimes been characterized with the adjectives "modal," "normative," or "nomothetic" if the concepts relate to a large proportion of the population. Like the statistical concept of mode, these concepts denote the most common type of occurrence.

Almost all writers have utilized developmental tasks as a nomothetic concept. Developmental tasks represent general learnings required of individuals in a given culture. Havighurst notes, for example (4, p. 4): "The tasks an individual must learn—the developmental tasks of life—are those things that constitute healthy and satisfactory growth in our society. They are the things a person must learn if he is to be judged and to judge himself to be reasonably happy and successful." By definition, the developmental task concept is a nomothetic one. The individual developmental task is also nomothetic, and this has often been stressed in the literature.

When developmental tasks are considered in terms of their implications for guidance, however, it would seem that in addition to this nomothetic dimension a new dimension should be considered—the idiographic dimension. While individuals within a culture or subculture tend to have some common traits among them, each individual is unique. It would appear to the writer that developmental tasks have an idiographic dimension in that the tasks vary from person to person. They vary as follows: First, a given task has a unique *meaning* to each individual. As the general task is internalized, it is interpreted by the individual and incorporated into his value, attitude, or need system, taking on a slightly different meaning for each person. Secondly, individuals vary with respect to their *general approach* to developmental tasks. Among the factors influencing the general approach would seem to be personal factors such as age, sex, temperament, values, attitudes, and social factors such as socioeconomic status. A developmental task may be approached hesitatingly or eagerly, methodically or casually.

The third idiographic dimension of developmental tasks is the *pattern of mastering* developmental tasks (12). LoCascio has identified three basic patterns for mastering developmental tasks (6). In the *continuous developmental pattern,* the individual proceeds in the manner expected by society, by mastering the learning or behavioral change successfully at the time it is expected that he will do so. In the *delayed developmental pattern,* the individual masters the developmental tasks later than normally expected. Individuals exhibiting the *impaired developmental pattern* never successfully master the developmental task and are therefore in varying degrees maladjusted.

Developmental Tasks and the Goals of Guidance

Developmental tasks can be described at different levels of abstraction and then articulated with the goals of guidance.

Range of the Goal	Developmental Task
1. Ultimate goal	Self-actualization
2. Long-range goals	General developmental tasks
3. Intermediate-range goals	Basic developmental tasks
4. Short-term goals	Subdevelopmental tasks

Developmental tasks constitute some reference points in the course of human development upon which the guidance worker can focus his attention. Ultimate goals of guidance are helpful only in a very general way. Typically, there is little direct relationship between any particular guidance activity and these abstract goals. Developmental tasks are helpful not so much as terminal goals for guidance but as long-range, intermediate, and short-term goals. The developmental task concept provides the student and the guidance worker with relatively discrete criteria for evaluating the student's developmental progress in many areas. Thus, developmental tasks are steppingstones whereby the student, assisted by the guidance worker, can achieve the broader, more far-reaching goals of guidance.

Developmental tasks coupled with a theory of personality, moreover, can provide a more adequate formulation of the means-ends relationships. Guidance practices can then be geared directly to the short-term goals. The attainment or mastery of an adequate set of these short-term goals (subdevelopmental tasks) facilitates the realization of intermediate goals (basic developmental tasks). The achievement of basic developmental tasks results in greater happiness and satisfaction for the individual. Success in mastering developmental tasks also leads to societal approval and a chain of other events which cumulatively enhance personality integration, personal development, and the mastery of the general developmental tasks of each life stage. In short, it is only by mastering the subdevelopmental tasks that the individual can achieve basic developmental tasks, and only when he has mastered the basic and general developmental tasks that the individual can be said to have achieved ultimate goals of guidance.

The usefulness of this hierarchy of goals, however, is limited by the adequacy of the links—in this case, subdevelopmental tasks, basic developmental tasks, and general developmental tasks. As noted above, current formulations are imperfect and in need of extension and refinement. Nevertheless, it is possible to utilize what is now known in a gross manner and to look to future research for more adequate constructs (12).

SOME OPERATIONAL ASPECTS

Developmental guidance is one aspect of a comprehensive program for assisting the student with the many dimensions of his total development. Guidance is an outgrowth of the developmental philosophy described above, functioning throughout the school setting, and constituting the core of the pupil personnel program. There is no inherent organizational structure within the developmental guidance concept except that an integrated and coordinated functional structure is utilized. Mathewson (7, p. 206), for example, describes the following model organizational unit for guidance at all school levels. (See Figure 7-1.) The guidance counselor is the pivot of the structural guidance

FIGURE 7-1

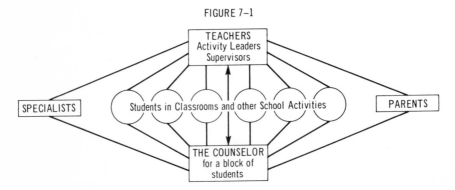

organizational unit, coordinating data for all of the students and coordinating guidance activities relating to any individual.

Although Mathewson's organizational model emphasizes the functional organization of developmental guidance, numerous formal organizational structures could be utilized for a systemwide structural framework for the formal aspects of the pupil personnel and guidance programs. The functions of developmental guidance as outlined by Mathewson are listed below:

FIVE FUNCTIONS OF GUIDANCE (7, p. 193)
1. Individual Case Work (and associated subfunctions): analysis, evaluation, interpretation, and description of the individual and his characteristics as applied to:
   a. Personal needs and problems of (1) academic adjustment and progress, (2) personal-social adjustment and orientation, and (3) educational-vocational orientation and planning.

    b. Institutional needs and problems: (1) classification, grouping and placement of pupil personnel; (2) educational adjustment and progress of pupil personnel; (3) educational-vocational orientation of pupil personnel; and (4) general and special educational development of all pupils.

2. Counseling and Related Group Work: including informal communication with pupils and interviewing of them as well as formal professional counseling and various types of group work particularly associated with guidance purposes.

3. Consultation: consultation and communication among teachers, parents, officials, staff members, community representatives, and others concerning guidance needs and problems of individuals or groups.

4. Coordination: coordination of data, casework activities, and procedures pertaining to guidance.

5. Programming: the planning and application of appropriate procedures and activities pertaining to the fulfillment of guidance purposes and functions.

RELATED OPERATIONAL PHASES (7, p. 198)

1. Classroom Activity. Informal interviewing of individual pupils; individual observations, appraisals, ratings, and record keeping; participation in case conferences by teacher; consultation with individual pupils for academic or social adjustment; individual adjustment, orientation, and development through classroom activities; referrals. All phases conducted on classroom level within teacher limitations of time, inclination, and competence. (Particularly applicable to elementary level, to class work in core programs, lab and shop courses, physical education,and special education and services.)

2. Cocurricular Activities. Individualized consultation incidental to leadership of cocurricular activities; also, individual adjustment, orientation, and development through these activities.

3. Group Work (instructional). Group activities led by classroom teachers, homeroom teachers, and part-time guidance workers dealing with common needs and problems of orientation on the informational level.

4. Special Instruction and Remedial Work. Including classes for the mentally retarded, physically handicapped, emotionally disturbed; academic remedial classes and speech correction.

5. Work Experience Programs. Organization and operation of cooperative work-study programs; evaluation of work experiences by students with counselors; group discussion of problems encountered; evaluation of employer satisfaction.

6. Parent Education. Discussion with parents of common adjustment, orientational, and developmental problems.

7. Community Activities and Public Relations. Utilization of services and resources of community agencies; fostering of school-community relationships; procurement of educational and occupational information; field trips and excursions; collaboration of parents and citizens in the life of the school.

The place of guidance functions and related functions in the total organizational pattern of the school system will depend upon a number of local factors such as the size of the program, personnel available, and finances. Pupil need, functional effectiveness, and operational simplicity and directness are three general principles which are helpful for determining where the functions should be allocated. While some aspects of the implementation of developmental guidance are similar to those of other orientations, others are unique to the developmental approach.

The orientation function, for example, in developmental guidance is similar to orientation in any other approach except that it is a key phase. Since the guidance process is a long-term endeavor, extending throughout the entire course of the student's academic life, and since there is a conscious effort to provide continuity to the developmental guidance process, orientation becomes a key step in providing the articulation and continuity deemed so important to the overall development of the student. Thus, the theme of the orientation tends to have broader and more encompassing overtones than the mere orientation of students to the physical plant, the curriculum, extracurricular activities, and school rules.

Individual casework has two major focuses: (*a*) the personal needs and problems of students and (*b*) the needs and problems of the institution. Individual casework focuses upon academic and personal development and adjustment of the individual in addition to vocational planning. This focus is supplemented by an attempt to assist the student in relation to his environment—e.g., the school. Individual casework also includes classifying, grouping, and placing students as well as the general and special educational development of the student.

Developmental guidance also involves consultation between guidance personnel and teachers, parents, administration, other staff members, and community representatives concerning the guidance needs and problems of individuals or groups of students. It is the consultative function that allows members of the pupil personnel team to communicate and collaborate with one another. It is through the consultative function that the specialists and generalists on the pupil personnel team can complement one another's unique perspectives and skills, thereby providing a balanced and coordinated effort to help the student to understand himself and his environment, and to relate with his environment more effectively.

The guidance worker at the secondary level of education has a dual role. Besides being a consultant, he is also a counselor. A comprehensive and well-balanced program of developmental guidance therefore emphasizes this dual role, calling the guidance worker a "guidance counselor" but realizing that he has the other important role as collaborator and consultant with the classroom teacher and other school personnel.

The individual and group developmental counseling have two functions. Some counseling provides the student with long-term, cumulative, incremental assistance in increasing self-understanding and exploring distant goals in preparation for decisions to be made in the future. This is the preventive function. It is neither possible nor desirable, however, to prevent all problems or crises. The young adolescent will therefore need assistance at crisis points where decisions and choices will be required. Individual and group counseling would appear to be two useful approaches for helping the pupil at these crisis points. The counseling for "wise choices" from a developmental orientation is similar in a gross sense to that of any other orientation to guidance except that the pupil has had a long series of experiences paralleling his development to give him information, attitudes, and a general orientation favorable for making good choices and adequately mastering developmental tasks.

Long-range developmental counseling centers primarily upon several general goals. First, it assists the pupil in understanding his personal characteristics. Developmental counseling at choice points can also help the student to evaluate the total range of his experiences. Lastly, developmental counseling attempts to facilitate the formation and application of a flexible but integrated orientation toward the self and the environment.

Developmental counseling at choice points encourages self-analysis and evaluation of interests, attitudes, values, and self-concept as each of these relates to the decision to be made. The long-range cumulative goal of developing the student's recognition of these aspects of personality and their significance for vocational decisions is most meaningful at these critical choice points. Developmental counseling therefore assists the student to understand and consider all pertinent factors about himself and the environment relating to the decision-making process and his subsequent instrumental behavior in attempting to master developmental tasks and to attain those goals that he has chosen for his life.

Since many students will continue their formal education in some type of post–high school training or education, while others will enter the work force either after dropping out of high school or after graduation from high school, developmental guidance must deal with three types. The dropout, the high school graduate, and the college-bound student each faces developmental tasks in different ways.

The school is only one institution in the overall socialization of the child. The student is in the school for only a relatively brief period of time, and his contact with guidance and guidance-related activities constitutes a small fraction of that short period of time during which he is in school. The developmental tasks concept articulated with a comprehensive and well-articulated theory and program of developmental guidance is one approach for enhancing the overall effectiveness of guidance and its total impact upon the development of the individual.

SUMMARY

Two general purposes of education emerge if the role of the school is viewed in terms of a broad concept of mental health. These objectives are those of (*a*) facilitating optimum development by helping students to anticipate and prevent problems and (*b*) providing remedial help for students with problems. A characteristic common to all of the approaches to guidance except the developmental approach has been their almost exclusive emphasis of the remedial function. While the context for focusing upon the remedial role varies, other approaches to guidance are predominantly crisis-oriented and problem-centered.

The unique identifying characteristic of developmental guidance is its explicit focus on the prevention of problems by attempting to promote the positive growth and development of the individual. Drawing upon the vast fund of knowledge concerning the nature and dynamics of human development, developmental guidance emerges as a long-term, cumulative, multiphasic, and incremental process. Prevention, however, is complemented by a remedial focus. Thus, the developmental approach to guidance constitutes a balanced broad strategy for attempting to help the student. The movement toward a developmental orientation or the inclusion of a developmental component in the overall frame of reference of guidance programs represents a significant trend in contemporary education.

REFERENCES

1. E. H. Erikson, *Childhood and Society*. New York: W. W. Norton & Company, 1950.

2. E. H. Erikson, "Growth and Crises of the Healthy Personality," *Psychological Issues*, 1 (1959), 50–100.

3. R. J. Havinghurst, *Developmental Tasks and Education*. New York: Longmans, Green and Co., 1950.

4. R. J. Havinghurst, *Human Development and Education*. New York: Longmans, Green and Co., 1953.

5. W. B. Little and A. L. Chapman, *Developmental Guidance in the Secondary School*. New York: McGraw-Hill, 1953.

6. R. LoCascio, "Delayed and Impaired Vocational Development: A Neglected Aspect of Vocational Development Theory," *Personnel and Guidance Journal*, 42 (1964), 885–87.

7. R. H. Mathewson, *Guidance Policy and Practice*, 3d ed. New York: Harper & Row, 1962.

8. H. J. Peters and G. F. Farwell, *Guidance: A Developmental Approach*. Chicago: Rand McNally & Co., 1959.

9. D. E. Super, *et al.*, *Career Development: Self-Concept Theory*. New York: College Entrance Examination Board, 1963.

10. D. E. Super, *et al.*, *Vocational Development: A Framework for Research*. New York: Teachers College Press, Columbia University, 1957.

11. L. E. Tyler, *The Work of the Counselor*, 2d ed. New York: Appleton-Century-Crofts, 1961.

12. J. S. Zaccaria, "Developmental Tasks: Implications for the Goals of Guidance," *Personnel and Guidance Journal*, 44 (1965), 372–75.

chapter 8

The Integrative Approach
to Guidance

> In spite of the common goals of educators, cleavages have developed between personnel workers on the one hand and faculty members on the other. In a large number of institutions the faculty member, trained as a specialist in a particular subject matter area, has devoted himself to the classroom, to increased expertness in his field, to research, and to particular professional interests. In personnel work, developing specialism and concentration on particular skills have resulted in a multiplicity of "services" to the student, with the experts focusing upon their unique tasks within a highly coordinated, hierarchical system. As a result, the environment has been segmented and fragmented, organized and compartmentalized, so that the American student of today lives in a much divided world. (4, p. viii)

Increasing specialization and bureaucratization have accompanied the growth of American education, resulting in a sharp threefold division of the educational process into teaching, administration, and guidance. On the one hand, educators tend to agree that the individual is a "whole person" and interacts with a "whole environment," and yet the education in early America seems to have more nearly approximated a truly integrated environment than contemporary education. Whereas both elementary and secondary education were characterized by unification, education today is characterized by separation. This formalization and separation is a reflection of parallel developments in our general society.

Brunson has described the following divisive factors and their operation in both the general society and the educational system of our country (4, pp. 8-32): (a) the background of our increasingly complex society, (b) capitalism, with its emphasis on individualism, (c) intellectualism, (d) impersonalism, (e) curricular expansion and the growth of the elective system, (f) increasing enrollments, (g) increasing class size, (h) the impact of institutional organization producing a separation of guidance from the rest of the system, (i) variations in educational philosophy, (j) variations in training for guidance functions, (k) excessively heavy faculty loads, (l) lack of recognition of faculty for functions other than teaching, (m) inadequate facilities, (n) specialization, (o) administrative load for guidance personnel.

The integrative approach to guidance has emerged as a reaction against these trends. A major concern of the integrative approach is that the overspecialization and oversegmentation of interest and function has resulted in a widening distance among faculty members, subsequently followed by progressive disintegration of interfaculty relationships. The system must then rely largely upon formal mechanisms imposed by the administration for drawing together and unifying the various segmental interests of the faculty and the students.

THEORETICAL BASIS

In its fundamental view of the student, the integrative approach to guidance has its roots in holistic and Gestalt psychology. The student and his experience are viewed as a whole, and an educational system that operates in such a way as to destroy this unity is seen as dysfunctional to the individual. Much of contemporary thought in guidance is criticized because it suggests approaches to guidance that are overspecialized, impersonally scientific, segmented and proliferative (2). The guidance specialist finds it increasingly difficult to achieve a common meeting ground with other faculty members. Specialization has been viewed as the natural correlate of increasing size, and the greater the specialization, the greater is the centrifugal force which fosters separation and nonintegration.

Several hundred articles and books relating to integration have been published. Philosophers (3, 21), psychologists (13, 19), anthropologists and sociologists (2, 12, 16), and physiologists (5) have considered the concept of integration as it relates to their various fields of inquiry. Nine ways of using the concept have been summarized by Hanna and Lang (9):

1. *Integration as a goal:* directing efforts toward a state of perfect unity.
2. *Physiological integration:* a biochemical process occurring in a living organism.
3. *Integration of behavior:* a type of behavior characterized by a unified relation of a human being to his environment.
4. *Social integration:* a process by which a group of people or their culture becomes unified.
5. *Integrative curriculum:* a unified curriculum which attempts to promote integration.
6. *Integrated course:* subject matter from several related subjects are brought together to form a generalized subject.
7. *Integrated program:* an activity program in which there are no distinct subject-matter divisions.
8. *Integration movement:* an educational movement which reacted against formalism by attempting to approach "real life" education.
9. *Integration:* a process attempting to promote more effective interaction among the school staff.

The integrative approach to guidance stresses the diffusion of responsibility rather than the limitation of duties by sharply defined job descriptions. More important than the diffusion or dissemination of responsibility, however, is the necessity for interfusing ideas and efforts of all individuals concerned with the educational program. This permeation, diffusion, and interfusing cannot be achieved where there is strict adherence to a formal organization and organizational chart for the performance of tasks. Rather, individuals in the educational system must be free and challenged to cross structural lines in order that interests, concerns, and activities can be interwoven. Brunson has defined integration as follows (4, p. 73):

> Integration is a continuous process directed toward the achieving of functional unity of the college campus, with the objectives, functions, and activities of the administration, faculty, personnel staff, and students so interwoven, so interrelated, and so interacting as to form a complete whole. In such a process the focus is upon the whole student as he interacts with the total educational environment.

Whereas the services approach stresses coordination, the integrative approach emphasizes integration and organic unity. Reed has used the term "functional coordination," in which coordination is seen as follows (17, pp. 119-20):

> A reciprocal enterprise does not depend upon hierarchy of power and differentiation in the rights of officers. It requires instead a dissemination of joint responsibilities. Like the arc described by the pendulum these are spread over wide territory. Success in coordination depends not so much on unification as upon permeation. It includes all effort, whether this be professional, student or lay contribution. It is not a task to be performed administratively but it is an integral element throughout the educational program.

Implicit throughout the foregoing discussion are notions of guidance as (*a*) a process, (*b*) constantly evolving, (*c*) flexible, (*d*) sharing some common objectives with other faculty members, and (*e*) diverging in some ways from other faculty's interests and concerns. The theoretical basis of the integrative approach can be summarized by the following principles (4, pp. 65-89):

1. *The Principle of Reciprocal Activity*
   Integration is achieved in proportion to the degree and manner in which the parts have freedom and opportunity to interact with each other and with the whole. The parts must be so mutually relating and interpenetrating that the activity of each part reciprocally affects the activity of each of the other parts and, in turn, changes and is changed by the whole. The process is never completed because of the chain of reaction constantly in operation.
   . . . .
2. *The Principle of Responsible Participation*
   Where opportunity is provided for all members of the college (high school) community to participate in the functional whole, integration is fostered. Such participation is more than verbal agreement or approval; it is active and responsible contribution. It is a part of the process from its very beginnings. It satisfies human need in that it is accompanied by feelings of belongingness and self-esteem. Since men value that which they bring into being, they will appreciate the total enterprise to which they have contributed their beliefs, decisions, and energies.

3. *The Principle of Shared Concern*

If integration is to be achieved, concern for the total situation must pervade each member of the whole. Mutual concern is a dynamic quality which cements the relationships of men; furthermore, it evokes the free expression of their ideas and blends their efforts in a common loyalty.

. . . .

4. *The Principle of Mutual Respect*

Integration is possible where there is mutual respect among members of an organization. Respect for all members is imbedded in the conviction that each individual is a person of dignity and worth, that he differs from all others in interests and abilities, and that his contributions are both unique and worthy of consideration. The differences should be used to enhance the quality of the process.

. . . .

5. *The Principle of Communication*

If the maximum contribution of each individual is to be evoked, if men are to relate to each other in shared enterprises, then individuals must be free and able to communicate with one another, regardless of position in a social system. Communication is essential to interaction. Only as men are able to speak with others, to make themselves understood, and to listen to and understand what others are saying, can they unite in spontaneous give-and-take, merge their purposes, and form an integrated society.

. . . .

6. *The Principle of Cooperation*

A sense of we-ness, of working cooperatively with rather than competing against others, is necessary if integration is to be developed. This accrues in an environment conducive to implementation of the principles of reciprocal activity, responsible participation, shared concern, mutual respect, and communication. Cooperation brings together in creative collaboration those of similar and dissimilar backgrounds, abilities, and skills. It frees individuals to rise to their highest levels as individuals and as members of society as they work together toward mutually accepted goals.

THEORY OF ADMINISTRATION

In the integrative approach to guidance, the administrative organization of the school becomes a critical factor because of the interrelationships among staff roles and functions. All of the organizational charts in prior chapters depict a hierarchical arrangement of superintendent, principals, teachers, etc. Shown in Figure 8-1, for example, is the basic organizational pattern utilized in virtually every college and university. Like the basic pattern in elementary and secondary education, it has a number of functional variations based upon the general scheme.

Line and Staff Theory

Line and staff theory utilizes a sharp delineation of authority with prescribed "divisions" and "levels" of responsibility in the system. The advantages of the line-and-staff pattern have been summarized as follows (4, p. 28):

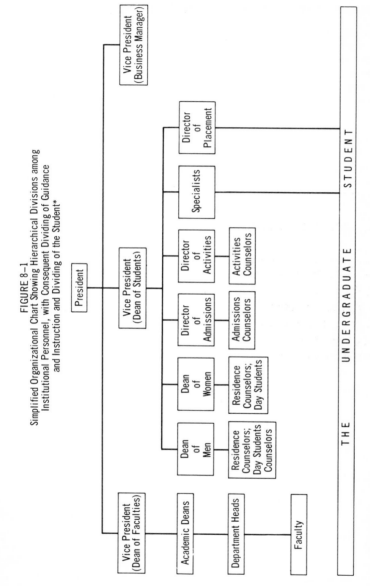

FIGURE 8–1
Simplified Organizational Chart Showing Hierarchical Divisions among
Institutional Personnel, with Consequent Dividing of Guidance
and Instruction and Dividing of the Student*

* Adapted from Brunson (4, p. 29).

It can be charted simply. Lines of communication and of authority are clearly evident. Areas of responsibility can be defined precisely. When staff work is completed at my level, administrative decisions can be made wisely.

Inherent in such organizational patterns, however (4, p. 30):

> ... are the advantages and disadvantages of any machine operation. The parts must work together smoothly; one must not get in the way of the others; each must perform its own part efficiently. A master mind is needed which can encompass the whole operation and maintain the desired efficiency of the services. Domination and autocratic control, while not the only methods for accomplishing this efficiency, sometimes are thought to be necessary and justifiable to keep the program operating smoothly.

Other criticisms of the line and staff organization have focused on its (*a*) highly compartmentalized superstructure with cleavages which divide rather than unite personnel services (4), (*b*) alignments that separate teachers and guidance-personnel workers (8, p. 517), (*c*) decision-making only by upper-level personnel, which may become detached from the lower rungs of the ladder (4, p. 30), (*d*) increased inflexibility (7, p. 321), (*e*) paradoxically releasing and binding the energy of the system (7, p. 321), (*f*) magnifying status differences and hindering vital channels of communication (20, p. 16), and (*g*) segmentation of interests and narrowing of behavior (11, p. 218).

Organic Administration

The concept of organic administration in the integrative approach to guidance focuses upon the *process* rather than the *structure*, and on *human relations* rather than *techniques*. The school is seen as a network of mutually interrelating people—people whose experience has both common and different elements. The daily activities of individuals in the school converge and fuse at some points and diverge at other points. Thus, the primary emphasis of organization and administration is on the relationship with and between people (20, p. 3). The advantages of organic administration (4, pp. 98–100, 154) are that it

1. Meets the needs of many rather than a few individuals.
2. Is powerful and dynamic.
3. Gives benefit of "pooled intelligence."
4. Moves effectively toward achieving the professed purposes of education.
5. Results in higher staff and student morale.
6. Encourages an essential unity of educational philosophy.
7. Facilitates mutual acceptance of educators from differing fields.

Responsibility for functions such as financing, housing, staffing, teaching, property maintenance, and medical care, must necessarily be centered in individuals and groups with the skills and knowledge required to insure effective performance. It is not suggested that all administrative functions can or should be shared among the total staff. Not only is general consultations on all matters excessively time-consuming, but it is imperative that some decisions must be made at the center of an educational organization by persons directly responsible for them. Within these limits, on the other hand, the integrative approach to guidance emphasizes administrators' demonstrating their confidence in groups of people to take joint responsibility and to contribute to their maximum creativity and support to the total educational effort.

Organic administration has been described as multicentered and circular. A structural representation of circular administration takes the form of circles centering around concerns, the circles representing groups of teachers, administrators, students, and guidance workers who collaborate on problems of genuine joint interest and concerns (see Figure 8-2). The intermeshing of ideas might begin, for

FIGURE 8-2
Circular Administration Centering Around a Shared Concern
General Administrative Policy

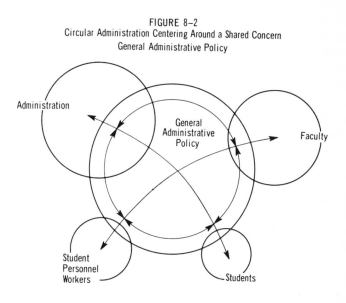

example, with a student group, proceed to a committee composed of representatives of teachers, administrators, students, and guidance personnel, and then flow outward to administrators. On the other hand, the initative might come from within the faculty and proceed to others. The process could begin with any group within the school. The process is a continuous one, setting off new configurations of relationships throughout the campus. Figure 8-2 shows a circular or organic administrative as it might center around general administrative policy. The circles vary from institution to institution with respect to configuration and relative size according to the extent of participation and interaction among administrators, teachers, guidance workers, and students.

Philosophy and Goals

The integrative approach to guidance, as the term implies, views the individual as a member of a network of interrelationships within the school. The individual is seen not as an inert object but as a dynamic entity interacting with his environment. Man both influences his environment and is influenced by it. The individual is seen as a total person. Being, thought, and feeling are fused, so that learning in this frame of reference, involves the total organism. A holistic view of man and interactional view of the individual and his environment result in a radically different philosophy of the role and function of guidance in the total school setting. Whereas all other approaches stress guidance as a process which focuses upon the individual student, the integrative approach envisions guidance as a process which involves and affects all members of the academic community.

The integrative approach is diametrically opposed to the services, counseling, and problem-centered/adjustment orientations to guidance. It is similar to the developmental approach in its emphasis on self-understanding and self-development. Unlike the developmental approach, however, it emphasizes self-understanding and self-development for all members of the academic community rather than only students. The integrative approach also differs from developmental guidance in regard to its primary emphasis on mutual understanding, respect, and interaction rather than introspection. It maintains that learnings derived from cooperative endeavors, democratic values, and mutual understanding can be applied to functioning as a member of the larger democratic society.

Since the integrative approach to guidance-personnel work has been systematically implemented only in student personnel work in higher education (1, 4), the goal statements in the literature are couched in the terms of student personnel work rather than guidance per se. General education and guidance-personnel work represent the two major movements in twentieth-century American education that have attempted to compensate for a fragmented and segmented educational process.

Assumptions

As in the case of other orientations to guidance, several unique assumptions underlie the integrative approach. The basic assumption is that the traditional approaches to school administration and guidance have unnecessarily fragmented the roles and functions of the academic community. Furthermore, it is assumed that the basic goals of education and the goals of guidance are quite similar and can, therefore, best be realized by a cooperative, group-centered effort. Functional groups should include administration, teachers, guidance workers, and students, and these groups will produce more desirable results than a strict division of labor according to formal line and staff patterns.

SOME OPERATIONAL ASPECTS

Formal Organization

Circular or organic administration relies on various councils, boards, and committees of various types as primary vehicles for promoting integration and

FIGURE 8–3
Circular Administration Through the Community Council

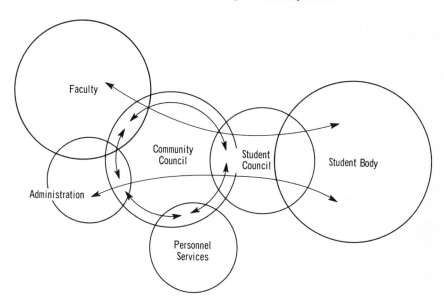

functional unity. Figures 8-3, 8-4, and 8-5 schematically depict the circular and multicentered organic organization of Muskingum College, which represents a high degree of integration of student personnel work with the total campus education program.

Brunson describes the program as follows: At Muskingum, the community

FIGURE 8–4
Student Personnel Services Committee as a Center of Circular Administration

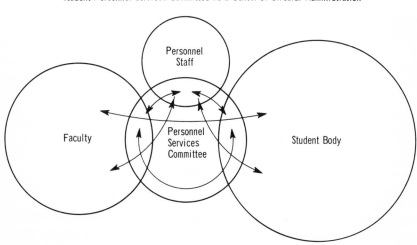

FIGURE 8–5
Student Council as a Center of Circular Administration

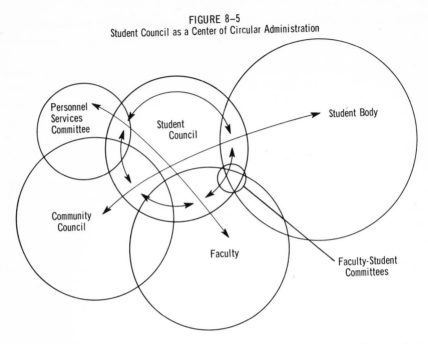

council is the campus governing group. Through the council, the college seeks to encourage (15, p. 33):

> ... each student to become an effective participant in the college community. It is hoped that this participation will enable the students to acquire those skills and attitudes which are essential to a democratic society. . . To a very great extent the responsibility for the development of democratic methods and procedure and of government of the student life is delegated to the Community Council.

Included in the membership of the council are the president and dean of the college, members of the personnel staff, faculty members, and the student council. The presidents of the college and of the student council chair the group jointly.

Integration of the community council with the administration is through membership of the president and the dean of the college. Through representation on the council, the personnel staff is able to stimulate the flow of ideas from and to the student personnel services committee. Articulation and interrelatedness with the faculty are accomplished through faculty representation and through faculty-student participation on eight committees which promote the extraclass program. Student relations are interfused with those of the staff through membership of the student council on the community council and through the eight joint faculty-student committees which provide for interfusing of understandings and activities. These committees, each of which is headed by a student and a faculty member, promote programs in eight extraclass areas: (*a*) executive and planning, (*b*) political action, (*c*) social, (*d*) publications and publicity, (*e*) community citizenship, (*f*) religious activities, (*g*) finances, and (*h*) student affairs.

At Muskingum, the personnel services committee is a policy-forming group composed of a representative of the faculty, president of the student body, chairman of the women student counselors, chairman of the men student counselors, the dean of students, the associate dean of students, and the assistant dean of students. Figure 8–4 shows the overlapping memberships through which communication, participation, and cooperation are stimulated from and through campus groups.

The student council at Muskingum is an elected body composed of representatives of the four college classes; it has the approval and support of the administration, faculty, and personnel staff as a vehicle through which student opinion and participation can be secured. Its stated purpose is (14, p. 33):

> to furnish a representative body which can reflect student opinion, control student conduct, encourage legitimate student activities, and foster and encourage the traditions and customs of the college . . . The organization aids in maintaining a complete understanding and establishing thoroughgoing cooperation throughout the institution.

Integration of the student council with the administration, faculty, and personnel staff is accomplished in several ways. (See Figure 8–5.) First, the entire council meets weekly with the community council to discuss problems and policies related to campus life; this provides for the interfusing of viewpoints with those of teaching, administrative, and personnel staffs. In addition, it functions with the faculty through the eight student-faculty committees that promote the extraclass program of the college; furthermore, it has representation on the policy-forming student personnel services committee. It is not represented on the administrative committee but functions with representatives of the administration on the community council, maintaining open channels of communication with the other group.

Other centers of organic administration of student life at Muskingum include the eight student-faculty committees and the interclub councils. Through the latter, close relationships between faculty members and students are stimulated. Each of the twelve social groups at Muskingum (six for men and six for women) is governed by a council composed of at least three student and one faculty representatives. Cooperation and communication among the clubs and between the clubs and the faculty is promoted through regular meetings of the interclub councils. Acting in an *ex-officio* relationship to the men's groups is the dean of men; the dean of women has a similar relationship to the clubs for women.

Whereas hierarchical organization centers administration at the upper levels and restricts active and responsible participation to a few officers, circular or organic administration spreads leadership and responsibility through many people of different orientations, skills, and interests. Compartmentalized organization may tend to become mechanistic in approach; organic administration provides for dynamic interaction among constantly changing people in a constantly changing environment. Strict line-and-level structure provides for communication on an up-and-down basis; organic administration interweaves communication through its many interrelated and interpenetrating centers of communication and activities. Vertical organization tends to encourage divisions among the staff as well as fragmentation of student and staff experience; integrated organizational arrangements foster opportunities for cooperation, understanding, and unification of experience.

Rigid heirarchical structure must frequently make use of administrative directives and exhortation; organic administration tends to develop self-direction and cooperative participation throughout the institution. Hierarchical organization places the student on the lower rungs of the organizational ladder; circular administration gives the student an opportunity to blend his ideas and values with those of others in a fully responsible way. Compartmentalized administration fosters a dualistic concept of the nature of human beings; organismic administration rests upon the dynamic concept of the interrelatedness of man and environment as wholes. Vertical organization gains its strength through structure; dynamic administration develops its effectiveness through the increasing cooperative skill and personal growth of many individuals as they interact with one another in their constantly changing social environment (4).

Roles and Functions

Somewhat similar programs of utilizing an integrative approach to student personnel work have been instituted at Allegheny College, Antioch College, and Stephens College. Stephens College for example, seeks faculty members who will act as counselors within the limits of their capacity and training (18). Each faculty adviser has a reciprocal relationship with other staff members. There is a continuous interchange of information among and between the staff members, all pertinent facts being coordinated through the faculty adviser. Table 8-1 summarizes the roles and functions of various staff members in relation to the program of student personnel work.

Brunson (4) notes the following programs and activities for promoting integrative unity (4, Chap. 4): (a) collaboration on admissions policies and problems, (b) cooperation in orienting new students, (c) cooperation in developing student records, (d) use of the case conference, (e) development of a faculty advisor program, (f) utilization of the academic program as a center for guidance-personnel activities, (g) utilization of extraclass activities as media for guidance, (h) utilization of residence halls as centers for integration, and (i) joint participation in budget planning. Translated into the high school setting, such programs require substitution of superintendent, principals, director of guidance, guidance counselors and teachers for the college president, deans, student personnel workers, and professors.

TABLE 8-1*

The Admissions Counselor Furnishes to the Adviser	The Adviser Furnishes to the Admissions Counselor
1. A confidential report on the advisees, gained from pre-college interviews with the advisee and her parents; 2. Additional information gained from interviews and not included in the Admissions Counselor's report; 3. Information with respect to senior colleges to which the advisee may transfer.	1. Copies of all letters and reports to the parents; 2. Notes of any unusual problems or achievements of individual counselee.

The Resistrar Furnishes to the Adviser	The Adviser Furnishes to the Registrar
1. A student plan sheet completed by the advisee, including background information, direction of interests, goals and plans; 2. A personal information sheet from the parents giving a subjective estimate of the daughter's needs, limitations, abilities, and future plans; 3. A transcript of credits from the advisee's secondary school; 4. A personal inquiry blank filled out by a competent person in the high school, giving his judgment as to needs of the advisee; 5. A data sheet showing results of standardized tests, with added comments regarding interests, abilities, and aptitudes; 6. An extra-class division inquiry of new students, including the student's statement concerning her extraclass participation in high school and the interests she would like to develop in college.	1. A copy of each letter to the parents; 2. A confidential report on each advisee at the end of the school year or when she is separated from the college.

The Classroom Teacher Furnishes to the Adviser	The Adviser Furnishes to the Classroom Teacher
1. An individualized progress report; 2. Information and recommendations as to courses, occupations, etc. which will assist the adviser in his contacts with the advisee.	1. Information concerning the advisee's background and significant experiences; 2. Information as to special limitations or handicaps of the advisee;

*Extracted from Brunson (4, pp. 194–96).

TABLE 8-1 (*continued*)

The Classroom Teacher Furnishes to the Adviser	The Adviser Furnishes to the Classroom Teacher
	3. Information which will facilitate to the teacher-student relationship, such as social, emotional, and occupational needs.

The Residence Counselor Furnishes to the Adviser	The Adviser Furnishes to the Residence Counselor
1. Significant information relating to the student as a resident in the dormitory;	1. Copies of letters to parents;
2. Information relating to adjustment when the student may be placed on probation or asked to withdraw because of citizenship;	2. Information concerning serious academic problems.
3. A confidential summary on the student at the end of the year;	
4. Information relating to physical or emotional problems;	
5. Information regarding a student's need for referral to specialists.	

The Student Health Center Furnishes to the Adviser	The Adviser Furnishes to the Health Center
1. A daily list of bedfast students;	1. Significant health information concerning his advisees;
2. Information, as far as ethics will permit, regarding mental or physical health problems of advisees.	2. Suggestions and criticisms of the Health Center.

The Sponsor of Extra-Class Activities Furnishes to the Adviser	The Adviser Furnishes to the Sponsor of Extra-Class Activities
1. Individualized progress reports on extra-class participation;	1. Names of advisees whose interest or ability indicates that they might profit from participation in specific organization.
2. Notes regarding special aspects of the advisee's activity.	

TABLE 8-1 (*continued*)

The Burrall Office (Religious Program) Furnishes to the Adviser	The Adviser Furnishes to the Burrall Office
1. Information concerning opportunities appropriate to needs of advisees; 2. Information concerning programs.	1. Suggestions of means by which the program may more fully achieve its objectives in assisting students; 2. Names of students who may profit from participation in particular phases of the program; 3. Names of potential student leaders; 4. Names of students needing religious counseling.

SUMMARY AND CONCLUSION

The integrative approach to guidance is the most visionary of the seven basic approaches to guidance—most visionary in the sense that it rests on the assumption that a very significant majority of the faculty and staff of the school are sensitive to and favorable toward the guidance program. Moreover, the integrative approach assumes that this significant majority will be willing to take an active part in the guidance process as envisioned by the integrative approach. A fully functional guidance program would also require parental cooperation and participation. While the above requisites have become somewhat more prevalent in recent years, it will take perhaps several decades before parents and faculty feel the necessary involvement in and commitment to the basic qualities of the integrative approach to guidance in order for such a program to be successfully operational.

When implemented in the college setting—e.g., Allegheny College, Antioch College, Muskingum College, and Stephens College—the results have been encouraging. Functional limitations of time and scheduling certainly represent some critical obstacles to overcome in implementing such a program in an elementary or secondary school setting. Careful planning and smooth implementation are also requisites.

Most important of all, however, may be the securing of staff interest and cooperation to develop a functionally expanded concept of their roles in the total educative process. The integrative approach to guidance has some elements of the educative and developmental strategies plus elements of thought which suggests a unique and comprehensive approach to guidance—an approach which has remained largely untested but nevertheless holds a great deal of promise for the future.

REFERENCES

1. R. Barry and B. Wolf, *Modern Issues in Guidance-Personnel Work*. New York: Teachers College Press, Columbia University, 1963.

2. Ruth Benedict, *Patterns of Culture*. New York: The American Library, 1934.

3. C. Bernard, "Introduction a la Medince Experimentale Paris," 1865, in George C. Homans, *The Human Group*. New York: Harcourt, Brace & Co., 1950.

4. M. A. Brunson, *Integrating Student Personnel Work with the Educational Program of the College Campus*. Doctoral Dissertation. New York: Teachers College, Columbia University, 1957.

5. W. Cannon, *The Wisdom of the Body*. New York: W. W. Norton & Company, 1932.

6. G. DeHuszar, *Practical Applications of Democracy*. New York: Harper & Row, 1945.

7. M. Dimock, *The Executive in Action*. New York: Harper & Row, 1945.

8. M. P. Gladfelter, "University Organization and Administration," *Journal of the American Association of Collegiate Registrars*, 21 (1946), 512–24.

9. P. R. Hanna and A. D. Lang, "Integration," in Walter S. Monroe, ed., *Encyclopedia of Educational Research*. New York: The Macmillan Co., 1950, pp. 588–600.

10. R. N. Hatch and B. Stefflre, *Administration of Guidance Services* . Englewood Cliffs, N.J.: Prentice-Hall, 1958.

11. M. E. Jones, *Basic Sociological Principles*. Boston: Ginn and Co., 1949.

12. G. Mead, *Mind, Self and Society*. Chicago: University of Chicago Press, 1934

13. G. Murphy, *General Psychology*. New York: Harper & Row, 1933.

14. Muskingum College, *Announcements for 1953-1954*. Bulletin, Series XLV, No. 1. New Concord, Ohio: Muskingum College, 1953.

15. Muskingum College, "On Going to College." Bulletin, Vol. XLV, No. 3. New Concord, Ohio: Muskingum College, 1953.

16. W. F. Ogburn and M. F. Nimroff, *Sociology*. Boston: Houghton Mifflin Co., 1946.

17. C. Reed, "A Functional Coordination of Personnel Services." Report, Sixteenth Annual Meeting of the American College Personnel Association, 1939.

18. Stephens College, Board of Advising Chairmen, *Workbook for Faculty Advisors*, 1950-51. Columbia, Mo.: Stephens College, 1950.

19. D. V. Tiedeman and R. P. O'Hara, *Career Development: Choice and Adjustment*. New York: College Entrance Examination Board, 1963.

20. H. B. Trecker, *Group Process in Administration*. New York: Woman's Press, 1950.

21. A. N. Whitehead, *Science and the Modern World*. New York: The Macmillan Co., 1927.

chapter *9*

An Overview of Contemporary Guidance Theory

Theories. . . are useful in integrating and abstracting the interrelatedness of natural phenomena. They often suggest the next steps in systematic inquiry–relationships that are postulated as existing in nature but which have never been described or detailed. They serve as a lure and a spur to the scientist's indigenous and acquired curiosity. Like a treasure map they whet his appetite for quest of the unknown and the uncertain. They satisfy his desire for understanding by permitting him to predict future events and in some instances to control the forces of nature. And finally they provide him the aesthetic pleasures of his own creation. (32, p. 9)

Guidance-personnel work arose as a response to certain needs in our society at the turn of the century, and during its first fifty years the movement has taken on a largely pragmatic flavor. Functioning almost exclusively within the context of secondary education, school guidance has placed its major emphasis on providing service to the individual student. The reason for introducing guidance into secondary education has been to adapt the community-prescribed curriculum to the unique needs of the student. Guidance has evolved as a means for individualizing the experience of the student within an educational system that has increasingly moved toward the mass production of graduates.

The formal academic preparation of school counselors and the general literature of the field also reflect this pragmatic, technique-oriented emphasis. A very limited exposure to educational philosophy and a fleeting review of a few general principles from the behavioral sciences, coupled with some study of psychology and counseling theory, has in the main represented virtually the entire theoretical basis for the work of the counselor.

This book utilizes the general framework suggested by Barry and Wolf (2), wherein the guidance process is described in terms of eight fundamentally different orientations. Other writers, however, have developed different types of conceptual frameworks for guidance, each a reflection of a different mode of thought. The conceptual approaches described below focus upon limited aspects of a total theoretical basis for guidance. In terms of the model outlined in Chapter 1, these efforts have occurred largely in related source fields rather than in the context of guidance per se. Thus, these theories are supplementary supporting theories in disciplines such as philosophy, psychology, and certain less well-explored behavioral sciences such as sociology and anthropology.

One of the basic premises of this book is that guidance practice should be derived at least in part from theory. Although most guidance practitioners do base a portion of their practice on some kind of theory, a major weakness in much of contemporary thought and practice in the field of guidance has resulted because many individuals have made philosophical and psychological assumptions but have neither examined nor tested them. It has been noted, for example, that few writers (and presumably practitioners, too) even pretend to possess a consistently operational philosophy or systematically psychological point of view (36). Shoben has also described the need for a more adequate conceptual framework for guidance, describing it as one of the dilemmas of the field (31). He notes that while guidance is a humane endeavor, it has faced the persistent problem of the lack of a clean-cut rationale and a well-developed set of methods for achieving the noble goals which it has set for itself. Not until quite recently has there been a concerted effort to investigate the theoretical basis for guidance, and only within the past few years more adequate conceptual approaches to guidance have begun to emerge.

THE NATURE AND FUNCTION OF THEORY

Among the plethora of definitions of the term *theory*, such as those advanced by Black (3), Fiegl (12), and others, is that of English and English (11, p. 197):

> A general principle, supported by considerable data, proposed as an explanation of a group of phenomena; a statement of the relations believed to prevail in a comprehensive body of facts. A theory is more solidly supported by evidence than a hypothesis. It is less firmly established than a law, which is usually limited to a single kind of relationship.

Some definitions of the term *theory* are less abstract. Broudy, for example, defines theory as "a set of ideas so related to each other that they account for or explain a set of facts" (6, pp. 16-17). Hall and Lindzey define a theory as "an unsubstantiated hypothesis or speculation concerning reality which is not yet definitely known to be so. When a theory is confirmed, it becomes fact" (15, p. 10). They summarize the following as the characteristics of theory generally agreed upon by methodologists and logicians (15, pp. 10-13):

1. A theory is a *set of conventions* created by a theorist.
2. A theory is a conventional choice, rather than something that is inevitable or prescribed by empirical relations.
3. A theory contains a cluster of relevant assumptions systematically related to each other and a set of empirical definitions.
4. The assumptions of a theory must bear upon the empirical events in which the theory is concerned.

5. There must be a systematic interaction between the assumptions and their embedded concepts.
6. The theory must come into contact with reality or observational data, this interaction occurring through the empirical definitions of a theory.

Many writers, including Tyler (34), have asserted that theory should be a guide for practice in education. Getzels writes, "Theories without practices like maps without routes may be empty, but practices without theories like routes without maps are blind" (13, p. 42). Theory can also provide a basis for research and conceptual and empirical tools for sound practice.

Hall and Lindzey have identified the following major functions of a theory (15, pp. 13–15): (*a*) a theory leads to the collection or observation of relevant empirical relations not yet observed, thus leading to a systematic expansion of knowledge; (*b*) a theory defines dimensions, variables, or parameters of empirical findings which will be observed and subsequently incorporated into the theory; and (*c*) a theory permits the incorporation of known empirical findings within a logically consistent and reasonable framework.

Theory does not seem to be a direct guide to practice in the sense that a handbook or manual is. Rather, it is a guide to thought and a way to think about fundamental problems.

SOME APPROACHES TO THEORY-BUILDING

A brief description of some processes of theory-building is included in order to point out (*a*) the general process of theory-building, (*b*) the alternative approaches to theory-building, and (*c*) the overall qualities of the end products resulting from these alternative approaches. Two types of theories have been described in literature. One type is a broad, all-inclusive, ' master" theory from which a very large number of empirically observed uniformities can be derived. *Toward a General Theory of Action* by Parsons and Shils (25) represents such an effort. These writers have developed a theory of social systems in which a society is not only a social system but also a complex network of interlocking and interdependent subsystems, each of which is equally authentically a social system.

In December 1955, the Society for the Advancement of General Systems Theory was organized in Berkeley, California. One year later the first yearbook of this organization was published. Research is being conducted at the Center for Advanced Study in the Behavioral Sciences at Stanford University, and at the University of Michigan's Mental Health Research Institute. A journal entitled *Behavioral Science*, first published in 1956, is also devoted to general systems theory.

Hearn notes that scientists from diverse fields are working together for a twofold purpose (17). It is hoped that by examining what has been learned in other fields, they can discover paths to new knowledge in their own spheres.

They hope also that through their collaborative efforts they can contribute to a growing body of unified theory. Merton however, argues against this general approach (23). He favors developing special theories adequate to limited ranges of social data and the subsequent consolidating of groups of special theories into more general conceptual schemes.

Northrop suggests an approach to inquiry or problem-solving in its most abstract sense and, while he does not focus directly upon theory-building, his discussion is relevant to the formulation of theory and research. He notes three stages of inquiry. The first consists of reducing the problematic situation to the relevant factual situation or, in Northrop's words, the question or problem "must, by means of the analysis, be translated over into a more specific question which can be answered by means of the determination of certain facts to which the analysis of the problem guides one" (24, p. 34). The first stage of inquiry ends when the analysis of the problem has pointed out which facts must be known in order to resolve the problem.

The second stage of inquiry focuses upon an inspection of the relevant facts which in turn have been designated by the analysis in the first stage of inquiry. Northrop believes that Bacon's inductive method is appropriate. The inductive method, sometimes called the natural history method, is composed of three separate methods: observation, description, and classification. Northrop notes that "the second stage of inquiry comes to an end when facts designated by the analysis of the problem in the first stage are immediately apprehended by observation, expressed in terms of concepts with carefully controlled denotative meanings by description, and systematized by classification" (24, p. 35).

Northrop believes that only after the first two stages of inquiry is it possible to proceed efficiently to the fruitful and relevant hypotheses, instead of laboriously developing and testing among an infinite number of possible hypotheses which can be evolved. This third stage of inquiry is based upon the deductive method.

A PERSPECTIVE ON GUIDANCE THEORY

If guidance theory is viewed in light of the foregoing discussion, some discomfort may be felt. While many hypotheses can be identified, they seem to lack the meaningful organization into coherent and well-articulated formulations typical of well-developed theories. To paraphrase Merton (23), one finds many points of view, but few theorems: many "approaches" but few arrivals; many concepts, but few confirmed theories. The more highly developed theories in the biological and physical sciences approximate the definition of a true theory. It must be remembered, however, that these theories have been evolved from a long tradition of centuries of cumulative diligent effort directed toward research and theory-building. But the entire life span of the formal guidance movement can be measured in terms of relatively few decades. Furthermore, the theory-building effort in guidance appears to be de-emphasized in favor of largely isolated, descriptive, experimental, and historical research. The theoretical basis of contemporary guidance can be summarized as follows:

1. Since guidance has elements of both an art and a science, guidance will be considered to be a scientifically based art. (The interested reader is referred to Hearn (17) for the underlying rationale.)
2. Contemporary theoretical approaches to guidance are too fragmentary, too poorly articulated, and too deficient in depth and scope to warrant their being called theories in the strict sense of the term.
3. Although they can be thought of as *embryonic theories* of guidance, this writer chooses to call them approaches to guidance because they appear to lack the fundamental substantive and organizational qualities of theory even in its embryonic form.

Aside from those criticisms relating to the nature and quality of research and theory-building in guidance, the two major limitations of contemporary guidance theory are (*a*) a lack of development of existing formulations and (*b*) a need for broader theoretical bases for research, practice, and counselor education.

DEVELOPING MORE ADEQUATE THEORIES OF GUIDANCE

The time is now ripe for a number of potentially fruitful lines of research to be initiated in terms of developing more adequate theories of guidance. The developmental approach to guidance will be utilized as an example to demonstrate some directions which future research might pursue. For purposes of exposition, the various types of studies are grouped under three categories: (*a*) those relating to developmental guidance, (*b*) those relating to the process of integrating knowledge from source fields into guidance, and (*c*) those relating to the expansion of knowledge in source fields which can in turn lead to more adequate theory in guidance.

Developmental Guidance

There is a need to set up and evaluate model programs for each of the approaches of guidance. In the case of developmental guidance, for example, operational programs of developmental guidance should be initiated and evaluated on a longitudinal basis at both elementary and secondary levels of education. Such a project constitutes a difficult and complex undertaking, but the rewards might be very great indeed.

A fairly substantial amount of descriptive research and theoretical discussion have laid down certain general guidelines for the operation of such a program. It would seem that the time is ripe for a rather comprehensive effort to plan, organize, and implement such an initial program in order to be able to observe the general characteristics of an operational developmental guidance program. Such a program could be a steppingstone to a long-term preliminary evaluation of developmental guidance and to further empirical research.

Among the requirements for such a project would seem to be the following: (*a*) one or more competent researchers, (*b*) a clear conception of the nature and function of developmental guidance at the various levels of education by the researchers, (*c*) a school system willing to cooperate, and (*d*) a fairly substantial grant from the federal government or a private source.

Since much of the writing about developmental guidance to date has been rather global in its orientation, it would seem profitable for some future studies to focus upon more specific aspects. These additional studies of limited scope might profitably focus upon some of the following typical areas: (*a*) theory; (*b*) philosophy; (*c*) goals; (*d*) organization and administration; (*e*) records; (*f*) counseling; (*g*) working with parents; (*h*) evaluation; (*i*) facilities; (*j*) educational requirements for personnel; (*k*) roles and functions of personnel; (*l*) policies.

The Process of Integrating Knowledge

Before a potentially useful concept, hypothetical construct, principle, or any other kind of knowledge can be incorporated into an orientation to guidance, the knowledge must first be identified. Methods of identifying potentially useful knowledge need to be devised so that knowledge from related source fields can be incorporated into guidance by a systematic, valid, and reliable process. A trial-and-error approach is obviously inadequate. Intuition of a single investigator is also probably inadequate. Any "shotgun" type of approach is bound to produce less than maximally effective results.

Although virtually nothing has been done to develop a rigorous and systematic method of identifying potentially useful knowledge to be integrated into guidance thought, there have been several attempts to integrate what intuitively appears to be useful knowledge into the field of guidance. In 1962, for example, the National Institute for Mental Health made a five-year grant for what was called The Project for Upgrading the Training of Guidance Workers Through Research in the Foundations of Guidance. In this project, guidance educators and behavioral scientists from different disciplines cooperated through joint study and research to identify relevant issues and problems in their fields. An outgrowth of this project led to the Arden House Conference in 1963, which investigated the applications of scientific knowledge in the behavioral disciplines to guidance. Several studies by Zaccaria (38, 39, 40) have also looked at the general process for integrating a concept into guidance thought, and a number of journal articles have focused upon a broad range of concepts and their implications for guidance-personnel work (2, 16, 37, 38).

It is important to understand the significance of one's guidance stance when new knowledge is to be incorporated into a guidance orientation. One's guidance orientation provides the frame of reference for looking at new knowledge. It also provides a certain amount of selective perception, influencing the kind of knowledge that will be incorporated. The orientation to guidance constitutes the point of departure in the integrative process, the point of entry for new knowledge, and the framework into which the new knowledge will be incorporated.

The second major factor in the integrative process is the concept itself. The general qualities of the concept, the utility of that concept for the guidance orientation, its philosophical and psychological assumptions and implications are other factors to be considered in this integrative process. Among the important qualities of a concept is a factor which can be called its "transplantability." The transplantability of a concept refers to the characteristics of the theoretical rootings of the concept which must be transferred along with it in order for it to convey its adequate meaning and thus function properly in the guidance setting. Concepts vary considerably in this regard.

The individual or group of individuals performing the integration cannot be overlooked as important factors in the integrative process. The background, experience, creativity, insight, and theoretical bias of the integrator are extremely important. Another important factor is the position the concept will assume within the guidance orientation. A concept can take a position on the periphery of an orientation or it can assume a position toward the center. Closely related to its position in the orientation is the functional relationship of the concept with other aspects of the orientation to guidance.

Broadening the Theoretical Basis for Guidance

In his description of the indifferent intercourse between guidance and sociology, Hansen portrays guidance as the monogamous mistress of psychology (16). Although a review of the literature in guidance-personnel work does not reveal any substantial change in the relationship between guidance and sociology or any of the other behavioral sciences, there appears to be an emerging trend toward seeking to harness the growing power of all the behavioral sciences for developing a broader theoretical basis for guidance and for evolving more adequate practices. Thus, a small but increasingly potent mode of thought in the field of guidance-personnel work is beginning to focus upon the individual and his development within a societal and cultural context.

Anthropology and sociology, for example, study the behavior of human beings in society, but so do other behavioral sciences, such as psychology, social psychology, economics, history, and political science. The unique focuses of anthropology and sociology, however, are the investigation of culture, social institutions, human groups, and human interaction.

The first step in understanding a behavioral science or any other scientific discipline is the mastery of its basic concepts. Concepts provide the intellectual tools with which the behavioral scientist works; concepts define the phenomena to be studied; concepts differentiate and delineate one behavioral science from another. Indeed, the term "science" has been defined as "an interconnected series of concepts and conceptual schemes" (9, p. 25).

There appear to be two general approaches for integrating a concept with guidance. Integrating the implications of a given concept for guidance in general constitutes one strategy. It would appear, however, that only some very gross implications can be drawn if they must apply to the field of guidance as a whole. Because of the wide variety of alternative strategies to guidance described in the preceding chapters it would appear more fruitful to consider the implications of a given concept, principle, or construct for a specific approach to guidance. If the latter approach is used, it is then possible to follow either one of two sub-approaches. The first subapproach consists in selecting one concept as described by one proponent and subsequently integrating that concept with an approach to guidance. The second subapproach consists in taking a number of writers' views of the selected concept and synthesizing these views into some kind of master synthetic formulation prior to integrating it with guidance theory and practice of a specific orientation. Some general dimensions of the integrative process might include the following (39, pp. 139–40):

1. Identifying a specific theoretical orientation to guidance.
2. Selecting a potentially useful concept, principle, construct, etc.
3. Identifying alternative formulations of that concept–e.g., developmental tasks, psychosocial crises, and vocational developmental tasks.
4. Assimilating homologous components of the alternative formulations into a master eclectic formulation.
5. Integrating the synthetic formulation of, for example, a concept with a specific orientation to guidance.
6. Considering the implications of the orientation to guidance that has been expanded by the incorporation of the new knowledge in terms of practices and techniques.

Broadening the Theoretical Basis for Counselor Education

Many individuals have urged that guidance should utilize the growing power of the behavioral sciences for a more adequate theoretical basis for counselor education. The behavioral sciences have been lauded as vehicles for gaining a broader perspective and a more adequate understanding of the dynamics of cultural and societal forces on human development. Thus, the behavioral sciences seem to have an important place in both theoretical discussions and in suggested guidelines for counselor education. At a superficial level, therefore, counselor educators appear to have relative unanimity with respect to the place of the behavioral sciences in programs of study. An analysis of the programs of study at a number of leading institutions, however, suggests that the actual course offerings in the behavioral sciences are surprisingly limited (37).

There is reason to question the extent to which the behavioral sciences (other than psychology) have really begun to take a meaningful place in the total program of study. Contemporary programs do not, in general, reflect the opportunity for broad advanced study in the behavioral sciences but rather reflect an emphasis upon advanced psychology, testing, and counseling even during the second year of graduate study in guidance. While the usefulness of additional course work in psychology should not be underestimated, it seems highly questionable whether most current programs are really giving the advanced graduate student "broader perspective," "a better understanding of the cultural and societal forces," or "an interdisciplinary approach," so often stated as the purposes for the second year of graduate study.

Apart from counselor education programs per se, there are some indications that the field of guidance is taking more cognizance of the potential contributions of all the behavioral sciences. Some books, a few recent journal articles, some American Personnel and Guidance Association convention papers and panel discussions, and a limited amount of research supported by private and federal agencies are focusing upon guidance in a behavioral science context. Perhaps the time has arrived when the indifferent intercourse between the field of guidance and the behavioral sciences is ending. Perhaps the bridges of communication between guidance and the behavioral sciences, so often described in the literature, are now beginning to be built. Perhaps the field of guidance can now really begin to harness the growing power of the behavioral sciences for building a more adequate theoretical basis for the work of the counselor educator and the guidance practitioner.

TYPES OF MODELS

A model is a convenient way of representing a complex structure or process. There are three major types of models: verbal or work models, mathematical models, and schematic or symbolic models. Verbal or word models are synoptic hypothetical constructs. Sheldon's familiar typologies of human anatomical types (endomorph, ectomorph, and mesomorph) and the correlative personality constructs of viscerotonia, cerebrotonia and somatotonia represent some examples of word models. Some additional work models include Bloom's taxonomical model of educational objectives (4), Scheffler's three philosophical models of teaching (30), Mathewson's three grand strategies of guidance (22), Barry and Wolf's eight approaches or views of guidance (2), and a variety of other examples (1, 7, 27, 29, 35).

There are a number of familiar mathematical models such as the mathematical formulas shown below:

1. Circumference of a circle: $C = 2\pi r$ (Circumference equals 2 times 3.1416 times the radius)
2. Area of a rectangle: $A = LW$ (Area equals length times width)
3. Length of a hypotenuse of a right triangle: $L = \sqrt{a^2 + b^2}$ (Length equals the square root of the sums of the squares of the lengths of the legs of the triangle)

A regression equation in statistics is another kind of mathematical model. Similarly, the formulas for computing the mean, median, standard deviation, etc., represent models for some other processes. Cattell in the area of personality theory (8) and Hull in the field of learning (18, 19, 20) have proposed mathematical models for predicting human behavior.

Schematic models utilize drawings and/or symbols to represent a structure or a process. Guilford's model of personality (14), Roe's model for describing the influence of early parent-child relationships on occupational choice (26), Tiedeman and O'Hara's model of the process of occupational choice (33), Lewin's model of personality, i.e., life space (21), and Rogers' model of personality (28) represent a few of the more commonly known schematic models.

SCHEMATIC MODELS OF GUIDANCE

Various kinds of models have been used in a number of fields as clear and concise representations of complex structures and processes. Good models are helpful in summarizing over-all processes and for providing a convenient frame of reference for understanding and describing processes, without having to go through a laborious verbal description. The use of schematic models in guidance has been rather limited. The most well-known schematic model of guidance has been described by Mathewson, who notes the possibility of defining almost any professional philosophy, any position, or any approach to guidance as a profile or pattern on the following scale of dimensions (22, pp. 97-99):

Educative. . . . . . . Directive
Cumulative . . . . . . Problem Point
Self-Evaluative . . . . Mentor-Evaluated
Personal Value . . . . Social Value
Subjective Focus . . Objective Focus
Multiphasic . . . . . Uniphasic
Coordinative . . . . . Specialized

Within this framework, Mathewson feels that developmental guidance, for example, is educative rather than directive because it is conceived as a learning process whereby the student develops the capacity for making his own choices and decisions and for directing his own behavior, rather than being conceived as diagnosis followed by prescriptive or recommendatory report by the guidance worker and then problem-solving by the student. Mathewson clearly indicates that developmental guidance is a relatively continuous, cumulative, and incremental process for all students, rather than a process which occurs only at problem points or decision points required by only a few pupils needing special assistance at those points.

Both the personal needs of the individual and the values of the society are considered whenever a decision or choice is made. Thus, personal values and social values are considered. Similarly developmental guidance, as described by Mathewson, focuses upon those subjective aspects of development such as psychological states and events having to do with self-defining and self-conceptualizing processes, together with a complementary focus upon results of tests, ratings, achievement assessment, etc. Mathewson clearly states that developmental guidance is multiphasic rather than uniphasic. It focuses upon all needs and problems in the normal range, rather than a singular concentration upon vocational, educational, or personal development. He stresses not only the importance of a multiphasic approach, but also the interrelatedness of the various aspects of development. Lastly, Mathewson describes developmental guidance as coordinative rather than specialized. Guidance should permeate the entire school. It should involve all staff. It should be a cooperative effort and not limited chiefly to professional specialists, with only supplementary contributary help from teachers. Mathewson's view of developmental guidance could be summarized as shown in Figure 9-1, using his profile pattern approach and his own description of developmental guidance.

FIGURE 9–1

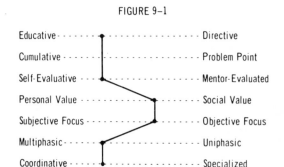

ANOTHER MODEL OF GUIDANCE

An adequate model of guidance should describe each of the major dimensions of guidance. Shown in Figure 9-2 is a schematic model of guidance process including: (*a*) the theoretical orientation, (*b*) the goal orientation, (*c*) the focal orientation, and (*d*) the process orientation. The model is a four-sided figure in which each of the four sides consists of a series of subdimensions in the form of scales which are used to depict the degree of emphasis placed upon that subdimension of the overall guidance process. As in the case of Mathewson's

FIGURE 9–2
A Model of Guidance

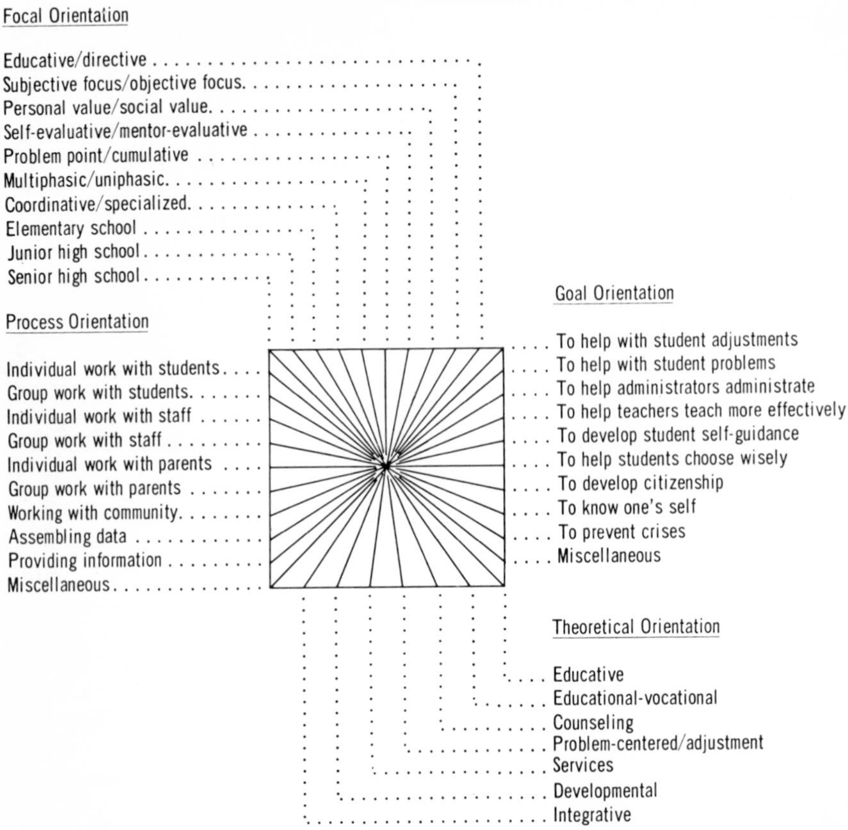

Focal Orientation

Educative/directive . . . .
Subjective focus/objective focus. . . . .
Personal value/social value. . . . .
Self-evaluative/mentor-evaluative . . . .
Problem point/cumulative . . . .
Multiphasic/uniphasic. . . . .
Coordinative/specialized. . . . .
Elementary school . . . .
Junior high school. . . . .
Senior high school . . . .

Process Orientation

Individual work with students. . . .
Group work with students. . . . . . .
Individual work with staff . . . . . .
Group work with staff . . . .
Individual work with parents . . . .
Group work with parents . . . .
Working with community. . . . .
Assembling data . . . .
Providing information . . . .
Miscellaneous. . . . .

Goal Orientation

. . . . To help with student adjustments
. . . . To help with student problems
. . . . To help administrators administrate
. . . . To help teachers teach more effectively
. . . . To develop student self-guidance
. . . . To help students choose wisely
. . . . To develop citizenship
. . . . To know one's self
. . . . To prevent crises
. . . . Miscellaneous

Theoretical Orientation

. . . . Educative
. . . . . . Educational-vocational
. . . . Counseling
. . . . Problem-centered/adjustment
. . . . Services
. . . . Developmental
. . . . Integrative

model, the general formulation is similar to the semantic differential in which the meaning of a concept for an individual is indicated by his placing an X on each of a series of continua of thought with respect to that concept.

When each of the subdimensions has been plotted and the points on each of the scales have been connected by a series of lines, an irregular polygon is formed, schematically representing the significant dimensions of an orientation to guidance. The four basic dimensions are summarized below:

1. *The theoretical orientation*: Barry and Wolf's classification (2) that has been utilized throughout this book constitutes the theoretical context for the guidance process.
2. *The goal orientation*: Cribbin's analysis of the goals of guidance (10) has been used for this major dimension of guidance. An additional goal from existential thought has been added.
3. *The focal orientation*: The focal orientation is closely related to both the

theoretical orientation and the goal orientation of a guidance program. Mathewson's basic model is adapted to include some significant sub-dimensions which are not included within theory or goals.

4. *The process orientation*: This dimension refers to the techniques and practices utilized to achieve the goals of the guidance process.

SUMMARY

The field of guidance-personnel work has two growing edges—its program of research and its program of counselor education. There has been a definite trend in recent years to carry on writing, research, and counselor education within a broader theoretical context and to present this new thinking to practitioners in the field through various media such as conventions, conferences, symposia, interdisciplinary seminars, and textbooks. While it is not true that the field as a whole can be characterized as having a broad interdisciplinary point of view or frame of reference for its work, the foregoing developments suggest that guidance is moving in the direction of a more broadly based theoretical basis for research, education, and practice.

REFERENCES

1. G. W. Allport, *Becoming.* New Haven, Conn.: Yale University Press, 1955.

2. R. Barry and B. Wolf, *Modern Issues in Guidance-Personnel Work.* New York: Teachers College Press, Columbia University, 1957.

3. M. Black, *Dictionary of Philosophy.* New York: Philosophical Library, 1942.

4. B. S. Bloom *et al.*, *Taxonomy of Educational Objectives.* New York: David McKay Co., 1956.

5. D. Brady, *An Analytical Study of Counseling Theory and Practice with Recommendations for the Philosophy of Counseling.* Washington, D.C.: Catholic University Press, 1952.

6. H. S. Broudy, *Building a Philosophy of Education.* Englewood Cliffs, N.J.: Prentice-Hall, 1961.

7. T. Caplow, *The Sociology of Work.* Minneapolis: University of Minnesota Press, 1954.

8. R. B. Cattell, *Personality: A Systematic Theoretical and Factual Study.* New York: McGraw-Hill, 1950.

9. J. B. Conant, *Science and Common Sense.* New Haven, Conn.: Yale University Press, 1951.

10. J. Cribbin, "Critique of the Philosophy of Modern Guidance," *Catholic Educational Review*, 53 (1953), 73–91.

11. H. B. English and A. C. English, *A Comprehensive Dictionary of Psychological and Psychoanalytic Terms*. New York: Longmans, Green and Co., 1958.

12. H. Fiegl, "Principles and Problems of Theory Construction in Psychology," in W. Dennis, ed., *Current Trends of Psychological Theory*. Pittsburgh: University of Pittsburgh Press, 1951.

13. J. W. Getzels, "Theory and Practice in Educational Administration: An Old Question Revisited," in R. F. Campbell and J. M. Lupham, ed., *Administration Theory as a Guide to Action*. Chicago: Midwest Administration Center, 1960.

14. J. P. Guilford, *Review of Educational Research*. Washington, D.C.: National Education Association, 1959.

15. C. S. Hall and G. Lindzey, *Theories of Personality*. New York: John Wiley & Sons, 1957.

16. D. A. Hansen, "The Indifferent Intercourse of Counseling and Sociology," *Journal of Counseling Psychology*, 10 (1963), 3-13.

17. G. Hearn, *Theory Building in Social Work*. Toronto: University of Toronto Press, 1958.

18. C. L. Hull, *A Behavior System*. New Haven, Conn.: Yale University Press, 1952.

19. C. L. Hull, *Essentials of Behavior*. New Haven, Conn.: Yale University Press, 1951.

20. C. L. Hull, *Principles of Behavior*. New York: Appleton-Century-Crofts, 1943.

21. K. Lewin, *Field Theory in Social Science: Selected Theoretical Papers*. New York: Harper & Row, 1951.

22. R. H. Mathewson, *Guidance Policy and Practice*, 3d ed. New York: Harper & Row, 1962.

23. R. K. Merton, *Social Theory and Social Structure*. Glencoe, N.Y.: Free Press of Glencoe, 1949.

24. F. S. C. Northrop, *The Logic of the Sciences and the Humanities*. New York; The World Publishing Company, 1959.

25. T. Parsons and E. Shils, *Toward a General Theory of Action*. Cambridge: Harvard University Press, 1951.

26. A. Roe, "Early Determinants of Vocational Choice," *Journal of Counseling Psychology*, 4 (1957), 212-17.

27. A. Roe, *The Psychology of Occupations*. New York: John Wiley & Sons, 1956.

28. C. R. Rogers, *Client-Centered Therapy*. Boston: Houghton Mifflin Co., 1951.

29. C. R. Rogers, "The Place of the Person in the New World of the Behavioral Sciences," *Personnel and Guidance Journal*, 6 (1961), 442-51.

30. I. Scheffler, "Philosophical Models of Teaching," *Harvard Educational Review*, 35 (1965), 131-43.

31. E. J. Shoeben, "Dilemmas of Guidance," *Teachers College Record,* 64 (1963), 719-22.

32. G. G. Thompson, *Child Psychology.* Boston: Houghton Mifflin Co., 1962.

33. D. V. Tiedeman and R. O. O'Hara, *Career Development: Choice and Adjustment.* New York: College Entrance Examination Board, 1963.

34. R. W. Tyler, "Specific Contributions of Research to Education," *Theory in Practice,* 1 (1963), 75-80.

35. R. W. White, *Lives in Progress.* New York: Holt, Rinehart & Winston, 1952.

36. C. G. Wrenn, "Philosophical and Psychological Bases of Guidance and Personnel Work," *Personnel Services in Education, Yearbook of the National Society for the Study of Education,* Part II, 1959.

37. J. S. Zaccaria, "The Behavioral Sciences in Programs of Counselor Education," *College of Education Record,* University of North Dakota, 6 (1966), 48-52.

38. J. S. Zaccaria, *Concepts from Sociology and Anthropology: Implications for Guidance-Personnel Work.* Unpublished paper read at APGA convention, Washington, D.C., 1966.

39. J. S. Zaccaria, *Developmental Tasks and Developmental Guidance: An Exploration of the Integration of a Concept from the Behavioral Sciences with an Orientation to Guidance.* Unpublished Doctoral Dissertation, Teachers College, Columbia University, 1965.

40. J. S. Zaccaria, "Guidance and the Behavioral Sciences: Broadening the Theoretical Foundations of Guidance," *The College of Education Record,* University of North Dakota, 5 (1965), 67-69.

part **II**

Guidance Within the Context of Contemporary Society

Part II consists of seven chapters, each of which focuses upon a specific aspect of the total process of guidance. These are:

Chapter 10. Elementary School Guidance: Background and Overview
Chapter 11. Architectural and Financial Aspects of Guidance
Chapter 12. Automation and the Field of Guidance
Chapter 13. Legal Aspects of Guidance
Chapter 14. Professional and Ethical Aspects of Guidance
Chapter 15. Issues and Problems in the Field of Guidance
Chapter 16. Trends in the Field of Guidance

The traditional topics are described in light of their historical and contemporary significance. Each chapter in Part II is, in effect, self-contained. Taken together, however, the seven chapters consider the role and function of the guidance worker in the broad context of the entire educational venture and against the backdrop of our contemporary society.

An expanded treatment of the topics in Chapters 10, 11, and 12 provide the reader with a broad understanding of these aspects of the guidance process. The chapters on issues and trends in guidance discuss the unresolved problems and issues facing the field of guidance with some indications of the directions in which the field is moving. The chapters on the legal and ethical aspects of guidance view the work of the guidance practitioner in terms of his duties and responsibilities to society, to the educational system, to the student, and to himself.

In summary, Part II complements the relative specificity of Part I with a more global perspective of the ongoing guidance process as it relates to education and society in the broad context.

chapter 10

Elementary School Guidance:
Background and Overview

It is estimated that public elementary enrollments, grades K through 6, will increase from 24,372,610 in 1962-63 to 34,125,000 in 1969-70. During 1965-66 12,350 counselors will be needed to achieve a ratio of 1 to 600. . . . To extend guidance services to the elementary school level, where these services are presently extremely limited and where many of the problems of children could be identified earlier and resolved much more easily, would require nearly 54,000 elementary school counselors by 1969-70. (52 pp. 43-44)

From a number of mutually reinforcing trends in our society has emerged a uniquely American phenomenon—the elementary school guidance movement. As is the case with all societal phenomena, however, elementary school guidance has not just suddenly occurred. Rather, it is a reflection of the *Zeitgeist* of our times against the backdrop of a number of earlier historical antecedents. Current thought and practice in elementary school guidance stems from related developments such as the mental hygiene movement, the emergence of standardized tests, the many advances in counseling, and particularly the child guidance bureaus and clinics.

Some writers have viewed elementary school guidance as a natural downward extension of the now fairly well established secondary school guidance movement. On the other hand, it is really quite surprising that it was not in the elementary school that guidance first appeared in education. A growing concern over the necessarily remedial emphasis of secondary school guidance (when not balanced with guidance in the elementary school) led to the original introduction of guidance personnel into elementary education. It has been the changing conception of the nature of elementary education, however, that has enabled elementary school guidance to flourish.

The theoretical basis for the functioning of the modern elementary school rests upon a broad educational philosophy which stresses the creation of an environment in which each pupil can develop to the fullest of his potential. Thus, the general goals of the elementary school are (4, p. 56):

1. To protect and foster the physical and mental health of each child.

2. To help the child learn those basic skills (reading, writing, numbers, listening, observing) which are a prime necessity for his all-around development.
3. To foster creativeness in each child.

The above goals reflect the tremendous increase in the breadth of elementary school curriculum occurring within the past quarter century. Subject matter areas have been extended. More significant, however, has been the increased attention given to the personal life of the pupil. An emphasis upon the "whole child" has resulted from the impact of Gestalt psychology upon educational thought in the elementary school. When translated into practice, Gestalt psychology, with its primary stress upon the totality of human development in an orderly and unified manner, results in learning that is meaningful rather than repetitive and integrative rather than segmental. In contrast with earlier emphasis on a circumscribed and rigid curriculum reflecting the influence of behavioristic schools of thought, the contemporary elementary school curriculum is broad, diversified, and flexible.

ELEMENTARY VS. SECONDARY SCHOOL SETTINGS

Until quite recently there has been marked contrast between the elementary school and the secondary school. The secondary school, for example, is typically a larger building with many more students than the typical elementary school. Guidance in the secondary school attempts to adapt the community-prescribed curriculum to the unique needs of each student by individualizing his experience, providing a place where the student himself, rather than subject matter or groups of students, is the focus.

FIGURE 10-1
The Organization of the Typical Secondary School

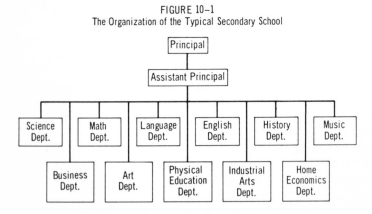

The secondary school has an organization of departmentalization by subject matter areas and a specialization of teachers by subject matter area. No one teacher assumes the responsibility for the major portion of the adolescent's education. The organization of a typical junior high school or senior high school is shown in Figure 10-1.

The fragmentization of the individual's experience produced by departmentalization has constituted one of the major reasons for guidance workers being introduced into the secondary school.

The elementary school, on the other hand, has for the most part continued to be organized by grade within a self-contained classroom pattern as pictured below in Figure 10-2. Coupled with the integrative approach to education de-

FIGURE 10-2
The Organization of the Typical Elementary School

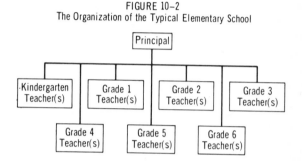

scribed above, the self-contained classroom unit has continued to be a unifying force in the life of the elementary school pupil.

There has also been a traditional differentiation of emphasis in elementary school and secondary school settings. In the secondary school, the teachers have been trained in one or two subject matter areas and emphasize the mastery of subject matter in their classes. The climate of the secondary school is an academic one, with each teacher focusing upon the subject matter in a particular course of study. Because of the resulting fragmentization of the student's experience, the primary concern for his total development—i.e., the integrating force in the student's experience—has become the province of guidance. Other differences between elementary and secondary school settings have been discussed by Peters and Shertzer (70, pp. 65-74). These differences are summarized in Table 10-1.

Patterns of education in the elementary school and the secondary school have differed in goals, organizational structure, and curriculums, as well as in the developmental status of the students themselves. Until quite recently the unity of the pupil's experience has been fostered by the self-contained classroom and other unique features of the elementary school. But a series of new forces is beginning to operate within the elementary school. These changes within the school, acting in conjunction with certain changes within the general society, are bringing about a metamorphosis in the content of the curriculum, the organization of the school, and hence, the needs of pupils in the elementary school setting.

TABLE 10-1*

Differential Factors of Elementary and Secondary Guidance

Factor	Elementary	Secondary
Personnel	Considerable, sometimes complete, reliance placed on teacher to perform guidance.	Greater use of counseling specialists with teachers.
Services	More emphasis on individual inventory, orientation, and information services.	More emphasis upon individual counseling, step-up of career information, and personal-social information.
Readiness for guidance	Fewer choice or decision points in the school for pupils, thereby less encouragement for self-study.	A number of critical stages encourages self-study and readiness for guidance.
Counselor's contacts	Conducted chiefly with teachers and parents.	Many more contacts between counselor and individual.
Pupil appraisal	Greater stress on teacher or counselor-centered instruments.	Use made of self reports or pupil-centered instruments.
Problem areas	Problems more often centered in learning areas or home relationships.	Problems involved not only learning areas but also heterosexual relationships, career and educational planning.
Referral of pupils	Referrals mainly from teachers and parents.	Increase of self-referrals.
Concept of time	More "now-oriented."	More "future-oriented."
Counselor-pupil ratio	One full-time counselor for every 600 pupils.	One full-time counselor for every 250 pupils.
Cost of guidance programs	Estimated cost of $20.00 per pupil.	Estimated cost of $30.00 per pupil.

*From H. J. Peters and B. Shertzer, *Program Development and Management* (Columbus, Ohio: Charles E. Merrill Books, Inc., 1963), p. 74. Used by permission of the publisher.

SOME TRENDS IN CONTEMPORARY ELEMENTARY EDUCATION

A number of recent trends in elementary education have begun to revolutionize the traditional pupil-centered self-contained classroom pattern of earlier decades. Taken cumulatively, these trends have caused the elementary school setting to become more complex, more fragmentized, and in general more similar to the pattern of education in the secondary school. In summary form these trends are:

1. An increase in the size of the school and an increase in the number of pupils in the total school environment.

2. An increasing emphasis upon subject matter.
3. An increase in the amount of departmentalization, especially in the upper grades, i.e., grades 4, 5, and 6.
4. An increased use of specialists to teach specific subject matter areas, e.g., science, art, music, physical education, etc.
5. An increased use of advanced approaches to teaching
   a. Team teaching
   b. Programmed instruction
   c. Educational television
   d. Homogeneous grouping
6. An increase in the number remedial specialists
   a. Remedial reading specialist
   b. Speech therapist
7. Increasing mobility in the school when, as a result of departmentalization and homogeneous grouping by subject areas, students must move from classroom to classroom.

The dynamic and emerging quality characteristic of our entire educational system, but especially of elementary education, is a reflection of our dynamic and emerging society. Not only does the guidance worker (especially in secondary education) constitute an integral aspect of the total educational endeavor but guidance may be thought of as the *nouveau riche* of education. Many writers describe the three distinct but well-integrated aspects of the educational process as (*a*) the administrative function (planning, organizing, staffing, and directing), (*b*) the instructional function (teaching), and (*c*) the personnel function (guidance).

Just as the advent of guidance in the secondary education reflected the emergent role of the secondary school in earlier decades, so does the elementary guidance movement reflect the emergent quality of contemporary elementary education. The school has accepted more and more responsibility as a socialization institution to the point where the school is attempting not only to consider the "whole child," but to influence his total development. It has become increasingly obvious that the elementary school cannot adequately perform its broadened role in the life and development of the child without including guidance as part of the school program.

Thus guidance in the elementary school is both ancient and recent, both old and new. The concept of the elementary school teacher as a guidance worker has dominated general thought in the field. Indeed, the idea that the teacher, regardless of level or subject matter area, should be concerned with the pupil's personal problems as well as his academic progress, has been one of the most cherished and pervasive themes throught the history of education. Guidance as a unique service offered by trained specialists was rejected by elementary education on the basis that the entire educational process is a guidance activity.

When the need for guidance specialists in elementary education became an obvious one, a major concern was that the process of guidance to be established in the elementary school setting might be patterned after models of secondary school guidance. It was generally felt that the unique qualities of the elementary school and its pupils required different strategies than those functioning in the secondary school. It was not until some of the team approaches to guidance were developed that the concept of elementary school guidance on a large scale was even entertained, except for some scattered systems in which the guidance specialist served as a referral agent, performing a remedial function. Not until the team approaches had been shown to be effective were guidance specialists introduced into elementary education in substantial numbers, giving rise to the elementary school guidance movement.

SOME CONCEPTUAL APPROACHES FOR DESCRIBING YOUTH

Whereas many approaches to secondary school guidance stemmed from theories of psychology, counseling, or administration, a continuing theme of elementary school guidance has been that guidance practices should be based upon the developmental status and needs of the elementary school child. The theoretical basis for elementary school guidance has been derived by mating an appropriately adapted model of secondary school guidance with a clear under-standing of the child and his needs. When placed in the context of the elemen-tary school setting, guidance then utilizes unique methods for achieving its goals. The starting point, however, has continued to be the child himself, rather than some pre-existent theory in an academic discipline.

A cluster of interrelated concepts permeate contemporary thought about the nature of child development and the role of the elementary school in the child's total growth and adjustment. Throughout the formative years of child-hood there is evident a shifting of the forces acting on the child. Although certain constitutional (genetic) forces determine and control much of the be-havior of infants, the immediate family, relatives, neighborhood friends, the school, and the community each in turn influence the experience of the child and hence his development. The society in which the child lives exerts an ever-increasing impact as he progresses through childhood and approaches adoles-cence.

Although the course of growth and development in continuous, development can be conveniently divided into periods called developmental stages. In any given developmental stage many individuals have many characteristics in com-mon. The general developmental stages of life have been summarized by Hurlock as follows (33, p. 5):

1. Prenatal: conception to birth.
2. Infancy: birth to end of second week.
3. Babyhood: end of second week to end of second year.

4. Early childhood: two to six years.
5. Late childhood: six to ten or twelve years.
6. Puberty or preadolescence: ten or twelve years to fourteen years.
7. Early adolescence: fourteen to sixteen or seventeen years.
8. Late adolescence: sixteen or seventeen to twenty-one years.
9. Maturity: twenty-one to sixty years.
10. Senescence: sixty years to death.

Descriptions of the elementary school child have been many (2, 11, 26, 33, 34, 73, 84). The general approach of developmental psychology and the sociology of child development has been to describe the typical or modal characteristics of children in each developmental stage in terms of various aspects of development, e.g., physical development, cognitive development, and social development. While most children go through a similar sequence of events in a general way, each child is unique. Consequently, summaries may or may not apply to a particular growth pattern in an individual child. Group norms are helpful in making comparisons and are also useful as general guidelines for action. Thus, the generalized summaries of child development serve as baselines—points of comparison and points of departure for studying, understanding, and helping individuals and groups of children.

SOME TRADITIONAL ROLES AND TECHNIQUES

Child Appraisal

A wide range of suggested techniques reflects the variety of general roles for the elementary school guidance worker (14, 16, 19, 54, 56, 71, 83, 91, 94). Studying the child through informal procedures includes the use of nonstandardized approaches such as questionnaires, autobiographies, diaries, and informal observations (e.g., rating scales, sociometric devices, and incidental observation). Other informal approaches suggest studying the product which the child produces. Wiley notes that certain product-evaluation devices can serve as a means of systematizing and organizing judgments concerning the products of various kinds of activities such as compositions, dancing, music, and especially the graphic arts (89, pp. 114-15). Similarly, the analysis of children's art productions has been suggested as another approach for studying the child (8, 13, 22, 24, 25, 30).

More formal approaches for child appraisal include the use of projective and expressive techniques such as sentence completion tests and oral and written storytelling (12, 28, 69, 74, 75, 77, 88). Sociodrama and psychodrama as originated by Moreno, the analysis of play (29), play therapy (3, 10, 52, 60, 61), and even psychoanalytic adaptations (23, 40) have been proposed and utilized as additional techniques for child appraisal. Although the use of standardized tests represents another avenue for studying the child, Wiley notes the following limitations of tests in the elementary school setting (89, pp. 167-70):

1. Tests can present a false picture of the child.
2. Tests are misleading in their ease of administration and interpretation.
3. Most of the older standardized tests are of limited educational significance.
4. Standardized testing can repress pupil and teacher initiative.
5. The use of "norms" in standardized tests has prevented the recognition of individual differences.

Individual Counseling

Although a growing body of literature and research has described and evaluated individual counseling with children, the effectiveness of counseling with this age continues to remain an unresolved issue (20, 58, 66, 72, 91). Some counselors have seriously questioned the use of contemporary counseling methods, even when they have been adapted for use with children. To date, empirical research efforts have not demonstrated in general that counseling is a useful approach for helping elementary school youth.

Play therapy represents an extension of individual counseling that may be more applicable to the elementary school setting than adapted traditional counseling methods.

Group Methods

Many of the methods and techniques described above—e.g., sociometry, psychodrama, and role playing—can be used in providing help for the child, as well as in diagnosis, appraisal, and understanding youth. Group counseling appears to be used with increasing frequency (62, 79). Another cluster of related group methods centers on the family as a focal point and includes family counseling (95), conjoint family therapy (78), home visitation, and parent conferences (89).

Classroom Methods

Although many of the above techniques can be utilized in the classroom and in related settings, several additional methods have been suggested in the literature.   In describing child guidance in the classroom, Driscoll makes many practical suggestions for teachers (21). He deals with helping students grow emotionally by adapting creative work, classroom routines, skills, and behavioral limits for guidance activities. Some basic considerations and techniques for helping children with particular problems—e.g., aggression, timidity, procrastination, laziness—are also discussed.

Research findings suggest that both elementary and secondary school children can learn and understand the basic dynamics of behavior (67). Furthermore, students can learn to apply this knowledge about human relations and general human behavior for increased self-understanding and for developing more healthy relationships with others.   Ojemann (67) describes the rationale and general methodology associated with integrating an understanding of human relations with regular academic subject matter in the elementary school. The emphasis is on understanding cause-effect (dynamic relationships) rather than surface approaches to behavior.

Vocational Guidance

Coupled with recent developments in vocational psychology and a general societal concern with vocational matters, vocational guidance has been increasingly emphasized in the elementary school setting. Such practice is developmental in quality and stresses the exploration of occupations rather than choice, per se. Norris (65) suggests the general focuses for vocational guidance exploration in the elementary school (see Table 10-2). The techniques for studying occu-

TABLE 10-2*

Major Topics in Social Studies in the Elementary School

Grade	Topics
Kindergarten	Work activities of mother, father, and other family members.
Grade 1	Emphasis is on work in the immediate home, church, school, and neighborhood environment.
Grade 2	The focus is on "community helpers" who serve and protect, e.g. stores and businesses.
Grade 3	The child studies the community from an expanded perspective on transportation, communication, and major industries.
Grade 4	Major industries in the state are stressed.
Grade 5	The United States is surveyed in terms of the major industries in various sections of the country.
Grade 6	Life and work in Canada, South America, and Central America are studied and contrasted with life and work in the United States.

*Adapted from Norris (65, p. 56).

pations in elementary education include the unit method, the use of class helpers, reading about the world of work, simple research written compositions, field trips, class discussion, audiovisual devices, art work, bulletin boards, experience stories, and the use of songs, poems, and riddles. Following is a brief outline of a first grade unit on the work in building and maintaining a home.

HOME AND FAMILY

Objectives
 a. To develop healthy attitudes towards family and home.
 b. To acquaint children with the fundamental facts about home and how it is constructed.

   c. To develop an appreciation of the work of the family.

   d. To help children realize their responsibility for helping at home.

   e. To develop an ability to appreciate working, playing, and living together as a family.

Content

   a. Family

     1. Father

      (a) Head of the family council

      (b) The provider

      (c) Keeps the yard neat

      (d) Repairs things

     2. Mother

      (a) Care of the family

      (b) Preparation of food

      (c) Care of clothing

      (d) Care of house

      (e) Helps children get ready for school

     3. Children

      (a) Chores

      (b) Personal care

   b. Types of homes

     1. House

     2. City

     3. Farm

     4. Apartment

     5. Summer homes

   c. Workers who build and protect the homes

     1. The architect who plans it

     2. The contractor who supervises the building

     3. The man who measures the ground

     4. The diggers

     5. The truck drivers who carry away the dirt

     6. The cement mixers

     7. The carpenters

     8. The electricians

     9. The plumber

    10. The brick layer

    11. The painters—inside and out

    12. The landscape men

    13. The family

   d. Living, working, and playing in the home with courtesy, kindness, and consideration of others

     1. Sharing work activities

    2. Happy evenings at home
    3. Music in the home
    4. Plays and games
    5. Birthdays
    6. Holidays
    7. Hobbies
    8. Trips
    9. Going to church together
  10. Safety
 e. Activities
    1. Bulletin boards
    2. Family group pictures from magazines
    3. Pictures of workers
    4. Make a scrapbook
    5. Sandtable of different size boxes made into models of homes
    6. Bring play furniture to furnish a room or rooms
    7. Make a yard
 f. Individual assignments
    1. Draw pictures of various workers
    2. Write a sentence about each worker
    3. Read poems about various workers

ELEMENTARY SCHOOL GUIDANCE: AN EMERGING FIELD

The contemporary field of elementary school guidance is a vigorous, dy-namic, and emerging one. Plagued with many of the problems of a new occupational speciality, individuals in the field are developing theory, evolving new practices, and attempting to resolve issues which have remained unsettled. The major issues facing elementary school guidance are a reflection of the general dilemmas of the general field of guidance. These major issues involve the nature of *goals, roles,* and *contexts* for elementary school guidance. The alternative statements of the goals of elementary school guidance are quite similar and in many cases identical to those of secondary school guidance (see pages 6 to 8). As in the case of secondary school guidance, a dilemma of the practitioner in the emerging field of elementary school guidance is that virtually all the goals are noble and worthy. Since it is impossible to achieve all of the suggested goals, the practitioner must pursue some of those goals which appear to be most realistic, worthwhile, and attainable by his particular guidance program and his personal philosophy. Other goals, on the other hand, must of necessity be rejected not because they are undesirable, but rather because they are deemed to be of lower priority by a practitioner whose efforts must be limited because of facilities, student load, time, institutional policies and/or personal philosophy.

The articulation between the goals of guidance and the subsequent role and function of guidance personnel is the second major issue in this area. Guidance personnel in the elementary school setting can operate from an almost infinite number of points of view in terms of what their general role should be (adapted from 41):

1. Working individually with students
    a. Remedial counseling
    b. Developmental (preventive, long-range) counseling
    c. Tests administration
2. Working with student groups
    a. General group guidance activities
        (1) Orientation
        (2) Study skills
        (3) Occupational information
    b. Group Counseling
        (1) Remedial
        (2) Developmental
    c. Tests administration
3. Working with teachers
    a. Identifying problem students
    b. Developing guidance units
    c. Providing guidance materials
    d. Working on curriculum changes
    e. Providing information about students
    f. Offering formal and/or informal in-service programs
    g. Serving on various educational committees
4. Working with parents
    a. Sensitizing parents to children's needs
    b. Participating in parent conferences and case conferences
    c. Providing parents with additional information about their children
5. Miscellaneous activities
    a. Working with the community
        (1) Providing community resources for children
        (2) Arranging for field trips, visitation, etc.
    b. Gathering data about pupils for the cumulative record
    c. Speaking to PTA and other groups
    d. Conducting evaluation, follow-up and other research studies
    e. Working with administrators
    f. Cooperating with other specialists
    g. Carrying out referrals

The elementary school guidance worker is a relative newcomer to the educational scene, and while a rapidly growing number of school systems are employing guidance workers, few model programs are described in the literature. The field is characterized by a searching—a searching for a professional identity. Literature and research either focus on highly generalized global approaches to elementary school guidance, or else represent experimental studies evaluating the effectiveness of counseling, testing, occupational information, etc. in the elementary school setting.

Until recently most elementary school guidance programs have been built upon the same general models of secondary school guidance described in Part I of this book. The 1960 White House Conference on Children and Youth provided the first of a series of important forces which helped to focus educational thought on the need for counseling and guidance for children as well as adolescents. For the most part, prior to about 1960 there were some isolated elementary school guidance personnel, but few organized and well-articulated elementary school guidance programs. As noted above, elementary school guidance was primarily a transplant of secondary school guidance with a few minor adaptations to the elementary school setting.

Counseling vs. Consulting

Gradually, however, it became quite apparent to most people that elementary school guidance required different models or strategies of guidance than the traditional ones that had been attempted to date. The issue of the role and function of the elementary school guidance worker has centered on whether the elementary school guidance worker should be primarily a counselor or a consultant (3, 53, 55, 59, 62). Few individuals still hold the position that it is undesirable to have guidance personnel in the elementary school setting. While there is a certain amount of disagreement concerning how much contact the guidance worker should have with students as opposed to teachers and parents, virtually all writers feel that the guidance worker should do some kind of work with individual students (e.g., 18, 32, 37, 42, 43, 57, 64, 81).

The issue per se of counseling vs. consulting has been pointed up most concisely by Nelson (63), Patterson (68), and Zaccaria (94). The consultant role of the guidance worker has been characterized as a blending of his psychological orientation with the educational viewpoints of the school. Consulting consists of (*a*) acting as a mediator between the child and his concerns and other significant people in the child's life and (*b*) helping the principal and the teachers to examine the impact and consequences of instructional procedures on the children (37). Although the specific nature of counseling has not been described in most of the literature, there appears to be increasing attention to the use of behavioral counseling at the elementary school level.

Recent studies have criticized other more traditional approaches to counseling (39), described the goals of behavioral counseling (46, 47), summarized the general rationale (44, 45, 49), and provided summaries of empirical research (6, 44, 86). Other studies have described the use of specific techniques such as systematic positive reinforcement (35, 48), tape recordings of students modeling certain behaviors (6, 49), programmed instruction (15), audiovisual materials (50), behavior contracts and role-playing (38), and systematic desensitization of anxieties (51, 92). Additional studies have described the utilization of behavioral counseling to control thumbsucking (5), eliminate tantrum behavior (90), control the amount of cooperation between children (4), influence the verbal behavior of children (76), and stimulate creative behavior in young children (1). Behavioral counseling or behavior modification is, in effect, a type of learning theory therapy and is based upon the fundamental principles of reinforcement and extinction developed by Skinner (80).

Nelson has outlined the advantages of both counseling and consulting in an attempt to place the basic issue facing elementary school guidance into a better perspective (63), and there have been several attempts to investigate the actual role and function of elementary school guidance workers. Smith and Eckerson's national study found the following (82, pp. 5-7):

1. Almost 13,000 or one-fourth of elementary schools *with enrollment over 100* had CDC's (Child Development Consultant) in 1962–63. No CDC's were employed in 41,000 elementary schools with 18,180,900 children. It is highly probable that very few of the remaining 34,500 elementary schools (with 4 per cent of elementary school pupils) with enrollment under 100 had CDC's.
   a. The proportion of schools with CDC's was found to be highest in the North Atlantic region (31 per cent) and the lowest in the Southeast (11 per cent).
   b. CDC's were employed in 40 per cent of schools with enrollment over 800 but in only 15 per cent of schools with 100 to 349 pupils.
   c. CDC's were found in schools with kindergartens two to three times as frequently as in schools without kindergartens.
   d. Schools located in advantaged and disadvantaged areas had CDC's more often than schools located in average communities. However, CDC services were available to children in only one-third of schools located in disadvantaged areas.
2. Three-fourths of principals in schools without CDC's expressed need for their services. CDC's were needed most in large schools, in disadvantaged areas, and in the Southeast region.
3. One-fifth of elementary schools with CDC's started their programs before 1948. Forty per cent of the programs with CDC's started during the period 1958–63.
4. CDC's described as having a background in psychology were more numerous than any other group of behavioral specialists; teachers with guidance preparation ranked second.
   a. Principals expressed a preference for psychologists (with courses or experience in elementary education) as CDC's; teachers with guidance preparation were a fairly close second choice.
   b. Teachers with preparation in guidance and social workers were preferred more frequently by principals in below-average and disadvantaged areas than by principals in higher socioeconomic areas.
5. About two-thirds of CDC's had master's or doctoral degrees, while 83 per cent of principals favored graduate degrees for their CDC's; one-fourth had less than a master's degree (non-response, 8 per cent).
6. Three-fourths of elementary school principals expressed no preference as to the sex of their CDC's.
7. By far the largest number of elementary school principals reported that their CDC's worked more with children than with teachers or parents.
8. Three-fourths of principals mentioned children with emotional-social problems as one of the three groups receiving the most attention from CDC's. Ninety-

one per cent of principals in advantaged areas reported that their CDC's gave high priority to children with emotional-social problems, with 81 per cent in disadvantàged areas so reporting.

9. Consultation with parents, consultation with teachers, and counseling of children were included among the six most important functions of a CDC by about 8 out of 10 principals.

10. The median number of CDC days needed (3.6 days) per week according to the principals was almost twice the median number provided (2.0 days) in their schools.

   a. CDC services were available only one day a week (criterion for inclusion in the survey) in 43 per cent of elementary schools.

   b. Schools in disadvantaged communities ranked first in the median amount of CDC time provided (3.4 days) for pupils. The median number of CDC days needed by these schools was 5.7 days, which exceeded the needs of schools in other socioeconomic areas.

   c. Principals in 41 per cent of schools reported that their schools needed one full-time CDC or more. Only 17 per cent of the schools had the equivalent of at least one full-time CDC. The gap between CDC services provided and needed was largest in the underprivileged communities.

   d. Principals in schools in the most privileged areas indicated a slightly greater need of CDC time than did principals in above-average and average socioeconomic areas.

11. The median number of pupils per CDC was 789 in schools that had CDC's. The median number cited by principals as needed for adequate service was 609 pupils per CDC.

Developing Roles and Functions

More recently, Greising made an intensive study of one large unified school district and summarized the guidance worker's role and function as follows (27):

Use of Counselor's Time

Item	Suggested	Actual
Administration	10%	9%
Individual counseling	15	23
Group counseling	15	3
Teacher consultation	30	30
Group guidance	15	0
Other	10	35

Hill concluded from his survey of the statements of state departments of education that there is no unanimity, some actual differences of opinion, and a good deal of uncertainty in regard to who should do what in the name of elementary school guidance (31). The literature and research cited above certainly corroborate Hill's findings. Resulting from and in part reflecting the role and function controversy are the many titles for the guidance functionary in the elementary school setting: counselor, elementary school counselor, guidance counselor, child development counselor, guidance specialist, child guidance specialist, consultant, child development consultant, etc.

To date, the role and function of the typical guidance worker has evolved as a response to the idiosyncratic needs of the school setting in which he works. The most prevalent pattern has been for guidance personnel to serve as remedial referral agents for the classroom teacher. Yet many theorists and practitioners alike realize that the remedial-referral role, while necessary to a certain extent, is inadequate as a global strategy. Consequently, contemporary elementary school guidance is moving toward complementing the remedial emphasis with a more longitudinal, preventive, developmental approach.

Although the work of the guidance practitioner should reflect the unique characteristics of the setting in which he works, a theory of guidance should constitute a meaningful point of reference within which guidance practices can be adapted to meet the needs of individual work settings. The eventual role of the guidance worker can be a function of both a theory of or an orientation to guidance and certain idiosyncratic environmental factors, such as school size, school facilities and resources, the climate of the school, and the needs of students.

A growing concern over the lack of clear-cut roles and functions of elementary school guidance personnel led a joint committee to make a preliminary statement which identifies and provides guidelines for the development of the role of the elementary school guidance worker as perceived by the membership of the Association for Counselor Education and Supervision (ACES) and the American School Counselor Association (ASCA). The essence of the ACES-ASCA recommendation is summarized by three key statements of this committee's report (36, pp. 658–61):

1. We believe that guidance for all children is an essential component of the total educational experience in the elementary school.
2. We envision a "counselor" as a member of the staff of each elementary school.
3. The "counselor" will have three major responsibilities: counseling, consultation, and coordination.

SUMMARY

Although guidance workers have been functioning in a few isolated settings for several decades, elementary school guidance as a movement in education is quite recent. Within the past few years the number of elementary school guidance workers has increased greatly. In fact, the elementary school guidance movement has been described as one of the major trends in the field of guidance-personnel work (70, 93). As a correlate to increased growth, however, several unresolved issues have continued to plague the field. Although in many areas of our country the number of guidance workers in elementary education has increased by as much as thirtyfold in the last ten years (87), there has been surprisingly little empirical research to support the effectiveness of guidance services (83).

There appears to be a definite trend toward supporting the remedial function with a developmental approach. Counseling, consultation with parents and teachers, testing, and coordination appear to be the major methods for implementing the guidance program by specialists in the elementary school setting. The Elementary and Secondary School Act and the National Defense Education Act have provided an additional impetus to the movement, and the projected growth in the number of elementary school guidance programs represents an encouraging trend for the field.

REFERENCES

1. R. C. Anderson and R. M. Anderson, "The Transfer of Originality Training," *Journal of Educational Psychology*, 54 (1963), 300-304.

2. D. P. Ausubel, *Theory and Problems of Child Development.* New York: Grune & Stratton, 1958.

3. V. Axline, *Play Therapy*. New York: Houghton Mifflin Co., 1947.

4. N. H. Azrin and O. R. Lindsley, "The Reinforcement of Cooperation between Children," *Journal of Abnormal and Social Psychology* 52, (1956), 100-102.

5. D. M. Baer, "Laboratory Control of Thumbsucking by Withdrawal and Re-presentation of Reinforcement," *Journal of the Experimental Analysis of Behavior,* 5 (1962), 525-28.

6. A. Bandura, "Behavior Modifications through Modeling Procedures," in L. Krasner and L. P. Ullmann, eds., *Research in Behavior Modification.* New York: Holt, Rinehart & Winston, 1965.

7. A. Bandura, "Psychotherapy as a Learning Process," *Psychological Bulletin*, 58 (1961), 143-59.

8. L. Bender and J. Rappaport, "Animal Drawings of Children," *American Journal of Orthopsychiatry*, 14 (1944), 521-27.

9. D. Berger, "Guidance in the Elementary School," *Teachers College Record*, 49 (1947), 44-50.

10. R. H. Bixler, "Limits are Therapy," *Journal of Consulting Psychology,* 13 (1949), 1-11.

11. J. H. Bossard and E. S. Ball, *The Sociology of Child Development.* New York: Harper & Row, 1960.

12. G. A. Boyd, "Role-Playing," *Social Education*, 21 (1957), 267-69.

13. M. Brick, "Mental Hygiene Value of Children's Art Work," *American Journal of Orthopsychiatry*, 14 (1944), 136-46.

14. D. W. Brison, "The Role of the Elementary School Counselor," *The National Elementary Principals' Journal*, 63 (1964), 41-47.

15. F. Bruner, *The Effect of Programmed Instruction on Information-Seeking Behavior in Tenth-Grade Students*. Unpublished Doctoral Dissertation, Stanford University, (1966).

16. H. F. Cattingham, "National-Level Projection for Elementary School Guidance," *Personnel and Guidance Journal*, 44 (1956), 499–502.

17. J. H. Conn, "Play Interview as an Investigative Therapeutic Procedure," *Nervous Child*, 7 (1948), 257–86.

18. D. Dinkmeyer, "Elementary School Guidance and the Classroom Teacher," *Elementary School Guidance and Counseling*, 1 (1967), 15–26.

19. D. C. Dinkmeyer, "The Consultant in Elementary School Guidance," *Guidance*, 1 (1962) 95–101.

20. E. Dorfman, "Personality Outcomes of Client-centered Child Therapy," *Psychological Monograph*, Vol. 72, No. 3 (1955).

21. G. P. Driscoll, *Child Guidance in the Classroom*. New York: Teachers College Press, Columbia University, 1955.

22. P. Elkisch, "Scribbling Games, Projective Method," *Nervous Child*, 7 (1948), 247–56.

23. A. Freud, *Introduction to the Techniques of Child Analysis*. Translated by L. P. Clark, Nervous Mental Disorders Monograph No. 48, 1928.

24. E. O. Gonder, *Art and Play Therapy*. New York: Doubleday & Co., 1954.

25. F. L. Goodenough, *Measurement of Intelligence by Drawings*. New York: The Publishing World Company, 1926.

26. F. L. Goodenough and L. E. Tyler, *Developmental Psychology*. New York: Appleton-Century-Crofts, 1959.

27. R. A. Greising, "A Pilot Program in Elementary School Guidance: A Study of Teacher Reactions," *Elementary School Guidance and Counseling*, 1 (1967), 126–39.

28. D. B. Harris and S. C. Tseng, "Children's Attitudes toward Peers and Parents as Revealed by Sentence Completions," *Child Development*, 28 (1957), 401–7.

29. R. E. Hartley, *Understanding Children's Play*. New York: Columbia University Press, 1952.

30. R. Henkes, "Art Expressions and Adolescence," *School Arts*, 57 (1958), 21–23.

31. G. E. Hill, "Elementary School Guidance: Criteria for Approval by State Departments of Education," *Counselor Education and Supervision*, 2 (1963), 137–43.

32. K. B. Hoyt, "Some Thoughts on Elementary School Guidance," *Elementary School Guidance and Counseling*, 1 (1967), 91–102.

33. E. Hurlock, *Developmental Psychology*. New York: McGraw-Hill, 1953.

34. A. T. Jersild, *Child Psychology*. Englewood Cliffs, N.J.: Prentice-Hall, 1960.

35. C. J. Johnson, *The Transfer Effect of Treatment Group Composition on Pupil's Classroom Participation.* Unpublished Doctoral Dissertation, Stanford University, 1964.

36. Joint ACES-ASCA Committee on the Elementary School Counselor, "Preliminary Statement," *Personnel and Guidance Journal,* 44 (1966), 659-61.

37. H. R. Kaczkowski, "The Elementary School Counselor as a Consultant," *Elementary School Guidance and Counseling,* 1 (1967), 103-11.

38. D. W. Keirsey, "Transactional Casework: A Technology for Inducing Behavior Change," Unpublished paper read at California Association of School Psychologists and Psychometrists, San Francisco, 1965.

39. D. A. Kennedy, "A Behavioral Approach to Elementary School Counseling," *Elementary School Guidance and Counseling,* 1 (1967), 118-25.

40. M. Klein, *The Psychoanalysis of Children.* London: Hogarth Press, 1932.

41. G. J. Klopf *et al., Interns in Guidance.* New York: Teachers College Press, Columbia University, 1963.

42. R. P. Koeppe, "Issues in Initiating and Implementing the Services of an Elementary School Counselor," *Elementary School Guidance and Counseling* 1 (1967), 41-46.

43. R. P. Koeppe and J. Bancroft, "Elementary and Secondary School Programs," *Review of Educational Research.* Washington, D.C.: American Educational Research Association, 1966.

44. J. D. Krumboltz, "Behavioral Counseling: Rationale and Research," *Personnel and Guidance Journal,* 44 (1965), 383-87.

45. J. D. Krumboltz, "Parable of a Good Counselor," *Personnel and Guidance Journal,* 43 (1964), 118-23.

46. J. D. Krumboltz, *Stating the Goals of Counseling.* Monograph No. 1, California Counseling and Guidance Association, 1966.

47. J. D. Krumboltz and R. E. Hosford, "Behavioral Counseling in the Elementary School," *Elementary School Guidance and Counseling,* 1 (1967), 27-40.

48. J. D. Krumboltz and W. W. Schroeder, "Promoting Career Exploration through Reinforcement," *Personnel and Guidance Journal,* 44 (1965), 19-26.

49. J. D. Krumboltz and C. E. Thoresen, "The Effect of Behavioral Counseling in Group and Individual Settings on Information-Seeking Behavior," *Journal of Counseling Psychology,* 11 (1964), 324-33.

50. J. D. Krumboltz *et al.,* "Non-Verbal Factors in the Effectiveness of Models in Counseling," *Journal of Counseling Psychology,* on press.

51. A. A. Lazarus, "Group Therapy of Phobic Disorders by Systematic Desensitization," *Journal of Abnormal and Social Psychology,* 63 (1961), 504-10.

52. D. Lebo, "The Expressive Value of Toys Recommended for Nondirective Play Therapy," *Journal of Clinical Psychology,* 11 (1955), 144-48.

53. W. H. McCleary and G. Miller, "Elementary School Counselors in California," *Personnel and Guidance Journal,* 44 (1966), 494–98.

54. F. Macomber, *Guiding Child Development in the Elementary School* New York: American Book Co., 1941.

55. T. Magoon, "Innovations in Counseling," *Journal of Counseling Psychology,* 11 (1964), 343–47.

56. R. Martinson and H. Smallenberg, *Guidance in Elementary Schools,* Englewood Cliffs, N.J.: Prentice-Hall, 1958.

57. A. Meeks, "Elementary School Counseling," *The School Counselor,* 10 (1963), 108–11.

58. A. R. Meeks, "Guidance in the Elementary School," *National Education Association Journal,* 51 (1962), 30–32.

59. J. Michael and L. Meyerson, "A Behavioral Approach to Counseling and Guidance," in R. L. Mosher *et al.,* eds., *Guidance: An Examination.* New York: Harcourt, Brace World, 1965.

60. C. E. Moustakas, *Children in Play Therapy.* New York: McGraw-Hill, 1953.

61. C. E. Moustakas, "Spoiled Behavior in the School-Age Child," *Education Digest,* 23 (1958), 36-38.

62. P. Munger, *et al., Counseling and Guidance for Underachieving Fourth Grade Students.* Cooperative Research Project, University of North Dakota, Grand Forks, N.D., 1964.

63. R. C. Nelson, "Counseling Versus Consulting," *Elementary School Guidance and Counseling,* 1 (1967), 146-51.

64. R. G. Nelson, "The Task Ahead," *Elementary School Guidance and Counseling,* 1 (1967), 56-62.

65. W. Norris, *Occupational Information in the Elementary School.* Chicago: Science Reasearch Associates, 1963.

66. M. M. Ohlsen, *Guidance Services in the Modern School.* New York: Harcourt, Brace & World, 1964.

67. R. H. Ojemann, "Basic Approaches to Mental Health: The Human Relations Program," *Personnel and Guidance Journal,* 37 (1958) 198-206.

68. C. H. Patterson, "Elementary School Counselor or Child Development Consultant?" Unpublished mimeographed paper, 1967.

69. A. F. Payne, *Sentence Completions.* New York: Guidance Clinic, 1928.

70. H. J. Peters and B. Shertzer, *Guidance: Program Development and Management.* Columbus, Ohio: Charles E. Merrill Books, 1963.

71. H. J. Peters *et al., Guidance in Elementary Schools.* Chicago: Rand McNally & Co., 1965.

72. E. Purkey, "Elementary School Counseling," *National Education Journal* 51, (1962), 18-20.

73. O. W. Ritchie and M. R. Koller, *Sociology of Childhood*. New York: Appleton-Century-Crofts, 1964.

74. A. R. Rhode, "Exploration in Personality by the Sentence Completion Method," *Journal of Applied Psychology*, 30 (1946), 169-81.

75. S. I. Roody, "Plot Completion Test," *The English Journal*, 34 (1945), 260-65.

76. S. Salzinger, et al., "Operant Conditioning of Continuous Speech in Young Children," *Child Development*, 33 (1962), 683-95.

77. H. Sargent, "An Experimental Application of Projective Principles to a Paper and Pencil Personality Test," *Psychological Monograph*, 57, No. 5 (1944).

78. V. M. Satir, *Conjoint Family Therapy*. Palo Alto, Calif.: Science and Behavior Books, 1964.

79. B. Shertzer and S. Stone, *Fundamentals of Guidance*. Boston: Houghton-Mifflin Co., 1966.

80. B. F. Skinner, *Science and Human Behavior*. New York: The Macmillan Co., 1953.

81. H. M. Smith, "Preventing Difficulties through Elementary School Guidance," *Elementary School Guidance and Counseling*, 1 (1967), 8-14.

82. H. M. Smith and L. O. Eckerson, *Guidance Services in Elementary Schools: A National Survey*. Washington, D.C.: U.S. Government Printing Office, 1966.

83. B. Stefflre, "Research in Guidance: Horizons for the Future," *Theory in Practice*, 2 (1963), 44-50.

84. G. G. Thompson, *Child Psychology*. Boston: Houghton Mifflin Co., 1962.

85. J. M. Thompson, "Current Issues and Problems in Elementary School Guidance," *The School Counselor*, 13 (1965), 77-81.

86. L. P. Ullmann and L. Krasner, eds., *Case Studies in Behavior Modification*. New York: Holt, Rinehart & Winston, 1965.

87. O. R. Warner, *Commitment to Youth*. Washington, D.C.: U.S. Office of Education, 1964.

88. M. J. Weiss, *Guidance Through Drama*. New York: William Morrow & Co., 1954.

89. R. D. Wiley, *Guidance in Elementary Education*. New York: Harper & Row, 1960.

90. C. D. Williams, "The Elimination of Tantrum Behavior by Extinction Procedures," *Journal of Abnormal and Social Psychology*, 59 (1959), 269-70.

91. F. M. Wilson, "Guidance in the Elementary Schools," *Occupations*, 29 (1951), 168–73.

92. J. Wolpe, *Psychotherapy by Reciprocal Inhibition*. Palo Alto, Calif.: Stanford University Press, 1958.

93. C. G. Wrenn, *The Counselor in a Changing World*. Washington, D.C.: American Personnel and Guidance Association, 1962.

94. J. S. Zaccaria, "Varied Contributions of Guidance," *Education*, 86 (1965), 75-77.

95. E. T. Zwetschke and J. E. Grenfell, "Family Group Consultation: A Description and a Rationale," *Personnel and Guidance Journal*, 43 (1965), 974-80.

chapter 11

Architectural and Financial Aspects
of Guidance

All new secondary schools have an area labeled guidance. Here again we have recognition of an emphasis on program. There seems, however, to be a lack of imagination and information regarding the amount and character of space needed for specialized guidance services . . . . It is felt that the lack of definitive information concerning the purpose and character of guidance areas will continue to hamper their design. Continued and detailed study of these areas will provide much needed information for school planners. (3, pp. 185-86)

ARCHITECTURAL ASPECTS OF GUIDANCE

A basic principle of architecture is that form follows function. If one takes the position that school guidance should reflect a philosophy of education and that it should be derived at least in part from theory, then it follows that the physical facilities for the guidance program should flow from the general philosophy and theoretical basis for the program. A search of the literature, however, reveals relatively little writing and research in this area. It was not until 1940 that the first definitive statement was made concerning the required facilities for a counseling program in the school setting (8). During the late 1940's and the early 1950's several additional articles appeared (12, 20, 22, 24, 27). Despite the generally acknowledged importance of the physical facilities for guidance services, most guidance programs have not been housed in adequately planned guidance suites.

Among the more recent over-all considerations of the necessary facilities for guidance (9, 19, 29) is a U. S. Office of Education publication which considers a variety of the relevant requirements in this area. The minimum requirements for an adequate guidance area include the following (25, pp. 8-12):

1. *Waiting area*: room for secretary-receptionist, one student for each counselor, and three or four additional students.
2. *Counselor office(s)*: private, soundproof rooms with enough space for counselor, counselee, and two other persons; access to hall other than through the waiting room.

3. *Small conference room*: large enough for about ten persons, to be used for conferences, consultation, small group testing.
4. *Multipurpose guidance room*: about the size of a regular classroom; to be used for group guidance, group testing, staff sessions, guidance information, etc.
5. *Storage room*: either one fairly large room or several smaller closets.
6. Adequate furnishings for each room.

Munson found the following items listed as essential by varying percentages of supervisors of guidance and administrators (16):

Item	Per cent
Private interviewing rooms	100
Individual testing facilities	99
Health rooms	95
Clerical facilities	94
Special social rooms	92
Reception room	87
Nearness to central office	87
Centralized location	77
Nearness to library	76
Social atmosphere	76
Location on first floor	68
Group testing facilities	54

Space Requirements

There is a wide range in terms of the space required for guidance by various orientations and the space allocated for guidance in various school systems. In actual practice the space available for guidance services is often determined by such factors as finances, age and size of the school plant, the prevailing philosophy of the board of education and the administration, and the general architectural style of the school, rather than the theoretical orientation of the guidance program. The educative approach to guidance requires the least amount of space, for when the guidance functionary is the classroom teacher or the homeroom teacher no special room is required for guidance aside from a modest storage area for materials.

When a teacher-counselor approach to guidance is utilized, a special room for counseling is desirable. In general, 9 ft by 10 ft is a minimal size for a counseling office. Sometimes a plan is employed wherein the counseling offices for two teacher-counselors are placed adjacent to each other and to the respective classrooms in which these staff members teach. Other orientations to guidance require a special guidance suite with substantially larger space requirements than the educative approach.

In general the pupil personnel services approach needs the largest amount of space because of the offices and special requirements of the various specialists. Although there are no general rules of thumb concerning square feet for guidance per student, the following typical allocations have been suggested (9, p. 234):

Purpose	Square Feet Needed
Counselor's office	100-125
Conference room	400-500
Reception area	200-250
Additional for receptionist	100
Space for guidance records	3 per 200 students
Space for information service files	25
Placement coordinator's office	125
Individual testing room	100-125

Floor Plans

There are obvious financial and educational advantages in carefully planned guidance facilities at the time the school plant is constructed. If the guidance suite is to reflect the philosophy of the school system, it may be desirable to utilize administrators, counselors, and teachers in a cooperative effort to plan the guidance area of the building in conjunction with the architect. Twiford notes, for example (25, p. 5):

> Committees with responsibility for participating in the planning process should help the architect by describing the philosophy and function of the particular educational program or service which they represent, and point up the educational specifications which should be considered in developing building plans. Committees which attempt to work out actual building plans often arrive at plans which are architecturally unsound and which cannot be fitted into a cohesive pattern with the plans developed by each of the other committees dealing with various aspects of the total building program.

While floor plans are available from many sources, inherent in these specific designs is the limitation that comes from attempting to adapt a preconceived plan to the unique needs of the school. Because of the difficulties of utilizing traditional floor plans for guidance facilities, a recent publication suggests the use of diagrammatic schemes such as those in Figure 11-1. These diagrams are, in effect, models representing the general relationships among the guidance facilities and various aspects of guidance-related and other facilities such as the library, records, administration, etc. From these general models of the guidance facilities, the relevant school personnel can, in conjunction with the school architect, evolve floor plans to fit their unique needs.

Location

There are advantages and disadvantages to every location for the guidance facilities. A survey by Parker (18) revealed that secondary school counselors, high school principals, counselor educators, and state guidance supervisors expressed significantly different attitudes in regard to where guidance facilities should be located. While administrators preferred to have guidance facilities near the administrative offices, the other groups of respondents preferred to have guidance facilities separated from the administrative offices. Interestingly, ap-

FIGURE 11–1
Diagrammatic Schemes Reflecting Plan for Guidance Facilities*

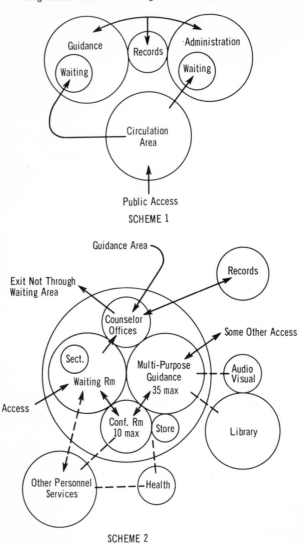

SCHEME 2

*Adapted from 25, p. 5.

proximately three-fourths of the respondents were dissatisfied with their present guidance facilities.

Some critical questions need to be resolved before the location of guidance services can be determined:

1. What should be the architectural relationship between the administrative offices and the guidance facilities?

2. On which floor should the guidance program be housed when the school plant has more than one floor?
3. What should be the relationship of the guidance facilities to other special services—e.g., health services, psychological services, the library?
4. How close to the main entrance of the school should the guidance facilities be located?

Table 11-1 summarizes the suggestions of a number of writers in regard to location of guidance facilities and reveals substantial agreement.

TABLE 11-1

Characteristics of Ideal Location for Guidance Services

Twiford (25)	Peters and Shertzer (19)	Stoops (23)	Roeber *et al.* (20)
Separate from but near the administrative offices		Adjacent to the administrative offices	Close to the central office
Accessible by a direct entrance from the corridor			
Exits from counseling that are separate from entrance to counseling			
Near main flow of student traffic	Centrally located	Centrally located	
Readily accessible from main entrance	Convenient location for parents		Accessible to parents
Reasonably near accounting, health and psychological services	Near other special services		Near other personnel offices and health clinic
Reasonably near library	Near or adjacent to school record files	Near library	Near library Near record storage

Furnishings for Guidance Facilities

There is general agreement that the guidance office should be pleasant and inviting, creating a comfortable atmosphere for general conversation and for counseling. Some writers suggest that the counselor's office should be made to look as much as possible like a livingroom or a den (1). In general, however, it is felt that if the furnishings in the guidance area become too elaborate the overall effect on the other members of the school staff will be adverse in terms of their general morale and cooperation with guidance personnel. Elaborate furnishings, such as, a rug, paintings, or upholstered furniture, may easily be interpreted as status symbols creating a psychological barrier between guidance personnel and the other faculty members.

Therefore, the best general plan seems to be to furnish the guidance office in a manner similar to that of the other offices in the school. The minimal furnishings include a desk, a chair for the counselor, several chairs for visitors, a telephone, and a bookcase and filing cabinets for easy access to pertinent references and records. Optional items such as table lamps, a rug, drapes, and pictures may also be included at the discretion of the counselor and the principal.

FINANCIAL EXPENDITURES FOR GUIDANCE

An Overview

The operational expenses for an adequate guidance program have continued to rise as a function of the general increase in the cost of goods and services and because of our increasingly high standards for guidance programs. Some of the major factors influencing the cost for guidance services include (*a*) the counselor-pupil ratio, (*b*) the availability of clerical assistance for counselors, (*c*) the socioeconomic status of the community, (*d*) the tax base, (*e*) the level of preparation of the guidance staff, (*f*) the length of time the guidance personnel are employed (*g*) the school system's salary schedule, (*h*) the community's interest in making provision for the guidance services, and (*i*) the types of services provided (26, p. 2).

There are a number of difficulties in accurately estimating the total cost of operating a guidance program. Often when guidance services are newly initiated it is impossible to estimate what the actual cost will be over an extended period of time. Different types of accounting systems place the cost for various items such as records, tests, and clerical expenses into different categories. When part-time counselors are used, they frequently spend varying amounts of time among guidance activities and other responsibilities such as teaching or administration, and an accurate assessment of the proportion of their time allocated for guidance becomes difficult. Sometimes the definition of what constitutes guidance services is not clear.

The cost of guidance services have been classified in many ways. Emery utilizes a twofold classification (6): of total cost and per pupil cost. Crosby utilizes a threefold classification of guidance costs (5): personnel, materials, and optional costs such as books, special materials, and tests. Mathewson divides the expenses for guidance into the four categories (15): counselor salary, part-time clerk, supplies, and an administrative overhead of twenty-five per cent. An almost identical breakdown of guidance costs into the following seven categories was employed in another study (14): salaries of personnel, facilities, equipment, repair, materials for guidance, travel expenses, and other expenses. Hill identifies seven somewhat different categories (10): staff personnel costs, materials and supplies, equipment and its maintenance, travel and other out-of-school expenses, service charges, research evaluation costs, and administrative costs.

A Review of the Research

It is clear that the calculated cost for the overall operation of the guidance program depends upon such a wide range of factors, including the definition of guidance services and the accounting system used, that the research in this area must be interpreted with caution. The findings are also complicated by the fact that cost is influenced by the year in which the study is completed. Table 11-2 summarizes studies of the expenditure for guidance over the fourteen years of 1950-1964. Table 11-3 summarizes Warner's (26) findings. In general, there appears to be a trend toward a larger annual expenditure per pupil for guidance services and for the expenditures for guidance to represent a greater proportion of the total cost of the educative process.

TABLE 11-2

The Cost of Guidance Services: A Survey of Recent Studies

Investigator	Year	Level of Education			Number of Schools	Annual per Pupil Expenditure	Per Cent of Total Budget
		Elementary	Jr. H.S.	Sr. H.S.			
Crosby (5)	1950			X	10	$10.48	1.4-5.9 (Avg. = 3.4)
Emery (6)	1952			X	16	$12.66–15.74	0.31-3.4 (Avg. = 3.4)
Mathewson (15)	1954		X			$12.02	4.0
				X		$19.08	4.0
Costa (4)	1960			X	64	$13.88–38.37 (Avg. = $22.88)	2.28-6.60 (Avg. = 4.6)
Kansas State Department of Public Instruction (13)	1960			X	199	$12-34	1.0-3.6
Palm (17)	1960			X	6	$24.98	5.3
Schreiner (21)	1964			X		$25.20	
California State Department of Public Instruction (2)	1964			X	151	$29.29-37.58 (Avg. = $32.90)	

TABLE 11-3

Nationwide Survey Results, 1965: Per Pupil Cost as a Function of School District Size (26)

Size of District (ADA of secondary pupils)	Number of Districts	Secondary Enrollments	Percentile Values of Per Pupil Cost			Cost Per Pupil (average)
			25th	50th	75th	
All districts	5,718	8,860,000	$10.60	$15.90	$22.10	$17.80
10,000+	108	2,353,000	9.50	15.70	26.20	18.40
6,000-9,999	108	825,000	11.20	17.10	22.00	18.70
3,000-5,999	383	1,578,000	9.20	16.90	24.30	18.60
1,000-2,999	1,365	2,195,000	8.30	14.80	23.90	17.40
500-999	1,716	1,231,000	9.90	14.60	20.70	15.90
150-499	2,040	678,000	13.10	17.00	22.10	17.20

A PROGRAM OF GUIDANCE: ECONOMIC LIABILITY OR INVESTMENT FOR THE FUTURE

There have been recent descriptions of school guidance both as an economic liability and as an investment for the future. At a theoretical level, a formal program of counseling and guidance can be part of any school regardless of its implicit or explicit philosophy of education. Is guidance an asset or liability? It is both. An effective guidance program staffed with adequate personnel does cost the taxpayer money. School administrators must allocate funds for guidance services which might have been channeled into other areas of education were it not for the presence of a guidance program.

There is no hard empirical evidence that the cost of guidance services are in the long run self-liquidating ones. Studies summarized in Appendices A and B suggest, however, that potentially an effective program of guidance can make significant contributions to students' development. The real question may not be "Can the school afford guidance?" but rather "Can the school afford *not* to have guidance?" As the school continues to assume a more important role in contributing to nonacademic areas of the individual's development, it is becoming increasingly apparent that there is a need for a staff member who can help the individual in the nonacademic areas, provide psychological remedial help in the academic areas when necessary, and help the student to integrate and incorporate the many-faceted experiences he has in the school into his self-structure. An impending danger, however, is that as guidance has become more widely accepted it may fall victim to the unrealistic demands that have been placed upon its personnel to achieve goals which are attainable through the use of its comtemporary techniques.

REFERENCES

1. A. V. Boy and G. J. Pine, *Client-Centered Counseling in the Secondary School.* Boston: Houghton Mifflin Co., 1963.
2. California State Department of Education, Bureau of Pupil Personnel Services. Research Brief No. 11. Sacramento: California Department of Education, 1964.
3. W. D. Cocking, "Secondary School Design Since World War II," *American School and University,* 27 (1955-56), 185-91.
4. A. S. Costa, "Minnesota Guidance Research," *Minnesota Guidance Cues and Views.* Saint Paul: Minnesota State Department of Education, 1961.
5. J. W. Crosby, "The Cost of Guidance Services in Selected High Schools," *Report E.* Los Angeles: California Test Bureau, 1956.
6. C. Emery, "The Cost of Guidance," *Occupations* 30 (1952), 525-26.
7. The Guidance Center, *Suggestions to the Teacher of Occupations.* Toronto: Ontario College of Education, University of Toronto, 1956.

8. G. E. Harris, "A Special Room for Counseling," *Occupations* 19 (1940), 106-10.

9. R. N. Hatch and B. Stefflre, *Administration of Guidance Services.* Englewood Cliffs, New Jersey: Prentice-Hall, 1958.

10. G. E. Hill, *Management and Improvement of Guidance.* New York: Appleton-Century-Crofts, 1965.

11. *It Takes More than Talk To Make a Good Guidance Program.* Sacramento: California Department of Education, 1956.

12. W. F. Johnson, "Physical Aspects of the Guidance Program," *Encyclopedia of Vocational Guidance,* 2 (1948), 1069-70.

13. Kansas State Department of Education, *Cost of Guidance in Kansas Secondary Schools.* Statistical Report. Topeka: The Department of Education, 1962.

14. M. McQueen, "Budget for Guidance Services," *Research Report.* Chicago: Science Research Assocaites, undated.

15. R. H. Mathewson, *Guidance Policy and Practice,* 3d ed. New York: Harper & Row, 1962.

16. J. B. Munson, *Physical Facilities for Guidance in Large Public Schools.* Lansing, Michigan: Department of Guidance and Placement, Lansing Public Schools, mimeographed, 1949.

17. H. J. Palm, "High School Guidance: What Does It Cost Today," *Vocational Guidance Quarterly* 9 (1961), 168-72.

18. E. H. Parker, "Location of Guidance Facilities within the School Plant," *Personnel and Guidance Journal* 36 (1957), 251-54.

19. H. J. Peters and B. Shertzer, *Guidance: Program Development and Management.* Columbus, Ohio: Charles E. Merrill Books, 1963.

20. E. C. Roeber, G. E. Smith, and C. E. Erickson, *Organization and Administration of Guidance Services.* New York: McGraw-Hill, 1955.

21. P. J. Schreiner, "A Cost Analysis of Public Senior High School Program," *Newsletter.* Harrisburg, Pa.: Pennsylvania State Department of Public Instruction, 1965.

22. B. Shear, "Physical Facilities for Pupil Personnel Services," *American School Board Journal,* 120 (1950), 25-27.

23. E. Stoops, ed., *Guidance Service: Organization and Administration.* New York: McGraw-Hill, 1959.

24. R. O. Stripling, "How about Physical Facilities—Are We Selling Student Personnel Services Short on Space," *Personnel and Guidance Journal,* 33 (1954), 170-71.

25. D. D. Twiford, *Physical Facilities for School Guidance Services.* Washington, D.C.: U.S. Office of Education, 1960.

26. O. R. Warner, *Cost of Secondary School Guidance Services.* Washington, D.C.: U.S. Office of Education, 1965.

27. G. L. Weaver, "Suggestions for Counseling in High Schools," *Bulletin*

of the Division of Vocational Education. Oregon State Department of Education, 1954.

28. F. E. Wellman, "The Cost of Guidance Services," *Guidance Services Newsletter.* Columbus, Ohio: 10, (1957), 279-80.

29. F. R. Zeran and A. C. Ricco, *Organization and Administration of Guidance Services.* Chicago: Rand McNally & Co., 1962.

chapter 12

Automation and the Field
of Guidance

When looms weave by themselves, man's slavery will end.. (Aristotle, 384–322 B.C.)

The purpose of the machine (automation) is to liberate man from the indignity of having to behave like one. (Wiener, in 1950, 71, p. 37)

On the average every electronic computer puts 35 people out of work and changes the kind of work for 105 additional workers. Since the United States alone is producing over 10,000 computers per year this multiplies out to 350,000 jobs disappearing every year and another 1,050,000 that will require retraining. (Buckingham, in 1963, 11, p. 20)

Some individuals feel that automation is merely an extension of the historical process of technological change which had its inception with fire, the wheel, and the lever. Most writers, on the other hand, describe automation as distinctly different from the process comprised of the innovations of traditional technology. Phrases such as the Second Industrial Revolution (22), the Age of Automation (9, 55), and Age of the New Technology (9) have characterized the pervasive influence of automation on our daily lives. Automation has begun to make an increasingly significant impact upon business, industry, and education. It has altered work at the very time that psychologists and sociologists had studied work sufficiently to produce significant breakthroughs in our understanding of the nature of work, the dynamics of human interaction in work settings, and, most important of all, the meaning of work in contemporary society. The purpose of this chapter is to survey applications of automation in industry, business, and education, and to consider some of the significant implications of automation for the general educator and the guidance counselor.

Harder has defined automation as a philosophy of manufacturing wherein machines are hitched together so that they feed each other without human intervention to produce either a completed product or a major component of a final product (10, p. 5). Diebold notes that the distinctive feature of automation is *feedback*, through which machines control and correct themselves through information fed to them by computers (20, p. 3). Similarly, Hart and

Lifton define an automated machine as one "that does man's mechanical work, and at the same time regulates and controls the work" (31, p. 282).

There are three major dimensions to automation. First, the direct control of the process is taken out of the hands of the worker. No longer does the worker watch dials, push buttons, pull levers, etc. Hydraulic and electronic devices control the machines. Automated machines have built-in, automatic self-correcting (feedback control) devices that alter the rate of output without any assistance from the worker. A second important aspect of automation is the utilization of electronic computers to store, manipulate, and record data which have been fed into them. Lastly, production can be automatic and constant.

Buckingham notes that automation has been called (10, pp. 5-18): (*a*) an intellectual revolution, (*b*) a new system of thought, (*c*) the mechanization of judgment, (*d*) machine control by nonhumans, (*e*) a state of mind, and (*f*) the substitution of mechanical, hydraulic, pneumatic, electric, and electronic devices for human organs of decision and effort. He identifies the following four principles as those that underlie automation: mechanization, continuous process, automatic control, and rationalization. The major difference between the new technology of automation and the conventional machinery of the old eighteenth-century industrial revolution is that in the new technology electronic devices perform the decision-making and control functions whereas traditionally machines merely did physical labor. It has been noted that, like other technological innovations, automation was born when necessary and sufficient conditions were united by the catalyst of motivation (34, p. 16).

THE IMPACT OF AUTOMATION ON INDUSTRY AND BUSINESS

A few brief descriptions will illustrate the nature of automation (10, 55):

1. Automated machines working in conjunction with transfer equipment move engine blocks through a complete manufacturing process. A total of 530 precision cutting and drilling operations are performed in 14½ minutes as compared to nine hours in a conventional plant.

2. An automatic lathe can gauge each part as it is produced, automatically resetting cutting tools to compensate for tool wear. In addition, when the cutting tools have been worn down to a predetermined limit, the machine automatically replaces them with sharp tools. Loading and unloading of parts is done automatically, and the lathes can operate for five to eight hours without attention, except for an occasional inspection.

3. A computer in an oil refinery automatically controls 26 flow rates, 72 temperatures, three pressure levels, and three gas combinations.

4. An electronic "salesgirl" can dispense 36 different items in 10 separate styles and sizes. It accepts one and five dollar bills in addition to coins, and returns the correct change, plus rejecting counterfeit currency.

5. In a radio plant 1000 radios a day are now assembled by two men where 200 had been required before automation.

6. A chemical company uses a computer for 30 hours to solve a problem that would have required one man working 40 hours a week 20 years to do the arithmetic.
7. A computer in a guided missile system receives 963 instructions, makes 1,100,000 calculations in two minutes, and then gives information for determining the path of a missile in time to change its course in flight.
8. A president of a large airline company receives a complete up-to-date profit-and-loss statement every morning.
9. A telephone company uses computers for payrolls, billing customers, and automatically making over 30 kinds of regular reports to management.

The impact of automation in industry has been substantial, and the future will hold even more extensive and far-reaching innovations. An increasing number of empirical studies provide the basis for making some generalizations which are pertinent to the guidance worker as he counsels youth planning to enter the industrial sector of the world of work.

The Physical Setting

In general, automation seems to improve the quality of the physical setting (47). Working conditions tend to become cleaner, neater, and generally more pleasant. Buckingham notes, for instance, that there are foundry workers who never touch sand and oil refinery workers who could wear dinner jackets and white gloves on the job and never get them soiled (10, p. 16). Automation also tends to bring about more safety in the work setting, since the materials are handled and tended by automatic machinery rather than by workers themselves. Temperatures tend to be more comfortable in automated settings, and air-conditioning is not uncommon.

Job Skills Required

Although the case for automation's improving the physical working environment is quite strong, whether or not automation generally requires workers to have more skill is still uncertain. In the absence of a substantial body of adequate research, opinions prevail, and the opinions differ. Some experts view automation as an innovation that upgrades workers and requires, on the whole, a higher level of skill. Others argue that automation downgrades work as skilled craftsmen are replaced by semiskilled operators, inspectors, and a few low-level technicians. Buckingham, reviewing a number of studies in this confusing area, notes, for example, that according to testimony given at Congressional Hearings on Automation, 23 new activities have been created by automation in one industry, but that only four of these new jobs require special training (10). Similarly, he states that in a survey made by the *American Machinist* magazine of a cross-section of automated metal-working firms, 43 per cent of the firms reported that the new machinery required less skill than the old equipment, 30 per cent reported no change in the skill requirements, and only 27 per cent reported that higher skills were required.

Gross describes one firm in which a major project included only three kinds of workers (26): scientists (persons with M.A.s, Ph.D.s), technicians (persons with some college—e.g., draftsmen and the like), and secretaries. Gross likens this automated company to a rigid caste system with technicians, secretaries, and only two levels of supervision (foremen and top management). No one can move up in the company because in effect rigid caste-like occupational levels and job categories have been set up.

Buckingham summarizes another study of a plant that prior to automation had 450 employees performing 140 different tasks in its central accounting area (10). It was estimated that 50 per cent of the tasks were eliminated by automation and that 30 per cent more were substantially changed. Buckingham's conclusion from this and other studies is that in most cases the effect on skill requirements is a transfer from one job to another of similar grade and that in some cases there is a definite downgrading of jobs, as in the case of an oil refinery in which nearly half of the factory workers ended up in maintenance work.

Retraining of workers for the new technology represents a crucial challenge. Gross examines the apparent lack of success of retraining programs, citing a number of cases where the net impact of the retraining programs was quite small in comparison with the need (26). In Bridgeport, Conn., for example, there were 12,000 job seekers in 1961 when a Manpower Development and Training Act program for retraining workers was initiated. Because of a need for 2,900 semi-skilled workers, the program focused upon this type of retraining. In the initial screening, 3,500 applicants were evaluated and 1,264 were selected for interviews. An additional 879 unemployed workers looked like good candidates on the basis of written records. Thus, the screening process produced 2,143 potential candidates from those unemployed workers who had applied. Of this total group, 1,550 appeared for the retraining, and 650 of these were rejected as unsuitable. Another 401 said that they were not interested in retraining, and the other 589 were recommended for machinist aptitude testing. Of 589 recommended candidates, 201 failed to appear for the test and an additional 248 failed the test. At this phase of the program, 140 of a total population of 12,000 possible unemployed workers were scheduled to be retrained. Failure to start or to complete the course accounted for another 56, with a net result of 84 completing the course. Gross reviews a number of prevalent conditions and worker attitudes that hinder the retraining efforts.

Worker Relationships

Although in isolated cases automation results in the centralization of controls, with workers spending more time in the company of other workers (47), there is in general a greater physical distance between work stations and less social contact among workers in automated settings. In most cases where a group of workers are together (e.g., in front of massive control panels), conversation among them is limited to immediate job matters because of the pace of the work, the accuracy required in the performance of their tasks, and the responsibility of the jobs. In some cases the worker may be as far as a quarter of a mile from his nearest companion, resulting in loneliness. The members of one British labor union who are physically isolated from other workers have begun to receive "lonesome" pay. Boredom can stem from two causes: isolation and the performance of repetitive tasks.

Worker Satisfaction

The degree of worker satisfaction and dissatisfaction resulting from automation is also somewhat unclear, but the fragmentary research to date suggests that, in general, automation involves a series of conditions which result in predominantly greater worker satisfaction. Physical conditions, prestige, status, higher pay (in some cases), ability for self-development, and job security constitute a few of the sources of worker satisfaction, while shift-work, interruption of family living patterns, and loneliness may in certain cases result in increased dissatisfaction.

On the whole, workers in automated settings tend to be satisfied. Mann and Hoffman report 25 per cent of the workers in automated settings describing their work conditions as "about average," 43 per cent reporting "quite satisfactory," and 18 per cent "very satisfactory" (47). Similarly, Buckingham notes that despite dissatisfaction with certain aspects of their jobs, 72 per cent of the workers preferred their new jobs in automated departments over their previous factory work (10).

Dunlop, reviewing a number of case studies of automation in industrial settings and its impact, arrived at the following conclusions (21):

1. Basic changes in technology mean major changes in the division of labor and the content of jobs.
2. Change in the structure of jobs affects social relations among workers.
3. Working conditions are typically better.
4. Technologically advanced plants demand different supervisory skills.
5. Changes in the structure of jobs mean changes in career patterns, channels of promotion, and job security.
6. Work in more advanced technological plants is generally rewarded with higher pay.
7. Work in new plants generally carries more prestige.
8. Work in the most technologically advanced plants is likely to require round-the-clock operations.

Although to date the most spectacular and far-reaching effects of automation have occurred in industrial situations, a number of thoughtful and knowledgeable individuals foresee that the biggest ultimate impact of automation may be in the office. Dunlop reviews case studies by Hardin (30), Mann and Williams (46), Hoos (37), and Weinberg (69) and summarizes the impact of automation in the office setting in an analogous manner to his analysis of automation in the industrial setting (21):

1. Developments in the theory of information and electronic data processing mean major changes in the organizational structure and division of labor in the office.
2. Automation in the office increases the volume of work that can be done with a work force, causes extensive reassignment of personnel, but has led directly to few layoffs.
3. Extensive changes in the division of labor in the office affect both social relations among workers and career patterns.
4. Automation in the office means higher pay for a few, but essentially the same pay for most employees.
5. Office automation leads to additional shifts.

While some general trends concerning automation in industry and business are quite evident and clear-cut, other trends continue to be ill defined or obscured by mythmakers. One of the continuing arenas of controversy has been the issue of whether or not automation causes technological unemployment. Other issues focus upon its ultimate impact upon various occupational groups, teen-agers, and civil rights (17, 34). It is beyond the scope of this chapter to delve into the intricacies of the many debates, issues, and myths, but the interested reader can find a voluminous amount of literature attempting to shed light upon current developments. More clearly than anyone else, Buckingham appears to have been able to cut through the maze of claims and counterclaims to identify some basic trends resulting from automation in industry and business (10, pp. vii–ix):

1. Automation is a force remolding our economy and many of its major institutions.
2. The high degree of automation existing today will continue to grow in scope and intensity.
3. The limits of automation can be overcome with intelligent planning.
4. The benefits of automation are enormous and varied.
5. New concepts and systems of management are necessary to cope with automation.
6. While working conditions are improved by automation, worker skills are not greatly upgraded.
7. Automation need not cause unemployment or depressions although it causes technological displacement.
8. Automation can raise living standards but tends to unstabilize the economy.
9. Much more rational planning for balanced economic and social growth will be required to meet the challenge of automation.

AUTOMATION IN EDUCATIONAL SETTINGS

Automation has not been as extensive in education as it has been in industrial and business settings. Automated equipment has been designed primarily for use in noneducational settings and has had to be adapted for use in education. Also, school budgets usually cannot finance data processing equipment. Most important of all, however, school operations are more fixed by tradition than those of business and industry. Thus, the use of automated systems in education has been limited to isolated schools and a few school systems.

Although the impact of automation on education has not been great, several pilot projects have utilized automated systems and a few school systems have continued to utilize the new technology (40, 42, 50, 58, 62, 63, 72). The guidance-personnel worker should be cognizant of the demonstrations of automation in education and should be sensitive to the far-reaching implications of these projects, for the use of this new equipment will certainly increase in the near future.

Automation touches the field of guidance in two ways. First, automation has entered the field of education and is beginning to change the day-to-day work of the guidance counselor, just as it has revolutionized work in other settings. Second, the impact of automation on the general world of work suggests a number of implications for guidance in terms of its goals, the new meaning of work and leisure, and the place of continuing education in the life of contemporary youth. The following sections will briefly describe the impact of automation upon guidance to date and suggest some possible future innovations that may be reasonably expected to influence guidance-personnel work and education in general.

Automation appears to be having two related but distinctly different lines of direct influence on the educative process. First, automated and partially automated systems are being utilized in the processes of teaching and counseling. Resulting from this type of application have been the emerging concepts of computerized teaching, computer-assisted teaching, and computerized counseling (14, 25, 44). The second major type of application of automation to the educative process consists of automatic data processing. Together, these two innovations have produced considerable change in the educative process (33).

Computerized Teaching and Counseling

The computer is basically a large complex electronic problem-solving machine. It is guided and controlled by the program that determines its entire problem-solving strategy. The program, in turn, is based upon a theory of learning and reflects the philosophy, goals, general psychology, etc., of the programmer.

Although a lack of understanding and a tradition-oriented frame of reference have retarded the use of automation in educational systems (66), perhaps the most important limiting factor has been cost. If the automated system is not fully utilized, the per-pupil cost becomes very high. One computerized teaching system, for example, if fully used, can handle up to 32 student learning stations interacting simultaneously with dozens of different courses at under two dollars per hour per student. In order to make automation economically feasible, many school systems have shared computer time with other school systems, rented computer time, or used a computer to handle both teaching and administrative duties.

In computerized or computer-assisted teaching and counseling, the student composes a solution or a request on an input device such as an electric typewriter connected with a computer. The student then calls the attention of the central processing unit by pressing a particular key. The computer in turn processes the electric representations of the student's solution or request by comparing it with anticipated answers previously stored in it by the author of a text, for example, or by applying a set of programmed rules. A reply is sent back to the student via a typewriter or some type of display device.

To date, computer-assisted teaching programs are available for such diverse areas of teaching such as typing (28), music (52), bookkeeping (29), chemistry (74), mathematics (36), reading (41), industrial education (56), and piano lessons (43). Elsewhere there have been descriptions of computers as tutors (51), lecture-demonstrations by computers (16), teaching the retarded by computers (45), and uses of a specific computer system called PLATO (8). Computers have also been utilized for grading both objective and subjective examinations (2, 18, 35).

Automatic Data Processing

Data processing has been defined as a series of planned actions and operations upon information (data) to achieve a desired result (70, p. 10). The various procedures and devices used constitute a data-processing system. A data-processing system may (a) be manual, (b) utilize key-driven machines—e.g., bookkeeping machines—or (c) utilize automatic data processing. It is the last category of data processing which has the greatest and most far-reaching implications for education. Automatic data processing may utilize punch-card equipment (electromechanical machines) or electronic data processing (electronic computers). Data placed on punch cards, paper tape, or magnetic tape are then fed into the processing equipment—e.g., electronic computer—which processes the data according to instructions—i.e., the program. Since it is beyond the scope of this chapter to deal with the details of the procedures in data processing, the interested reader is referred to Whitlock (70) for detailed consideration of automatic data processing as it relates to education. In addition to the guidance uses for automatic data processing to be described below, studies have described the impact of automation upon master scheduling for entire school systems (1, 3, 4, 19, 23, 39, 66), attendance processing (61), and the general impact of automation on education (7, 9, 22). Anderson (3) has outlined 100 uses for computers in educational settings.

Information Retrieval

Owing to the explosion of knowledge and the progress of research efforts, it has become increasingly difficult for the practitioner in education to keep abreast of research findings, new techniques, alternative solutions to various problems, etc. The U.S. Office of Education has recently developed an information system to supply practitioners with needed data. This system is called ERIC (Educational Research Information Center). Although there is a headquarters office (Central ERIC) in Washington, D. C., the most important functional units are thirteen ERIC clearinghouses in universities and other institutions throughout the country. Each clearinghouse is responsible for acquiring, selecting, abstracting, and indexing relevant information in a given area of education. The ERIC clearinghouse for counseling and personnel services is at the University of Michigan. The purpose of ERIC is to provide relevant research materials for practitioners who need them. Current plans call for an increase in the number of ERIC centers and for a broadening of the services they will provide.

Following is an ERIC scope statement (67, p. 3):

> The ERIC Information Center on Counseling and Personnel Services is responsible for acquiring, indexing, abstracting and analyzing materials and research reports relating to the preparation, practice, and supervision of counselors and other personnel workers at all educational levels and in all settings. Included are materials describing theoretical developments; the use and results of personnel procedures such as testing, interviewing, disseminating and analyzing personal and environmental information; group work and case work; and reports on program development and evaluation. The coverage will include materials which deal with the nature of pupil, student and adult characteristics; description of educational, occupational, and community settings; and discussions of the types of assistance provided by personnel workers in areas such as career planning, family consultation, and student orientation and activities.

The Cumulative Record

The cumulative record is a key vehicle for the work of the guidance counselor in the area of appraisal, child study, or the inventory service. Standardized test scores, subject matter grades, anecdotal reports, personality ratings, medical history, family background, a summary of the individual's extracurricular activities, constitute some of the kinds of information stored in the cumulative record. The hand recording of the information into the cumulative record represents one of the most routine and time-consuming duties of teachers and guidance workers.

Needless to say, the limitations of contemporary management of cumulative records include (*a*) inaccurate entires, (*b*) omissions of important data, (*c*) inefficient and uneconomical use of highly trained personnel, (*d*) multiplicity of formats of cumulative records among various schools and school systems, and (*e*) a lowering of the general morale of the staff resulting from their having to perform peripheral clerical functions.

Electronic data processing can enable the school to record pertinent information about the pupil automatically. Merz describes the inventory function of guidance in a medium-sized high school (Nyack, N. Y.) where data processing has been utilized since 1956. He discusses the following as some of the major advantages of automation (48):

1. Elimination of time-consuming clerical tasks.
2. Better service to students.
3. More legible records.
4. Increased accuracy of records.
5. Day-by-day absence reports are made available to staff.
6. Speedy preparation of failure lists, grade lists, failure percentages, special listings for departments.
7. Accurate and complete records of standardized aptitude and achievement tests.
8. Ability to mechanize additional processes as desired.
9. Availability of records to more people as a result of automated duplication.
10. Automatically calculated honor roll.

Grouping of Students

The guidance worker often becomes involved in the process of homogeneous grouping by making recommendations regarding which students should be placed into various groups and by taking part in the decision-making process of actually classifying students in to the various types of homogeneous groups.

Although intelligence, past achievement, teacher's recommendations, and general readiness have most often been utilized as criteria for homogeneous grouping, more than twenty variables, singly and in combination, have been utilized for determining the composition of homogeneous groups. One of the major difficulties in homogeneous grouping is the problem of manipulating the complex data and the unnecessarily large consumption of time needed for placing students into the correct groups. Because of its speed, accuracy, and economy, data processing has been utilized to automate the decision-making process in homogeneous grouping. Automation resulted in a more adequate means of recognizing individual differences through the development of a curriculum and the selection of individual students through a more adequate choice process (53).

Scheduling

Assisting the administration in the planning and organization of the master schedule of classes is a frequent peripheral guidance function. It has been estimated that class scheduling requires from 15 to 2,500 man-hours, depending upon the size of the school (13). Five basic factors go into making the master schedule: students, teachers, rooms, times, and courses. With increasingly complex curriculums, hand scheduling is becoming too complex, too time-consuming, and too inefficient. In the Flexible Scheduling Project (13), four high schools ranging in size from 160 to 2,500 have cooperated in an experiment to evaluate the usefulness of automation for setting the complex master class schedules. The findings of this experiment typify the general findings where automation has been introduced:

1. There were larger percentages of students with completed and satisfactory schedules.
2. There was a better utilization of staff and physical resources because the computer worked out a number of schedules and selected the most efficient one.
3. Scheduling was quickly performed just before the opening of school, reflecting any last-minute changes resulting from summer school, last-minute changes in personnel, or late enrollments.
4. Automated scheduling was cheaper than hand scheduling.

In California, a State Advisory Committee on Integrated Data Processing has initiated plans for a research and development center which will attempt to investigate and suggest solutions to data-processing problems in schools of varying sizes. The staff personnel at the center will also act as special consultants for schools to investigate the feasibility of introducing data processing where it is not currently used.

Grossman and Howe describe the proposed uses for electronic data processing as follows (27, p. 346):

1. *Conducting a school census*: Districts can obtain abundant and accurate information about the nature and location of school population, present and future.
2. *Setting up student programs and schedules*: Course programs and class schedules can be set up with a high degree of efficiency. As by-products of this process, class lists or reports are accurately compiled; these show the names of students and the classes in which they are enrolled, the time and locations of the classes, the teachers assigned, and the credit to be given.
3. *Reporting students' grades*: Quarterly and semester grades can be accurately and speedily recorded. Additional ratings and reports are by-products of this operation.
4. *Evaluating students*: Group and individual tests of achievement, intelligence, aptitude, and interest can be processed. Effective use of the data thus processed can be made in both guidance procedures and instruction.

5. *Identifying and placing students*: It is possible to identify and place students according to their abilities, interests, and objectives.
6. *Accounting for attendance (daily, monthly, and at other intervals)*: Evaluating, recording, summarizing, and reporting of attendance is both feasible and logical.
7. *Recording*: Gathering an analysis of information, the systematic testing of hypotheses, and the summarization of current information can be done successfully by data processing machines.
8. *Reporting*: Meaningful and accurate information can be readily provided to pupils, parents, teachers, school officials, and the community on appropriate data processing equipment.

Likewise, these investigators summarize the advantage of automated rather the manual manipulation of data (27, pp. 346-47):

1. *Speed*: For example, it is possible to alphabetize 1,000 names in eight minutes; to list 1,000 names in six or seven on conventional punched-card equipment, and in two minutes on new electronic equipment; to convert and make statistical summaries of eight test scores for 2,500 students in two hours.
2. *Accuracy*: Most electronic data processing systems include self-checking devices; but even when they do not, increased accessibility of data makes verification easier and more positive. Given correct instructions, not only will the machine make fewer errors than even the most conscientious clerk, but machine errors will be more easily detectable.
3. *Reproduction*: A test score, once it is punched on a card or recorded on magnetic tape, may be converted to a normative score and then used in a statistical summary, listed, posted on records, reproduced at other points, and collated with supplementary data—all from a single source.
4. *Accessibility, internal and external*: Data scored in machine data processing systems, unambiguously coded, may be located rapidly and easily by those who need them. In addition, such data are readily available for conferences, research, historical review, or transmittal.
5. *Collating*: Pupil test data, school marks, teacher ratings, and many other types of data can be rapidly assembled in convenient form from a variety of sources for any special purpose; mechanical reference to norm tables reduces errors in test-score conversion and makes possible the multiple use of tables. Class registration lists may be collated with test scores and other data to provide teachers with information relevant to their students.
6. *Compactness*: Data may be stored, transmitted, and referenced in a highly condensed form; reels of magnetic tape or magnetized discs can be used to store information that would otherwise require many cubic feet of storage space. Identification codes can be used to effect additional compression.
7. *Automatic processes*: Although it takes time to develop programs and other automated processes for handling data, once the process has been designed, it is repeatedly reusable and can be shared with other school districts. Programs for processing student data can be used in hundreds of school systems on repeated occasions without additional developmental cost. Automation not only makes it easier in the performance of traditional tasks, but also makes feasible a number of tasks formerly considered impossible, or perhaps not even conceived.
8. *Dividends*: Under this general heading must be included all the readily obtainable by-products of data-processing systems. The processing of semester grades

is more efficient in a mechanized system than it is in a manual system; in addition, it makes possible more effective summaries of marks by course, grade, department, teacher, or school and permits facile pursuit of research studies. Similarly, the availability of the punched cards that are needed to describe course registration makes possible additional uses of the same cards for grading, attendance, mailing lists, special groupings, selection and placement systems, the maintenance of essential student records, and the analysis of curriculum needs.

IMPLICATIONS FOR GUIDANCE

Although automation is a relatively new innovation in business and industry, and even though it has just begun to have an impact upon the educational setting, this new technology has a number of far-reaching implications for education in general and in particular for guidance-personnel work. As noted above, automation is influencing both the work setting of the counselor and the perspective required for his making a maximum contribution to the growth and development of contemporary American youth.

Guidance Role and Function

The direct impact of automation on education to date suggests that in the near future the very role and function of guidance will be influenced as data processing becomes increasingly utilized in the educational setting. The impact of automation for the immediate future will undoubtedly be greatest in terms of cumulative records, the preparation of programs of study for individual students and developing master schedules of courses for the entire school. Some preliminary work is being done in terms of programming counseling interviews, test interpretation, and the dissemination of occupational information.

In effect, the new technology is beginning to free the guidance counselor from some clerical and routine tasks and is allowing him to have a more flexible and productive role and function. Instead of spending a great deal of his time and energy gathering and recording pupil data, he can now redirect much of his effort toward more productive activities, such as testing, counseling, and consultation with teachers, The guidance counselor will also have more time to carry on such activities as follow-up, evaluation, and research, now almost nonexistent as parts of a typical guidance program.

Samler (55), reviewing a number of problems related to automation as they affect vocational guidance, notes that counselors need labor market data about the changing occupational structure and authoritative analyses about the nature of the job. Counselors need not only the data included in standard brochures but also the psychological and social characteristics of various occupations. The importance of psychosocial aspects of work are becoming increasingly evident. The culture of the work setting, the status associated with a given job, and ways of meeting personality needs in a given work setting, for example, are being studied with greater interest and intensity.

The need for greater skills in virtually all levels of work underlines the importance of the guidance counselor's focusing upon his goal of developing each person to his optimum level. The key to happiness and success is increasingly becoming linked to education. Therefore, guidance should attempt to help each student to derive the maximum benefit from his schooling. In his analysis of labor trends, manpower, and automation, Wolfbein notes that the following five points of general significance for guidance emerge (73, pp. 170–72):

1. We must make a better match between the jobs we now have and will have and the people available to fill them.
2. Change, the most difficult of all forces to assess and be responsive to, will continue to be an important dimension in the field of counseling.
3. The aspirations, expectations, and goals of education and guidance need to be refocused.
4. Guidance is and must be a developmental process over the lifetime of the individual.
5. The guidance profession must play a critical role in helping to increase and broaden the pathways along which students move.

Hoppock notes the following implications of automation for vocational guidance, stating that the counselor can (10, pp. 218–222):

1. Recognize that the future is not entirely unpredictable.
2. Reassure students that there will still be some life careers open for those who choose carefully and plan wisely.
3. Emphasize the stability of employment as a consideration in educational and occupational planning.
4. Implement an annual follow-up of graduates and dropouts.
5. Make similar follow-ups five and ten years after high school graduation.
6. Consult with various community people to learn more about automation and its impact on the life of the worker.
7. Prepare and distribute reports of automation and its implications for the school.
8. Make all of the above activities a part of the annual school program.
9. Adjust the occupational guidance of terminal students to learn about the effects of automation on local industries.

At the close of the 1950's "the identification of the gifted" and "the pursuit of excellence" became major themes in education and guidance. More recently "education for employment" has become a prevalent theme because American education found itself accused of a bias in favor of higher education and against vocational education. Automation requires personnel who work with ideas, basic problems, and continual adjustment rather than working with limited skills. Similarly, in industrial settings, for example, workers will have to be less "craft" and "job" oriented. Thus, automation is requiring a clearer distinction between *education*, i.e., teaching people to think, and *training*, i.e., preparing individuals with specific skills.

The goal of guidance workers should be to develop within each person the ability to "think logically, plan rationally, to understand himself in relation to his environment and to accumulate those basic intellectual tools necessary for a productive and meaningful life" (64, pp. 78–79). In its broadest context, therefore, guidance focuses upon the total development of student. Special emphasis, however, should be given to educational, vocational, and personal-social development. As vocational development and vocational adjustment become more and more important in terms of the general well-being of the individual, vocational guidance and related activities should assume a greater emphasis in the work of the counselor.

The Meaning of Work and Leisure

Traditionally there has been a dichotomy between work and leisure. Work has included those activities necessary for physical and economic survival while leisure, on the other hand, has been undertaken by choice rather than necessity. Work and leisure have tended to undergo a number of changes in recent decades (60, pp. 107-13):

1. Automation has increased productivity and economic growth.
2. Rising earnings coupled with more free time has changed styles of leisure.
3. In the perspective of several centuries, time at work increased before it decreased.
4. Recent increases in leisure have been unequally distributed by industry and occupational category.
5. Despite an increasing age of entry into the labor force and a decreasing age of exit, men today work more years over the life cycle than they did in 1900. (Length of working life has gone up about 15 percent and the length of retirement has doubled.)

Thus, the Judeo-Christian ethic of work being good and leisure being bad has been increasingly breaking down in recent decades. Automation is accelerating and intensifying this trend. The meaning of work and leisure are clearly changing. With increased productivity and economic growth due in large degree to automation (and advanced technology in general) have come changes in styles of both work and leisure. It has been observed that a "reversed pyramid" of work is emerging in our society, in which a relatively few people are working for the many, rather than the classical pattern of the many working for the few (34, p. 216).

Significantly, work and lesiure have different meanings for different occupational groups. The bulk of business and industrial workers have chosen to take part of the increased economic productivity in the form of time off from work rather than in increased pay. This group has become the new leisure class. The evidence is clear that bureaucratization, fragmentation of work, and alienation have decreased the capacity of work to be a meaningful activity in the lives of many workers. Many workers are now having more free time than they know what to do with. What often results from this is not leisure—i.e., free time spent in enjoyable relaxation and entertainment—but idleness, listlessness, and boredom.

Leisure for the professional and managerial strata tends to become fused with work. The individual's career becomes the central life interest and dining out, the game of bridge, the golf course, cocktail party, etc., become extensions of the work setting. Individuals in these occupational groups have continued to work very long hours, often as many as sixty or more per week, with only one day off per week for "leisure."

Thus, there is clearly emerging a new fragmentization of meaning in our already pluralistic society. Work, which once provided a stabilizing, meaningful structure for life, is also being changed by automation and is, in turn, influencing individuals' attitudes toward life in general (57).

Numerous writers have pointed out the various orientations to work. Rosenberg has identified three personal orientations (54): (a) people-oriented, (b) extrinsic-reward-oriented, and (c) self-expression-oriented patterns. Friedmann and Havighurst note that one group of workers derives such satisfactions as a challenging experience, feelings of creativity, feelings of service to people, and the reward of a prestigeful occupation, while another group derives such satisfactions as associations with friends and a pleasant or at least tolerable routine for passing time and avoiding boredom (24). Elsewhere, Havighurst notes that the three major orientations to work are (a) ego-involving, (b) society-maintaining, and (c) alienation (32).

In summary, the impact of automation and advanced technology in general has been to require fewer hours of effort per worker per week. One large group of workers have chosen to take more leisure time, but do not really enjoy the free time. A second group are so ego-involved in their work that they have chosen to continue to work long hours and fuse work and leisure into a fundamentally work-oriented life style. A third group has not found a meaningful place in the world of work. In Super's terms, it exhibits the multiple-trial-career pattern (65). This group has also been called disadvantaged, displaced, technologically unemployed, chronically unemployed, the alienated, etc.

As the length of the work week continues to shrink, and as an increasing proportion of the work force receives less satisfaction from work itself, both guidance counselors and other educators will have to examine the Cardinal Principles of Education (15) and focus upon worthy use of the individual's leisure time as a more important goal. The research on the meaning and implications of leisure time and boredom is quite meager. The relationships among leisure time, boredom, vocational development, and general personal-social development are rarely, if ever, discussed during counseling in the school setting. Yet, the bulk of the available research underlines the necessity and complexity of good mental health and general well-adjustment in future years. Automation is a prime determinant in the increasingly complex process of growth and development in our culture because it touches so many aspects of individuals' personal and vocational life.

The Emerging Concept of Continuing Education and Continuing Guidance

Automation has revolutionized our current concept of formal education. Guidance counselors and others have held forth the benefits of completing a high school education. A tacit assumption behind our thinking to date has been that the high school, the technical school, the community or junior college, the four-year college, and the university represent the alternative points for terminal formal education. But the new technology requires a new concept of education—a continuing education.

Many retraining programs resulting from the innovations of automation have failed because the workers have failed to grasp the significance of these programs. Other workers have not been successful in these programs because of negative attitudes toward education as a carry-over from earlier public school experience. Whereas most students feel that formal education ends at some graduation ceremony, the guidance worker must now begin to show students that a continuing education will become increasingly necessary as automation and other technological advances become felt in more and more sectors of our occupational structure.

Many people are used to routine work; when automation is introduced, then, the older workers and the less educated workers are those who have the most serious adjustment problems. Here, the basic aim for the guidance counselor is to help these individuals distribute themselves throughout the labor market and to influence their attitudes toward work learning, education, and leisure. The ability to hold a job will increasingly depend on continuing education throughout one's entire working life. The guidance counselor must understand the general social environment of the student as a potential worker and focus upon personal attitudes toward school and education if the idea of life-long learning is to be a major social realization.

SUMMARY

Automation is rapidly changing the nature of work and its meaning for the individual. Together, automation and cybernetics have opened up a scientific-technological-cybercultural revolution. The implications for education in general and guidance in particular are broad and pervasive. Perhaps the most significant implication of the new technology is that a profound psychological revolution is required for mankind to realize the attainable fruits of technological progress. Traditional attitudes toward education, minority ethnic groups, work and leisure must be reexamined and revised. Undoubtedly, it will become increasingly more desirable to educate rather than train, for in a rapidly evolving occupational structure and a dynamic and fluid society what is fashionable and required today may be outmoded and obsolescent tomorrow.

The challenge for education is to adequately implement the philosophy of education for total living required in an Age of Automation. Such an education is fundamentally developmental in character. Such an education includes guidance as an aid to the student searching for meaning in a pluralistic and evolving society. Such an education requires guidance personnel with a broad background and an adequate perspective on the individual and his multiplicity of relationships with other individuals and his sociocultural milieu. In a culture of shifting values, the goal of optimum development of the individual becomes noble, complex, and perhaps unattainable against the multiple backdrops of the morality of work, the morality of leisure, and the morality of the equivalence of work and leisure.

REFERENCES

1. D. W. Allen and D. Delay, "Stanford's Computer System Gives Scheduling Freedom to Twenty-Six Districts," *Nation's Schools*, 77 (1966), 124-25.

2. G. E. Anderson, "How to Use Computers in Grading Objective Tests," *Nation's Schools*, 78 (1966), 62-63.

3. G. E. Anderson, "Trends to Watch in Data Processing," *Nation's Schools*, 78 (1966), 101-3.

4. G. E. Anderson, "What You Should Know about Computerized Scheduling," *Nation's Schools*, 77 (1966), 84-85.

5. M. F. Baer and E. C. Roeber, *Occupational Information*. Chicago: Science Research Associates, 1964.

6. C. E. Bare, "Automated Data Processing in Education," *Educational Forum*, 30 (1966), 435-39.

7. R. A. Beaumont and R. B. Helfgott, *Management, Automation, and People*. Brattleboro, Vermont: The Book Press, 1964.

8. D. L. Bitzer *et al.*, "Uses of PLATO: A Computer Controlled Teaching System," *Audio Visual Instruction*, 11 (1966), 16-21.

9. W. W. Brickman and S. Lehrer, *Automation, Education, and Human Values*. New York: School and Society Books, 1966.

10. W. Buckingham, *Automation: Its Impact on Business and People*. New York: Harper & Row, 1961.

11. W. Buckingham, "The Impact of Automation on Skills and Employment," *Computers and Automation*, 6 (1963), 16-20.

12. L. G. Burchinal, *ERIC and the Need to Know*. Pamphlet (no notation of publisher or date).

13. R. N. Bush, "Decision for the Principal: Hand or Computer Scheduling," *National Association of Secondary Schools Principal's Bulletin*, 48 (1964), 141-46.

14. J. Cogswell and D. Estavan, "Explorations in Computer Assisted Counseling," *Technical Memorandum 2582*, Santa Monica, Calif.: System Development Corporation, August 6, 1965.

15. Commission of the Reorganization of Secondary Education, *Cardinal Principles of Secondary Education*, Bureau of Education, Bulletin 1918, No. 35. Washington, D.C.: U.S. Government Printing Office, 1918.

16. M. L. Corrin, "Lecture Demonstrations With an Analog Computer," *Journal of Chemical Education*, 43 (1966), 579-81.

17. J. Cunniff, "Negro Unemployment Rate at Root of Racial Unrest," *The News Gazette* (Newspaper). Champaign, Ill.: June 19, 1967, p. 13.

18. A. Daigon, "Computer Grading of English Compositions," *English Journal*, 55 (1966), 46-52.

19. A. D'Antuono and W. S. McCallum, "Constructing the Master Schedule by a Computer," *National Association of Secondary School Principal's Bulletin*, 49 (1965), 58-65.

20. J. Diebold, "The Application of Information Technology," *Annals of the American Academy of Political and Social Science*, March 1962.

21. J. T. Dunlop, *Automation and Technological Change*. Englewood Cliffs, N.J.: Prentice-Hall, 1962.

22. L. H. Evans and G. E. Arnstein, *Automation and The Challenge to Education*. Washington, D.C.: National Education Association, 1962.

23. R. L. Fleche, "County Computer Takes Tedium out of Testing and Scheduling," *Nation's Schools*, 76 (1965), 50-51.

24. E. A. Friedmann and R. J. Havighurst, *The Meaning of Work and Retirement*. Chicago: University of Chicago Press, 1954.

25. D. D. Friesen, *The Validation of an Automated Counseling System*. Unpublished Doctoral Dissertation, University of Oregon, 1965.

26. E. Gross, "Social Effects of Automation," *Automation: The Threat and the Promise*. Minneapolis-St. Paul: Twin City Vocational Guidance Association, 1964.

27. A. Grossman and R. Howe, "Human Economy and Data Processing," *The Personnel and Guidance Journal*, 43 (1964), 343-47.

28. E. J. Haga, "Get Ready for Automated Typing Instruction," *Journal of Business Education*, 41 (1966), 250-51.

29. E. J. Haga, "What Automation Means for Bookkeeping," *Business Education Forum*, 20 (1965), 14-16.

30. E. Hardin, "The Reactions of Employees to Office Automation," *Monthly Labor Review*, 83 (1960), 925-32.

31. D. S. Hart and W. M. Lifton, "Of Things to Come: Automation and Counseling," *Personnel and Guidance Journal*, 37 (1958), 282-87.

32. R. J. Havighurst, "Youth in Exploration and Man Emergent," in H. Borow, ed., *Man in a World at Work*. Boston: Houghton Mifflin Co., 1964.

33. W. L. Heckman, "The Renaissance of Teaching," *School and Society*, 94 (1966), 265-67.

34. A. M. Hilton, ed., *The Evolving Society*. New York: The Institute for Cybercultural Research, 1966.

35. C. C. Hinckley and J. J. Lagowski, "Versatile Computer Graded Examination," *Journal of Chemical Education*, 43 (1966), 575-78.

36. W. Hoffman, "Computers for School Math," *Mathematics Teacher*, 58 (1965), 393-401.

37. I. R. Hoos, "Impact of Automation on Office Workers," *International Labor Review*, 82 (1960), 363-88.

38. R. Hoppock, "Influence of Automation on Occupational Guidance," *High School Journal*, 49 (1966), 218-22.

39. L. E. Hull and D. A. McWhirter, "Scheduling with the Small Computer," *College and University*, 42 (1966), 60-62.

40. P. A. Jansen, "Where the New Technology Will Take Education," *Nation's Schools*, 78 (1966), 70-73.

41. J. Keene, "Computer at the School Helps Teach Students How To Read," *Nation's Schools*, 78 (1966), 81-83.

42. L. L. Kornfeld, "Mechanization of Data Processing," *Education Digest*, 32 (1967), 35-37.

43. P. Lewis, "Has Your District Evaluated these Electronic Products"? *Nation's Schools*, 78 (1966), 85-94.

44. J. W. Loughary *et al.*, "Autocoun: A Computer-Based Automated Counseling Simulation System," *Personnel and Guidance Journal*, 45 (1966), 6-15.

45. L. F. Malposs, *Automated Teaching Procedures for the Retarded*. Cooperative Research Project 1267, Tampa: University of South Florida, 1963.

46. F. C. Mann and L. K. Williams, "Organizational Impact of White Collar Automation," *Industrial Relations Research Association Annual Proceedings*, Publication No. 22 (1958), 56-59.

47. R. L. Mann and F. C. Hoffman, *Automation and the Worker*. New York: Holt, Rinehart & Winston, 1960.

48. A. F. Merz, "The Use of Processing Equipment for Educational Records," *National Association of Secondary School Principal's Bulletin*, 46 (1962), 7-16.

49. D. N. Michael, *Cybernation: The Silent Conquest*. Santa Barbara, Calif. Fund for the Republic, 1962.

50. F. Pollack, *The Economic and Social Consequences of Automation*. Oxford, England: B. Blackwell Publishing Co., 1957.

51. J. Ridgeway, "Computer-Tutor: Competition for Public Education," *Education Digest*, 32 (1966), 7-10.

52. G. Roller, "Development of a Method for Analysis of Musical Compositions Using an Electronic Digital Computer," *Journal for Research in Music Education*, 13 (1965), 249-52.

53. S. P. Rollins, "Automated Grouping," *Phi Delta Kappan*, 42 (1961), 212-14.

54. M. Rosenberg, *Occupations and Values*. Glencoe, N.Y.: Free Press of Glencoe, 1957.

55. J. Samler, "Technological Change and Vocational Counseling," *Automation: The Threat and the Promise*. Minneapolis-St. Paul: Twin City Vocational Guidance Association, 1964.

56. H. A. Schwartz and R. J. Haskell, "A Study of Computer-Assisted Instruction in Industrial Education," *Journal of Applied Psychology*, 50 (1966), 360-63.

57. B. B. Seligman, "Man, Work, and the Automated Feast," *Commentary*, 34 (1962), 9-19.

58. B. B. Seligman, *The Most Notorious Victory: Man in an Age of Automation*. Glencoe, N.Y.: Free Press of Glencoe, 1966.

59. C. E. Silberman, *The Myths of Automation*. New York: Harper & Row, 1966.

60. E. O. Smigel, ed., *Work and Leisure*. New Haven, Conn.: College and University Press, 1963.

61. A. E. Smith, "Innovation in Attendance Processing," *Balance Sheet*, 48 (1966), 164-65.

62. R. E. Stennett, "Control in Educational Programming," *Elementary School Journal*, 67 (1967), 317-22.

63. D. H. Stollar and J. Ray, "The Program Ahead for Data Processing System," *The American School Board Journal*, 152 (1966), 12-13.

64. Subcommittee on Employment and Manpower of the Committee on Labor and Public Welfare, U. S. Senate, *Toward Full Employment: Proposals for a Comprehensive Employment and Manpower Policy in the United States*. Washington, D.C.: U.S. Government Printing Office, 1964.

65. D. E. Super, *The Psychology of Careers*. New York: Harper & Row, 1957.

66. S. Tobias, "Lack of Knowledge and Fear of Automation as Factors in Teachers' Attitudes Toward Programmed Instruction and Other Media," *Audio Visual Communications Review*, 14 (1966), 99-109.

67. G. R. Walz, *News Brief*. Ann Arbor, Michigan: Counseling and Personnel Services Information Center, March 1967.

68. G. Watson, *No Room at the Bottom*. Washington, D.C.: National Education Association, 1963.

69. E. Weinberg, "Experiences with the Introduction of Office Automation," *Monthly Labor Review*, 83 (1960), 376-80.

70. J. W. Whitlock, *Automatic Data Processing in Education*. New York: The Macmillan Co., 1964.

71. N. Wiener, *The Human Use of Human Beings*. Boston: Houghton Mifflin Co., 1950.

72. H. L. Wilensky, "The Uneven Distribution of Leisure: The Impact of Economic Growth on Free Time," in E. O. Smigel, ed., *Work and Leisure*. New Haven, Conn.: College and University Press, 1963.

73. S. L. Wolfbein, "Labor Trends, Manpower, and Automation," in H. Borow, *Man in a World at Work*. Boston: Houghton Mifflin Co., 1964.

74. O. T. Zajicek, "A Computer Program for Use in Teaching Chemical Equilibria," *Journal of Chemical Education*, 42 (1965), 622-24.

75. K. L. Zinn, "What Computerized Instruction is All About," *Nation's Schools*, 78 (1966), 78-79.

chapter 13

Legal Aspects of Guidance Process

... a counselor must be cautious when applying general rules of law to specific cases. Every specific question which arises in the work of the counselor must be answered by reviewing all the specific known facts, the general principles of law, ... and the statutes and case of law of the jurisdiction in which the alleged action arises. (3, p. 82)

The United States differs from almost every other country in the world in that the federal government has no direct control or authority over public education. Since it is not mentioned in the U.S. Constitution, education has become one of the powers reserved for the states. Departments of education and departments of public instruction represent the typical responsible organizational structures at the state level. It is through these bodies that the standards for the operational aspects of public instruction are formulated, adopted, and implemented. Thus, each state enacts legislation that determines and controls the scope and content of education in that state. It is within this legal context that guidance services have become an integral part of education in our country (19).

The U.S. Supreme Court has made a number of relevant decisions whereby the Constitution has been interpreted to mean that parents have the right to select where and how their children are to be educated as long as the educational system or educational institution meets the minimum standards prescribed by the state. As the concept of public instruction has evolved, school attendance has become both a right and a duty. Pupils, however, cannot be required to attend a public school as long as their parents desire them to attend a private or parochial school and that school meets state standards. Although the general standards are determined by the state, five regional accrediting associations evaluate school programs. When the pupil enrolls in a school, the school and its staff become responsible for that pupil's conduct and general well-being under the concept of *in loco parentis*—i.e., the school then stands in place of parents.

GUIDANCE: DUTIES AND LIABILITIES

Butler notes that many states have enacted legislation that authorizes or requires local boards of education to establish and maintain guidance programs in public school systems and to employ qualified staff to provide educational and vocational guidance (5). The general activities of school guidance counselors have been described as follows by a counsel for the American Personnel and Guidance Association (4):

> ... They assist students in making appropriate educational and vocational choices and in developing self-understanding which contributes to more adequate personal and social adjustment. They are available to all students who seek their assistance. They maintain a counseling relationship to the extent their competence permits and as long as the students desire it. They utilize the interview, objective psychological tests, occupational information and other resources in contributing to student development. They are concerned with normal student growth toward the effective use of student capacities rather than with the diagnosis or alleviation of mental illness . . ., which is the proper field of other scientific disciplines and more specifically in the field of a highly technical medical specialty.

Similarly, the Code of Ethics of the American Personnel and Guidance Association notes the following (7, p. 207):

> ... A counseling relationship denotes that the person seeking help retain full freedom of choice and decision and that the helping person has no authority or responsibility to approve or disapprove of the choices or decisions of the counselee or client, [the primary obligation of the guidance counselor being] to respect the integrity and promote the welfare of the counselee or client with whom he is working.

The Counselor's Responsibility

The counselor has a twofold responsibility—(*a*) to the individual student and (*b*) to the student body, the educational system as a whole, and the general society. As the guidance worker performs his daily functions, situations almost invariably occur in which he must decide where his primary responsibility lies. In instances where the interests of an individual conflict with the interests of the larger group, the counselor must (32, p. 13):

1. Weigh the competing interests of both the individual and the group.
2. Balance the equities.
3. Act in good faith and in accordance with the standards of APGA.
4. Make a choice, possibly in consultation with a superior.

The key point here is that if the guidance worker acts in "good faith" according to the principles laid down by the professional organization of which he is a part, he has rather broad protection against any legal action taken against him. There is a presumption that school authorities have acted correctly and in good faith. The burden of proof, in most cases where legal action is brought against school authority, will lie with the person or persons bringing the action; this is generally also true where staff personnel are acting within the scope of their duties. Thus, the guidance worker should act in good faith both for ethical and legal reasons, good faith including: (*a*) being faithful to one's duty or obligation (14); (*b*) honestly refraining from taking an unconscionable advantage of another (12); (*c*) acting with good motives and interest (24); (*d*) making an honest effort to ascertain the facts (6); and (*e*) acting honestly, without fraud, collusion, or deceit (8). The behavior and actions of a guidance worker should relate to the educational process as it affects the individual, to the maintenance of good morale, discipline and order in the school, and to the general advancement and welfare of students in the school setting.

Counseling and Confidentiality

Both practitioners and the general literature describe counseling as an intimate, confidential relationship involving a counselor attempting to help a counselee with some type of problem. Indeed, it is difficult to envision effective counseling occurring without confidentiality. A study by Smith, for example, reveals that over 75 per cent of the surveyed guidance counselors felt that they should respect the confidence of pupils and not reveal information received directly from counselees (25). Undoubtedly, most students would be rather hesitant to discuss important personal aspects of educational, vocational, and personal difficulties if they felt that this information would not be kept confidential.

There are, however, legal limits to confidentiality of information communicated in the counseling interview, because the law recognizes two types of confidential relationships. Certain communications, between such parties as attorney and client, husband and wife, physician and patient, clergyman and confessor, have an absolute privilege and disclosure shall not be compelled to any third parties. Some states have also extended the doctrine of privileged communications to journalists, accountants, and psychologists. Most of these fall in the classification of a qualified privilege, to be referred to later.

There has been a tendency in recent decades to prevent the newer professions from having privileged communication. Thus, since the doctrine of privilege does not apply to school administrators, teachers, or counselors, they may be compelled in a court of law to reveal statements made to them by students even in confidence where such information would be admissible under the rules of evidence applicable in the particular jurisdiction. The school counselor should not divulge information received during the counseling interview to any third persons outside of court, however, except in order to further the best interests of the student or the school system. Fortunately, most of the communications of a client to a counselor fall within the hearsay rule (a court rule of evidence) and are therefore not admissible in court. Wrenn notes that since counselors seldom get more evidence than what the client says (primarily subject to the hearsay rule), counselors may be better off legally than most think they are (34, p. 165).

Legislation in Michigan, on the other hand, specifically provides that no teacher, guidance officer, school executive, or other professional person may disclose information obtained from records or communications or produce such records without the consent of the student if he is 21 years or older, or by his parent or legal guardian if the student is a minor. Wigmore summarizes the following basic conditions which must be met in order to establish a privilege against the disclosure of communications in court (9):

1. The communications must originate in a confidence that they will not be disclosed.
2. This element of confidentiality must be essential to the full and satisfactory maintenance of the relation between parties.
3. The relation must be one which in the opinion of the community ought to be sedulously fostered.
4. The injury that would inure to the relation by the disclosure of the communications must be greater than the benefit thereby gained for the correct disposal of litigation.

Some states specify that a public officer may not be examined as a witness to communications made to him in an official confidence when the public interest would suffer from the disclosure of that information. A clear distinction must be made in these cases between a public "officer" and a public "employee." School board members and superintendents of school systems are sometimes considered to be public officers, but principals, teachers, counselors, and other school personnel are generally classified as employees. While a guidance counselor does not in general benefit from the doctrine of privilege in communications, a broad aspect of the confidential relationship requires him to act in good faith and to both observe and protect the best interests of the counselee. In any case, the guidance counselor may submit a request for a meeting in chambers with the court as a means of establishing whether the interests of the counselee or society should prevail. The counselor should make every attempt to avoid the breaking of confidences in order to prevent the client's harming himself.

Although guidance counselors do not have absolute privilege, they are often protected by qualified or conditioned privilege. Thus, essential information may be divulged in court whenever it is reasonably necessary for the protection of one's own interest, the interests of third parties, or certain interests of the public. The purpose of qualified or conditional privilege is to facilitate the free giving of information in court. In order to give the court access to necessary free and complete information, most courts afford the school counselor protection against liability even if misinformation is unknowingly given. In order to qualify for conditional or qualified privilege, however, an honest and reasonable effort to protect or advance the interest in questions must have been made.

The breaking of every confidence (legally or illegally) jeopardizes the future effectiveness of the counselor. The counselor's obligation to confidentiality and secrecy lapses, however, when any one of the following conditions are met (20, p. 254):

1. The common welfare demands revelation, e.g., murder, suicide, treason.

2. The secret is invalid.
3. There is unjust aggression.
4. The client gives his consent to reveal the information.
5. There is publication of the secret.

The Counselor and Defamation

In his daily work, the counselor frequently learns information about students which fit the definition of defamation. Since he must often reveal information about the student to other people, the guidance counselor should be cognizant of the extent of permissible release of defamatory information. Although the specific definitions of what constitutes defamatory statements vary from state to state, Seitz notes that these statements are generally considered to be those communicated to third persons which tend to diminish esteem, confidence, goodwill, respect, or statements which excite adverse feelings or opinions against that person in the eyes of a substantial respectable minority (21, pp. 21-22). Defamation represents an invasion of the individual's interest in his own reputation and also contains an element of personal disgrace. Defamation can take two forms:

1. *Slander:* the defamation of an individual in the form of the spoken word.
   a. Imputation of serious crime.
   b. Imputation of a loathsome disease.
   c. Imputation of unchastity.
   d. Imputation affecting an individual's business, trade or profession.
2. *Libel*: the defamation of an individual by means of printed words, and sometimes utterances over radio or television. (In the latter cases it is often held that the resultant harm is equivalent to that produced when the written or printed medium is used.)

In some cases the law excuses and even sanctions defamatory remarks, statements, and writing, because of their general social importance. When a person can speak freely, knowing that he is immune to the recovery of damages through subsequent court action, he is said to have an absolute privilege. The doctrine of absolute privilege pertains to judges in connection with judicial proceedings, to comments by lawmakers during legislative sessions, and to the communications of certain executive officers of the government in the discharge of their duties (21, pp. 23-24).

As noted above, guidance personnel do not have an absolute privilege. Qualified or conditional privilege may apply to guidance personnel when the release of defamatory information is necessary for the protection of the guidance worker's own interest, the interest of third parties, or certain public interests. The protection of qualified privilege is given because, without it, court proceedings might not convey true information for fear of making defamatory statements that would subject the conveyor to libel or slander. Seitz notes, however, that an individual who states or publishes defamatory information about another person upon a qualified or conditionally privileged occasion is liable if he abuses the occasion by not honestly believing the truth of the defamatory information or if he does not have reasonable grounds for his beliefs. (21, p. 24).

While in some states truth of the defamatory statement is a defense, in many states truth does not give the individual an adequate justification for making defamatory statements unless the dissemination of the defamatory information is done with good intention and for justifiable ends. Rumors and suspicions about students often come to the attention of guidance personnel, and while these in general have no place in subsequent comments or communications by guidance personnel to third parties, there are some circumstances in which rumors may be communicated. If an interest is in great danger, the counselor may be justified in communicating defamatory rumors and suspicions even if these rumors and suspicions are not supported by evidence. Because of the risk involved, however, most counselor remarks should probably be limited to those based upon strong evidence that they are true (21, p. 26).

THE USE AND RELEASE OF RECORDS

The use and release of student records constitute another area with legal implications. School records are often considered as "public records"—i.e., records kept because of a statute, rule, or regulation of the state—as distinguished from private records. The cumulative folder and its contents may be considered public, and ordinarily any citizen has the right to inspect public records during reasonable hours at the office where they are kept. Absolute right of inspection exists, however, only if a statute, ordinance, rule, or regulation confers such a right. One court has ruled that "records are intended to serve as evidence of something written, said, or done and are not kept to gratify the curious or the suspicious" (15). If, on the other hand, an individual has an interest to maintain or defend in an action, and public records can furnish evidence or necessary information, the individual does have a right to inspect them (11, p. 10).

Release of Records to Parents and Students

Abels notes that since the public school authorities stand *in loco parentis* in regard to minor students (in the absence of statutes to the contrary), the student has no common-law right of inspection, even though he has an interest to maintain or defend in action, except through his parents or a duly appointed guardian (1, p. 30).

Whether or not school records should be released to parents constitutes another possible source of legal contention (17, 27, 28, 29, 33). A New York advisory commission recommended that there should be a distinction made between school records (permanent records that should be available to all staff members who work with pupils) and other information (background or technical data, communications with cooperating agencies, etc.), which should not become part of the school record (27). Thus, although the common law in this country seems to give the public the right to inspect public records (22), the right of inspection may be limited only to the "public record" and then only to those who show a special interest. Since parents obviously have a special interest in their children, the school record—i.e., the cumulative record—should be open to them.

A major question, however, is whether or not school records are public records. In general, public records must be (*a*) written memorials, (*b*) made by public officials, (*c*) made by officers authorized to do so, and (*d*) accurate and durable (21). Since the records are not kept by public officials—i.e., by the board of education or the superintendent of schools—they are not, strictly speaking, public records but rather quasi-public records.

Paradoxically, school records are both (quasi-) public—because they are kept by school districts supported by state tax funds—and private—because they are confidential except with the consent of the parent. A parent has the right to inspect school records not because he is a taxpayer but because of his or her relationship with the school authorities as a parent who, under compulsory education, has delegated to them the educational authority over his child. When a school counselor does release information from the school record to parents, he may defend his actions if sued on the basis that he disclosed only to authorized parties and that he has a qualified privilege. A formal opinion of a counsel for the New York State Department of Education made the following general statement concerning the release of information in the school records to parents (10):

> It is, therefore, my opinion that a carefully worded professional opinion rendered in line of duty by a physician, psychiatrist, psychologist, *guidance counselor,* principal or teacher, which is reasonably related to the educative process, made in good faith and with diligent regard for the rights of the person or persons involved, is protected by a qualified privilege against civil actions for damages based on libel. [Italics supplied.]

> Consequently, it would seem to me that such a law suit based *on such a professional opinion* against such persons would not be successful.

However, the New York State commission heretofore referred to also recommended that confidential, temporary, or background information should not become a part of the school record and should not be made available to parents. A counselor's notes fall into this category.

Release of Records to Nonschool Personnel and Agencies

Many people and agencies come to the school requesting information about students. This group includes prospective employers, P.T.A. officers, college representatives, the press, individuals planning to do research, governmental agency representatives, and law enforcement agencies. The procedure for providing the information, the form in which it should be transmitted, the conditions under which information should be given, and the issue of who is entitled to such information remain complex and rather ill-defined. These issues are discussed in some detail by Baumer (3).

The school counselor is clearly liable when he does not act as a reasonable and prudent man and in a manner in which a professional individual would be expected to act in the same situation. In the event that there is any question with respect to the release of the school record, a general rule of thumb would be for the counselor to consult with and obtain the written clearance of a superior, such as the principal or the director of guidance.

Abels notes the following general guidelines (1, pp. 33-34): (*a*) disclosures and releases that are clearly directed by state law or duly adopted rules of the local board of education constitute the best guides; (*b*) if there is any reasonable doubt in regard to the propriety of release or disclosure, the records should be kept in confidence unless the parents or guardians execute a covenant not to sue and provide a proper indemnifying release; (*c*) the record must be released when a staff member of the school is served a court order (subpoena) directing the disclosure of information in the record; and (*d*) rather than being a disgrace or cause for humiliation, a court order serves to provide the counselor with protection against financial liability.

The Release of Records to Staff Members and Other School Systems

School records also pose a problem in regard to which staff should have access to them. School practices vary all the way from keeping records under lock and key in the principal's office to a rather open policy allowing virtually all school personnel to inspect the records. The law is quite clear on this matter, however, for only those staff members who have an interest in the general welfare of the pupil should have access to the records (18, p. 53). Thus, any staff member who finds it necessary to use the information about the pupil in the school record to promote his general welfare should have access to the records. But a staff member who misuses that information or acts unprofessionally or unethically leaves himself open to valid criticism and possibly a law suit for slander or libel.

The problem of the use of records by the school staff is somewhat clarified in light of the general purpose of counseling and guidance and the use for which the school record is intended. Wrenn speaks to this point, noting, "It is clear that there is frequently a real question to whom the counselor's loyalty is due. It is due the client and not the employer, the client and not the colleague, the client and not the state" (34, p. 174).

While the school counselor's primary goal is to help the student, he also has an obligation to help the rest of the staff too. While meaningful and relevant information he gathers should be shared with other staff members, not all of that information should become a part of the cumulative record, thereby possibly becoming a part of the public or quasi-public record of the school. In the absence of clear-cut statutes, rules, or regulations, maximum accuracy of the information in the record and discretion on the part of the counselor will avoid most potential problems.

The transfer of records from one school system to another does not, in general, lead to legal difficulties. Since the purpose of records is to help the student, records are routinely transferred from one school system to another. In most states, however, there is no specific legislation in regard to the transfer of school records.

THE SEARCHING OF STUDENTS

School staff are sometimes placed in a position where the searching of students becomes a seemingly necessary course of action. These occasions arise most often because of a theft in the school, because of the alleged presence of a dangerous weapon, or because a student has been seen carrying some other objects or materials that should not be brought upon school property. The Constitution of the United States guarantees the individual the right of unwarranted interference, declaring in the Fourth Amendment:

> The right of the people to be secure in their persons, houses, papers, and effects, against unreasonable searches and seizures, shall not be violated, and no warrants shall issue, but upon probable cause, supported by Oath or affirmation, and particularly describing the place to be searched, and the persons or things to be seized.

The position of the teacher or the school counselor is a difficult one in cases where a search appears to be necessary, for the freedom from unwarranted search in such a situation is counterbalanced by the *in loco parentis* principle. The teacher or the guidance counselor stands in place of parents, this authority not being delegated by the parents but granted to him as an essential part of his educational responsibility.

One court found, "Search implies a probing into secret places for that which is hidden; it implies force, actual or constructive, or forceful dispossession of property of one by exploratory acts" (26). The guarantees of the U.S. Constitution related to search apply only to the search and seizure of material things and not to evidence that is secured by using the facilities of vision or sight. Thus, Paton notes that if smoking, for example, is prohibited on school grounds and a student had been seen smoking on school grounds by a staff member of that school, a package of cigarettes in a shirt pocket (in sight) could be seized as evidence for some subsequent disciplinary action (16, p. 135). Search and seizure represents a legal problem for school personnel because of the legal action which may result from such action. Paton further notes that while there have been relatively few court cases resulting from search on school premises, assault and battery charges stemming from search represent a real possibility if school personnel do not act "prudently" and in "good faith."

The following points should be kept in mind in dealing with cases of search and seizure:

1. An action for assault must establish a demonstration of an unlawful intent by one person to inflict injury on the person of another then present (16, p. 136).
2. A battery constitutes "any intentional touching of a person, his clothes, eyeglasses, etc., which is harmful or offensive when not consented to or privileged" (13, p. 34).
3. Any act, e.g., threat, which causes an apprehension or fear of a battery can be classified as an assault (13, p. 34).
4. *American Jurisprudence* (2) holds that the slightest unlawful touching of the person of another is sufficient, for the law cannot draw the line between degrees of violence and therefore totally prohibits the first and lowest stage, as every man's person is sacred and no other man has a right to touch it.

There are some indications that the charge of assault or battery cannot be found if consent has been given by one individual—e.g., a student—for another person—e.g., a school employee—to search him. Teachers and counselors in the school setting are almost invariably dealing with minors. Paton notes that if a student is able to understand the nature, extent, and consequences of the invasion (search), then his assent to be searched protects the teacher or the counselor from liability even if the parent or guardian does not give consent (16, p. 137).

The question of slander may also arise when the search of a student takes place. Slander can be shown if either direct or indirect charges are made. Thus, even the expression of opinions is actionable, as in cases where the individual precedes his statement by "I have every reason to believe," "I believe," "It is alleged," or "It is reported," etc. If the meaning is clear, then a mere insinuation is as actionable as a positive assertion.

Paton notes that there are two causes of action when a minor has been injured (16, p. 141): (*a*) the right of action by the child himself for personal injuries, and (*b*) the right of action by the parent for consequential damages for loss of services and expenses caused by the injury. Paton further notes that in the absence of any showing of loss of services, a parent cannot recover for defamation of his child and that if the child has no cause of action, neither has the parent. In cases where damages are to be paid, they are paid in accordance with the degree of harm suffered by the injured party. When the use of defamatory language is proved without proper justification nominal damages are typically awarded.

Some General Guidelines

The following general guidelines are suggested in relation to the issue of search and seizure of property or premises—e.g., lockers of students—by counselors and other school personnel.

1. The search should be performed only within the scope of his authority under his contract of employment.
2. The purpose of a search should be to:
   a. Protect the welfare of a particular student.
   b. Promote the good order and best interests of the school.
3. The methods of the search should be reasonable and prudent.
4. The search should be performed if possible in such a way as to protect the dignity of the individual.
5. The search should be exercised without caprice, malice, and in general with good motives and in "good faith."
6. Although search involves a calculated risk, school personnel involved in the search should be acquainted with school regulations and state statutes.
7. School personnel have broad protection if they act in light of school regulations and rules, provided that they act with reasonableness and in a way that any other prudent person would be expected to act.

THE GUIDANCE COUNSELOR AND CHILD LABOR LAWS

Reutter notes that in most states compulsory education laws work in conjunction with child labor laws which regulate the employment of minors (19, p. 50). These laws are complementary, protecting the best interests of both the individual child and the state by giving local school officials the authority to issue work permits to minors within the compulsory-education age bracket. Several pamphlets describe the Fair Labor Standards Act (30) and its child labor provisions (31) as they relate to such aspects of minors and their work as:

1. Basic minimum age for employment.
2. Minimum age for employment in an occupation declared hazardous by the Secretary of Labor.
3. Minimum age for specified occupations outside of school hours.
4. Exemptions from the child-labor provisions of the Act.
5. The number of hours a minor may work.

While the details of the child labor provisions of the Fair Labor Standards Act are beyond the scope of this book, guidance counselors should be aware of the details of these laws, since they relate closely to the placement function in guidance. They are even more important if the guidance counselor is the school functionary responsible for issuing working papers.

SUMMARY

The fact that in the past counselors have not been involved in many court actions serves as evidence for their prudent behavior. Obviously, the legal aspects of the guidance process are complex and vary from locale to locale. This chapter has merely summarized a few of the major legal principles with which the guidance counselor should be familiar. This chapter is intended not as a handbook but rather as a general guide for the guidance counselor in the school setting. The legal aspects of the guidance process complement and supplement the ethical aspects.

The best guides for making decisions are sensitivity, discretion, the Code of Ethics of the American Personnel and Guidance Association, and a knowledge of both general legal principles and the unique laws of the district in which the counselor works. If the counselor is honest and sincere in a decision made without malice—i.e., in good faith—he can practice without any fear of the consequences of legal action which might be brought against him.

REFERENCES

1. L. C. Abels, "Inspection and Release of Records to Students," in M. L. Ware, ed., *Law of Counseling and Guidance*. Cincinnati, Ohio: W. H. Anderson Co., 1964.

2. *American Jurisprudence.*

3. M. R. Baumer, "Inspection and Release of Records to Others," in M. L. Ware, ed., *Law of Guidance and Counseling*. Cincinnati, Ohio: W. H. Anderson Co., 1964.

4. Bogust *v.* Iverson, 10 Wis (2d) 129, 102 NW (2d) 228 (1960). Brief submitted by Arthur B. Hanson and Emmett E. Tucker, Jr., for American Personnel and Guidance Association as Amicus Curiae.

5. H. E. Butler, "Duties and Liabilities of Counselors," in M. E. Ware, ed., *Law of Guidance and Counseling.* Cincinnati, Ohio: W. H. Anderson Co., 1964.

6. Colket *v.* St. Louis Union Trust Co., 52 F (2d) 390 (8th Cir., 1931).

7. Committee on Ethics of the American Personnel and Guidance Association, "Code of Ethics," *Personnel and Guidance Journal*, 40 (1961), 206-9.

8. Docter *v.* Furch, 19 Wis 464, 65 NW 161 (1895).

9. Eight, Wigmore on Evidence, sec. 2285 (McNaughton Revision, 1961).

10. Formal Opinion of Counsel, No. 92. New York State Department of Education, November 17, 1960.

11. Forty-two Am. Jur., Public Administrative Law, 76, 23 Ruling Case Law 160.

12. Groh *v.* Viglet, 34 Ohio L Rep. 132.

13. R. R. Hamilton, *Legal Rights and Liabilities of Teachers.* Laramie, Wyoming: School Law Publications, 1956.

14. Hilker *v.* Western Auto Insurance Co. of Ft. Scott, 204 Wis 1, 235 NW 413 (1931).

15. Owens *v.* Woolridge, 22 Pa. County Ct. 237, 240.

16. W. F. Paton, "Search of Students," in M. L. Ware, ed., *Law of Guidance and Counseling.* Cincinnati, Ohio: W. H. Anderson Co., 1964.

17. C. H. Patterson, *Counseling the Emotionally Disturbed.* New York: Harper & Row, 1958.

18. E. E. Reutter, *Schools and the Law.* New York: Oceana Publications, 1960.

19. A. A. Rezny, "Inspection and Release of Records to Professional School Staff," in M. L. Ware, ed., *Law of Guidance and Counseling.* Cincinnati, Ohio: W. H. Anderson Co., 1964.

20. A. A. Schneider, "Problems of Confidentiality," *Personnel and Guidance Journal,* 42 (1963), 252-54.

21. R. C. Seitz, "Law of Slander and Libel," in M. L. Ware, ed., *Law of Guidance and Counseling.* Cincinnati, Ohio: W. H. Anderson Co., 1964.

22. Seventy-six C. J. S. 112.

23. Seventy-six C. J. S. 133.

24. Silliman *v.* International Life Ins. Co., 135 Tenn. 646, 188 SW 273 (1916).

25. C. E. Smith, *Development of Ethical Standards in the Secondary School Counseling Relationship for the Use of Counseling Information.* Doctoral Dissertation, University of Southern California, 1956.

26. Smith *v.* State (Alabama), 138 S (2d) 474 (1962).

27. Special Advisory Commission, "Should Student Records Be Made Available to Parents?" *American School Board Journal,* 143 (1961), 14-15.

28. R. Topp, "Let's Tell Parents Their Childrens' I.Q.'s," *Phi Delta Kappan,* 40 (1959), 342-43.

29. G. M. Trachtman, "Should Parents Know the Results of Intelligence?" *The P.T.A. Magazine,* 56 (1962), 4-6.

30. U.S. Department of Labor, *A Guide to Child Labor Provisions of the Fair Labor Standards Act.* Washington, D.C.: U.S. Government Printing Office, 1963.

31. U.S. Department of Labor, *Handy Reference Guide to the Fair Labor Standards Acts.* Washington, D.C.: U.S. Government Printing Office, 1965.

32. M. M. Volz, "Law of Confidentiality," in M. L. Ware, ed., *Law of Guidance and Counseling.* Cincinnati, Ohio: W. H. Anderson Co., 1964.

33. J. A. Wilson, "Let's Not Tell Parents Their Childrens' I.Q.'s," *Phi Delta Kappan,* 40 (1959), 343-45.

34. C. G. Wrenn, "The Ethics of Counseling," *Educational and Psychological Measurement,* 12 (1952), 161-77.

chapter 14

Professional and Ethical Aspects
of Guidance

Before a group can define its ethical standards, its members must come to some general agreement on a common set of underlying values and responsibilities. It must define, at least in general terms, some common goals and purposes that are important in fulfilling its obligations to society and the needs of its own members. As goals are formulated, the group members come to recognize that certain standards of conduct are essential for the carrying out of their professional responsibilities in a manner that builds public confidence in the profession. These standards of conduct are then formalized and set down in a professional code of ethics, which helps to clarify choices between alternatives so that individual members may react more in accordance with a group consensus on appropriate action in any specific situation. (28, p. 342)

During the first half century of its existence, the formal guidance movement has undergone tremendous growth and development. School guidance has matured to the point where it is seeking admission to the family of fully recognized traditional professions. As guidance has grown, it has assumed additional responsibilities in terms of service to individual students and to society as a whole. Especially within the past two decades, school guidance has turned its energy toward defining its scope and limits, as members of the field of counseling and guidance both individually and collectively have sought to mold the growing field into the general model of a profession.

The perception of counseling and guidance by general educators and parents has progressed through a number of stages. During the formative years of the guidance movement (the early 1900's) guidance counselors were practically unknown, for only a few schools utilized them on their staffs. Later, as more guidance counselors began to become a part of school staffs (the 1930's and 1940's), teachers and parents were still largely unaware of their contribution to the total school program. By the early 1950's the guidance function was emerging as a more widely recognized and accepted part of the secondary school. In the mid-1950's, however, there occurred a reaction against "unnecessary frills" in education. Due in part to the Sputnik scare, a sector of educational thought attempted to return to an essentialist philosophy, whereby only the "basic skills" would be stressed. Both implicitly and explicitly educators espousing this point of view stated that guidance services should be eliminated, along with several other frills.

At the same time, however, a counterforce was emerging. This force was being exerted to prevent the atrophy of a part of educational system that had matured to the point where it was beginning to make a contribution to the growth and development of a significant segment of the student population. For several years in the mid-1950's a debate occurred over which aspects of the curriculum were essentials and which aspects were frills. The National Defense Education Act (NDEA) of 1958 was the turning point in the emergence of counseling and guidance toward professional status. Under Title V, the act provided funds for testing and guidance programs in the public secondary schools and also for Counseling and Guidance Institutes in colleges and universities for improving the qualifications of secondary school counselors and of teachers preparing to be counselors. During the first five years (1958-1963), an estimated 13,800 individuals received training (30).

A subsequent amendment to the NDEA of 1958, coupled with additional legislation—e.g., the Vocational Education Act, the Elementary Education Act, and the Secondary Education Act—have helped the growth and development of the field of counseling and guidance. As noted in Chapter 10, a recent trend has seen the extension of guidance services into the elementary school. There is also an emerging concern over the lack of guidance services in junior colleges, community colleges, technical and trade schools, and adult education. Thus, the pendulum of the general educational and public opinion has completed its full course. The doubt and concern about guidance has changed to acceptance and, indeed, in many school systems a demand for more guidance services.

The guidance movement is in a developmental stage somewhat like late adolescence. Like the adolescent in this period of his life, the field of counseling and guidance is seeking to fill in the details of its professional identity. It is beginning to answer its questions of scope and purpose. It is attempting to define its role and function in the school setting more clearly. Wrenn notes that the youth of the guidance-personnel movement as a profession is a strength, enabling it to be aggressive without being too disturbed about making some mistakes (34). At the same time, however, he notes that guidance-personnel work sometimes lacks consistency and self-assurance.

TWO VIEWS OF EDUCATION

As one views the emerging guidance profession, a wide range of strategies, roles, and functions is apparent. Part I of this book has described the seven major approaches to guidance and has mentioned some other approaches, such as guidance as *quasi*-administration, guidance as social reconstruction, guidance as human engineering, guidance as an adjunct to national governmental policies, guidance as a parent surrogate, guidance as a role model for youth, guidance as character development, and guidance as an aid to "becoming." Within a broad context of education, two major modes of thought have been identified (13). The first is called the Theory of Freedom, flowing from the philosophy of Rousseau, the progressive education tradition, and permissive child rearing practices, and relating to client-centered (Rogerian) counseling. This view of education holds that the function of education is to free the naturally good and healthy growth-promoting tendencies of the student. Education is seen, in effect, as a drawing-out process.

The second major view of education has been called the Theory of Restraint. This view holds that the individual becomes humanized only through the socialization process. Socialization is viewed as a process of limiting and conforming behavior to fit in with societal modes of thought and action, and the school becomes a socializing institution. Whereas the former view of education stresses "drawing out," the latter approach emphasizes "pouring in." The Theory of Freedom emphasizes the individual, and the Theory of Restraint emphasizes the society.

While elements of both theories are evident in the functioning of most schools, the fundamentally antagonistic nature of these views of education constitutes a major source of strain for the entire school and the professional and ethical aspects of guidance. These two major theories of education have contributed to the dilemma, for there is a real issue with respect to the ethical and professional behavior of the counselor in terms of where his primary responsibility should lie—with the counselee or with the society.

ETHICAL AND GUIDANCE STANDARDS

One of the traditional criteria of a profession is that it possess a code of ethics. A code of ethics defines the scope and limits of the professional in broad terms and defines his responsibilities to the individual and to the society. Although there has always been a concern on the part of counselors regarding ethical versus unethical behavior, only quite recently has the field of counseling and guidance been sufficiently ready to develop a formal code of ethics. Some reasons for the relative recency of the American Personnel and Guidance Association Code of Ethics have been the following (28, pp. 331-57):

1. School counselors have only recently become self-conscious enough about their own identity to begin to develop ethical standards.
2. Professional standards require the existence of a professional group and it was only recently that such a group was formed.
3. In the past, an emphasis on local problems and a local definition of role and function obscured the broader framework of values and responsibility.
4. Narrow definitions of counselor roles resulted in success with particular tasks, providing little incentive for counselors to be critical of their work.
5. The growth of the guidance function was haphazard.
6. Only relatively recently have the communication media provided school coun-

selors with newer theories and the broader perspective required for a readiness to develop a code of ethics.

7. There has been a lack of agreement on values and responsibilities.

Purposes of a Code of Ethics

Codes of ethics serve a number of general functions. First, they serve to define the functions and duties of the practitioner. They help to define standards of training and performance. Codes of ethics protect the public against quacks and charlatans and also protect practitioners individually and as a profession (15). Codes of ethics provide a position on standards of ethical practice in order to help the practitioner to make decisions when conflict situations arise in his work. Although codes of ethics do not provide clear-cut solutions to these conflict situations, they do constitute guidelines to which the practitioner can refer for help in making judgments that would be generally acceptable to his colleagues.

More specifically, a code of ethics clarifies the counselor's responsibilities. The APGA Code of Ethics protects the counselee from the counselor's violation of or failure to meet his professional responsibilities. The code obliges the school counselor to respect the integrity of the student and to promote his general welfare. McGowan and Schmidt note in this regard that (*a*) clients should not be forced to avail themselves of counseling services, (*b*) the counselor should attempt to maintain the highest standards of competence in work, (*c*) the counselor should not work outside the area of his competence, (*d*) the counselor should not claim any qualifications he does not have, (*e*) counselees whose problems are beyond the counselor's ability to help should be referred, and (*f*) if divided loyalties arise—e.g., as between the student and the school or the society—the nature of that division should be worked out and made clear to all (20, pp. 583-86).

The code of ethics protects the profession from unethical practices of its members, simultaneously assuring society that the services of the counselor will demonstrate a sensible regard for social codes and the general moral expectations of the community in which he works. Too, ethical standards safeguard the privacy and integrity of the counselor from the extra-counseling demands sometimes made by clients. Because a code of ethics cannot be specific enough to cover all situations precisely, the personal needs and the value orientation of the counselor greatly affect his interpretation of its contents. Thus, it is necessary for ethical standards to be stated in fairly specific terms and for the counselor to have self-insight with respect to the motives operating in the interpretation of the code of ethics in any given conflict situation that may arise.

Types of Codes

Schwebel notes that while contemporary codes describe ethical behavior and provide machinery for dealing with violations, they do not provide information concerning the selection and training of counselors (25). The APGA Code of Ethics (5) and the earlier NVGA Code (6, 8) are *professional codes* in that they establish minimum standards for guidance services and approve agencies that meet those standards. The joint committee of the American Psychological Association, the American Educational Research Association, and the National Council of Measurement (16), on the other hand, developed a *technical code* with technical recommendations for preparing and publishing psychological tests and diagnostic techniques.

Codes of ethical practice for counselors are proposed by Gluck (11) and Hawkes (14). The American Psychological Association has also published an ethical code (4), and Wrenn has applied the APA code to counseling (33). Ohlsen has summarized existing codes as they relate to testing (21, pp. 214-16). Because the APGA Code of Ethics is not sensitive to all facets of the school counselor's work, the American School Counselor Association (ASCA) has been attempting to develop some possible modification of the APGA Code. One set of these proposed modifications have been presented by Flanagan and McGrew (9). Both Ohlsen (21) and Stewart and Warnath (28) suggest that the NEA Code (3), the APA code (4), and the APGA code (5) relate most significantly to the school counselor. While it is beyond the scope of this book to describe all of the relevant codes in detail, the APGA code is presented in Appendix C in full because, of all the codes, it is the most pertinent to the work of the guidance counselor.

Professional and Ethical Responsibilities of Guidance Counselors

Basic to any consideration of professional and ethical responsibilities is the fundamental issue of values. It is generally accepted that the counselor is entitled to his own value system and that part of his formal academic preparation should include an opportunity for his gaining self-understanding in regard to his value system. Aside from the questions of the place of values in counseling per se (10, 12, 22, 23, 31, 35) is the fundamental issue of the counselor's values in relation to the individual-versus-society problem in education. The school counselor's work with individual students touches upon and affects many significant people in the students' lives as well as the general society. A number of forces act on the counselor as he does his daily work.

First, there are legal concerns, which relate to the codified body of rules recognized by the state as binding on its members. Society formally expresses its expectations of the counselor in the form of enacted legislation and court rulings. There is a wide variety of potential problems in the legal area. Until quite recently there has been relatively little attention paid to the legal responsibilities of the counselor. In the past few years, however, there has been increasing interest in defining the counselor's responsibilities in the legal context more precisely (18, 26, 29) Chapter 13 described the role and function of the school counselor from a legal point of view. Society expresses itself in a somewhat more diffuse manner politically, electorally, through hiring policies, salaries, and through local efforts to define the role and function of counselor.

The profession of which the counselor is a part is also interested in and concerned about the counselor's meeting his responsibilities. The self-interest of the profession, coupled with its concern for the welfare of the members of society individually and collectively, motivates this concern. The profession influences the practitioner by (*a*) striving to enhance the status and function of counseling, (*b*) assisting and supporting its individual members, and (*c*) influencing or controlling within broad limits the nature and type of duties carried on by individual counselors (24, pp. 378-79).

Within counseling and guidance there is a continuum of thought ranging from "school counseling is a profession" and "school counseling is quickly becoming a profession" through "school counseling has a long way to go for professional status" to "school counseling can (should) never be a profession." Another group feels that the issue of professionalization is a pseudo-issue, in effect saying, "It isn't worth the time and energy discussing the matter."

The attempts to define the counselor's responsibilities in the legal context and by the various codes of ethics have been at best very general. In the last analysis, it is the counselor's own value system that is the final role determinant, with his own philosophy, values, attitudes, morals, and past experience constituting his eventual guides. The legal concern refers to what society expects from the counselor or to how it limits him in his work with counselees. Professional responsibilities are summarized by the code of ethics, representing what his colleagues expect of him. The third set of forces originates from the counselor himself, relating to what the counselor morally and philosophically expects from himself (24).

Several studies reveal that counselors have relative unanimity of thought in regard to what constitutes the proper discharge of their duties. Wiskoff investigated what counselors would do in the case of divided loyalties by asking counselors to respond to 22 incidents in which there were conflicts involving loyalty to the individual versus loyalty to the society (32). He found that industrial psychologists tended to stress the societal responsibilities, clinical psychologists emphasized their responsibilities to the individual, and counseling psychologists took a position between the two. Significantly, the differences between the three groups of counselors were very small.

Schwebel differentiates between unethical behavior which results from self-interest and unethical practice which is an act that is not within the accepted standards of ethical practice (25). Schwebel's point is that unethical practice refers to the act but not to the motivation, while unethical behavior includes the motivation and the underlying values of the person. He states that unethical behavior occurs only when conflicting personal interests of the practitioner lead to the unethical practice. Conversely, unethical practice resulting from ignorance, inadequate training, or poor supervision does not constitute unethical behavior.

Patterson notes the validity of this distinction, adding that it is sometimes difficult to make (22, p. 36). He describes the counselor's responsibilities to various others and to himself. Table 14-1 summarizes several writers' statements concerning counselor responsibilities. (2, 21, 22, 28).

TABLE 14-1

The Nature and Description of Counselor Responsibilities

Responsibility	Description
1. To client	*a.* Help client to achieve a more adequate life: self-direction; self-actualization.
	b. Help client to achieve his own end.
	c. Respect integrity and protect client's welfare.
	d. Do not impose services upon client.
	e. Do not urge unduly client to avail himself of services.
	f. Have professional and technical preparation.
	g. Recognize limits.
	h. Refer when necessary.
	i. Refrain from propaganding.
	j. Help each student to weigh all factors in making decisions.
	k. Be aware of his own needs—i.e., needs of the counselor; understand himself.
	l. Guard confidences and confidential information.
	m. Do not enter into clinical relationship with members of counselor's family, relatives, friends, intimate friends, or with other individuals which might jeopardize their welfare.
2. To client's family and friends	*a.* Have no contact with family or friends of client without client's permission, except where another person is clearly in danger or when client is clearly mentally irresponsible.
	b. Help parents understand what they can do to help their children and help them to understand factors affecting their children.
	c. Avoid using the technical language of your profession when talking with parents.
3. To employer and colleagues	*a.* Accept and work with only those clients who are eligible for services of the agency—i.e., the school.
	b. Be responsible to the entire institution.
	c. Define yourself in terms of role, function, responsibilities, and commitments.
	d. Don't use student cases for social conversation.
	e. When necessary or advisable to exchange information with colleagues, do it in a professional manner.
	f. Keep files—i.e., notes of counseling—completely confidential and under lock and key.
	g. Avoid using student clerks in guidance office, because it may lead to a loss of confidentiality of information in files.
4. To referring source	*a.* Treat nonprofessional referrals similar to those of parents and friends.
	b. Consult client before transmitting confidential information.

TABLE 14-1 (*continued*)

Responsibility	Description
5. To the profession	*a.* Represent the profession so that it does not suffer in the eyes of clients or the general public. *b.* Maintain high standards of service. *c.* Avoid condemnation or disapproval of other people's approaches or methods. *d.* Inform appropriate professional body or organization when you have evidence of unprofessional or unethical practice.

6. To society	*a.* Give primary responsibility to the client.
	b. Give ultimate allegiance to society.
	c. Protect client as member of society.
	d. Guard professional confidences and reveal them:
	  1. only after careful deliberation;
	  2. when there is clear and imminent danger to an individual or society.

7. To self	*a.* Protect your own reputation. *b.* Protect your private life from excessive demands of clients. *c.* Don't conform to assumed needs or demands of clients. *d.* Don't yield to clients in regard to the counseling method he prefers. *e.* Leave clients' problems at the office. *f.* Avoid becoming overly involved in the problems of clients.

THE GROWTH OF GUIDANCE IN SCHOOLS

The field of counseling and guidance in schools has grown at an unprecedented rate in the last decade. As recently as 1954 a national survey of school guidance services and personnel found only about seven thousand counselors who were devoting half time or more to guidance responsibilities (17). The growth of guidance between 1958 and 1963 is summarized in Table 14-2. A recent study reveals that while the counselor-pupil ratio was 530:1 in 1963, the ratio has dropped from 520:1 in 1964 to 507:1 in 1965 (30). The factors relating to the demand for additional guidance services and the subsequent growth of guidance have been summarized as follows (7, pp. 5-6):

1. National concern for the early identification and development of talent.
2. Increasing professional and public acceptance of guidance services as normal and expected functions of the schools.
3. Support of educational leaders and professional organizations for an adequate ratio of counselors to students (ranging from 1 to 250 to 1 to 300).
4. Marked increase in total school population, forecasting, in turn, the need for as many as 100,000 new teachers and 5,000 new counselors each year through 1970.
5. Federal subsidies for the development of statewide testing programs, develop-

ment of school counseling services, and the preparation of a larger supply of secondary school counselors.

6. Recognition that much wastage of talent might be counteracted by guidance services through which teachers and counselors work more effectively together.

TABLE 14-2

A Summary of the Growth of Counseling and Guidance: 1958-1963*

Category	1958-59	1959-60	1960-61	1961-62	1962-63
Number of school counselors in USA	12,000	18,739	21,828	24,492	27,180
Ratio of FTE† counselors to all public secondary school students	1:960	1:640	1:570	1:550	1:530
Per cent of public secondary school students with programs: NDEA Title V-A programs	5-10%				75%
Limited counseling and guidance programs	40-45%				15%
No counseling and guidance programs	50%				10%
Total number of tests administered to public secondary school students	10,264,220				20,534,244
Students tested at least once: Number	5,228,007				9,756,915
Percentage	46%				68%
Professional guidance personnel in state departments of education: Number	99				257
FTE support personnel	78				203
FTE professional personnel	100				226
Ratio of FTE guidance supervisors to: Secondary school students	1:437,000				1:190,000
Elementary & secondary school students	1:147,000				1:71,000
Local secondary school guidance personnel	1:154				1:134

*(30, p. 8-44)
†FTE = Full-Time Equivalent

THE AMERICAN PERSONNEL AND GUIDANCE ASSOCIATION: THE PROFESSIONAL ORGANIZATION OF COUNSELING AND GUIDANCE

The American Personnel and Guidance Association (APGA) came into existence in 1951 through a merger of the National Vocational Guidance Association, the American College Personnel Association, the National Association of

Guidance Supervisors and Counselor Trainers, and the Student Personnel Association for Teacher Education. The American Personnel and Guidance Association is composed of seven divisions. The nature and function of these divisions are summarized in the following official descriptions of the various divisions (1):

ACPA: *The American College Personnel Association*

ACPA is the division of the American Personnel and Guidance Association that unites the various interest groups, specialties, and competencies of student personnel workers employed at a junior college, a four-year college, or a university level. Membership in ACPA links you with a nationwide community of student personnel workers who share your interests whether you are a college teacher, a counselor, dean, or director, engaged in research activity, or any combination of these.

Through the annual convention program and the commission and committee structure, members have an opportunity to participate in Association activities while the ACPA publications, including the *Journal of College Student Personnel* and the growing ACPA Monograph Series, are available to members at reduced rates. By joining ACPA, the college student personnel worker thus becomes an integral part of a national organization that seeks to identify and communicate the latest and best in current practice and research.

ACES: *The Association for Counselor Education and Supervision*

The objective of ACES is to advance counselor education and supervision in order to improve counseling and personnel services at all levels of education and in related settings.

This Division is made up of persons who hold leadership positions in the guidance and personnel field. The Association's regular membership is made up of three groups: local guidance directors or coordinators of elementary and secondary schools; state and national guidance supervisors or consultants; and counselor educators. These three groups work together to improve guidance and counseling by involvement in many projects and programs sponsored by the Association. Members participate in six regional meetings held each fall and in the national APGA convention each spring. *Counselor Education and Supervision* is published quarterly.

Associate membership is especially appropriate for graduate students preparing for work in counselor education or guidance supervision and for local guidance directors who supervise less than 10 full-time counselors.

NVGA: *The National Vocational Guidance Association*

Every APGA Member may also belong to NVGA. NVGA has drawn its viability from the fact that work is a critically important part of our lives. It has consistently provided leadership in the development of guidance theory and practice. NVGA promotes concern for the lifelong productive and profitable utilization of man's knowledges, abilities, and skills in the evolving pattern of society and culture. It has emphasized the close relationship and interdependence among personnel workers in schools, colleges, community agencies, business, industry, and government. It provides quality pamphlets on current issues.

The *Vocational Guidance Quarterly* covers practical developments, ideas, and applications of new techniques and procedures. Through the convention, committees, sections, interest groups, and local chapters, NVGA continuously promotes guidance as a responsible activity in the growth and development of each individual.

SPATE: *The Student Personnel Association for Teacher Education*

One third of all graduates from four-year college programs in the United

States in 1964 were prepared for elementary or secondary school teaching. It is for these students in private colleges, public colleges, and universities that SPATE has a special concern.

SPATE invites into membership those engaged in personnel services in teacher education, those teaching in the counseling or guidance and personnel areas, and those in supervision, placement, and other areas related to the student personnel program in teacher education. Graduate students are also eligible. Organization activities include publications, such as the quarterly *SPATE Journal* and a recent monograph, *The Role of the Student Personnel Worker in Teacher Education;* convention programs, cooperative sponsorship of publications, meetings, and projects with other national organizations in the field of teacher education; and a coordinated effort to improve preparation and standards among college personnel workers.

ASCA: *The American School Counselor Association*

Over 12,000 school counselors across the nation are members of ASCA, making it the largest division of APGA. Membership and active participation in ASCA helps each of them, as counselors, to continuously broaden and deepen their knowledge in the many areas encompassed by guidance and counseling. This in turn helps them to better serve youth.

Regular membership in ASCA is open to those who hold a bachelor's degree and are employed as elementary or secondary school counselors, teacher counselors, directors, supervisors, or coordinators of guidance services or those who are employed in an institution in which they have a major responsibility for guidance and counseling. Professional membership is available to those who hold a master's degree, valid certification in school counseling and guidance, have been employed for at least three years in the field and who are regularly employed in elementary and secondary school counseling or related fields.

ASCA publishes the *School Counselor* quarterly, a newsletter, and other publications to aid the counselor in his work with students and parents.

ARCA: *The American Rehabilitation Counseling Association*

Rehabilitation counseling is one of this country's newest and most rapidly growing professions. It emphasizes the social concept that the conservation of human resources merits a skillful and well-trained professional individual who desires the personal satisfaction that comes from helping disabled individuals achieve more productive and useful lives. The rehabilitation counselor works with those persons who are physically, mentally or emotionally disabled.

ARCA membership is open to all counselors interested in and concerned with the adjustment problems of the disabled and who wish to share in the professional growth and development of this field. Membership is available on a professional, associate, and student basis.

ARCA publishes the Rehabilitation Counseling Bulletin on a quarterly basis; makes an annual research award; and provides other services designed to aid the counselor in his work with the disabled.

AMEG: *The Association for Measurement and Evaluation in Guidance*

AMEG members are those who are engaged in planning, administering, and conducting testing programs; providing test scoring services; interpreting and using test results; developing evaluation instruments; teaching college-level courses in evaluation and measurement; or conducting research concerned with personal and guidance aspects of evaluation and measurement.

AMEG strives to provide a forum for the discussion of ethical, social, and technical problems related to measurement and evaluation in guidance, including the opportunity for communication between the producers and consumers of evaluation devices. AMEG members are concerned with improving standards of service by identifying problems in the use of tools of evaluation, stimulating research relating to these problems, and disseminating the results of such research. This Division promotes greater technical competency on the part of those who construct, use, and interpret measurement and evaluation instruments in guidance and personnel work. Graduate students are eligible.

NECA: *The National Employment Counselors Association*

Professional and regular membership in NECA is open to those who are engaged in administering, planning, and conducting employment counseling programs and related research. It is also open to those who help prepare counselors. Those who have an interest in the aims and objectives of NECA are invited to become associate members.

The major goal of employment counseling programs, whether in government, private agency, or industry is to assist the client to clarify his relationship to the world of work, to identify his vocational problem, and to plan a program to overcome this problem by means of insight and learning.

The employment counselor works with clients varying in age and occupational, social, and educational background. The client's vocational problem, whether it be in the nature of vocational planning or adjustment, is perceived by him as an immediate one. Most clients receive counseling at a time when they are either presently working or immediately interested in entering employment. No-vocational problems may also be present, but the primary focus is vocational. The employment counselor does not restrict his services to any select special interest group. He deals with an across-the-board variety of individuals.

NECA publishes the *Journal of Employment Counseling* quarterly.

SUMMARY

The growth of counseling and guidance in schools reflects the felt need and concern of our society for additional personalized services for youth. As our culture has become more complex, the pressures upon individuals have increased. Decisions and choices have become more crucial. Developing and implementing an identity (self-concept—constitute a major source of concern. America has increasingly turned to public education as a source for meeting its needs—an educational system which in turn has looked to guidance personnel for individualizing education, providing remedial help, and fostering the general development and well-being of the student. As the field of counseling and guidance has assumed an increasingly strategic role in the educational venture, it has attempted to cast itself in the mold of a profession, with a growing concern for its ethical standards, its responsibilities, and its limitations.

REFERENCES

1. *Add-A-Division.* Washington, D.C.: American Personnel and Guidance Association, 1966.

2. L. B. Brammer and E. L. Shostrum, *Therapeutic Psychology*. Englewood Cliffs, N. J.: Prentice-Hall, 1960.

3. *Code of Ethics.* Washington, D.C.: National Education Association, 1952.

4. Committee on Ethical Standards for Psychologists, *Ethical Standards of Psychologists.* Washington, D.C.: American Psychological Association, 1953.

5. Committee on Ethics of the American Personnel and Guidance Association, "Code of Ethics," *Personnel and Guidance Journal,* 40 (1961), 206-9.

6. *Directory of Approved Vocational Counseling Agencies.* Washington, D.C.: American Personnel and Guidance Association, 1954.

7. W. E. Dugan, "Critical Concerns of Counselor Education," *Counselor Education and Supervision,* (1961), 5-6.

8. Ethical Practices Committee, *Directory of Vocational Counseling Services.* Washington, D.C.: National Vocational Guidance Association, 1951.

9. M. Flanagan and D. R. McGrew, "A Suggested Code of Ethics for School Counselors," *The School Counselor,* 8 (1961), 137-41.

10. S. W. Ginsberg, *et al.,* "Values and Their Relationship to Psychiatric Principles and Practice," *American Journal of Psychotherapy,* (1953), 546-73.

11. S. Gluck, *et al.,* "A Proposed Code of Ethics for Counselors," *Occupations,* 30 (1952), 484-90.

12. A. W. Green, "Social Values and Psychotherapy," *Journal of Personality* 14 (1946), 199-228.

13. R. J. Havighurst, *Human Development and Education.* New York: David McKay Co., 1953.

14. A. L. Hawkes, *et al.,* "A Proposed Code of Ethics for Counselors Using Occupational Information," *Occupations,* 28 (1950), 464-68.

15. K. F. Heiser, "The Need for Legislation and the Complexity of the Problem," *American Psychologist,* 5 (1950), 103-7.

16. Joint Committee of the American Psychological Association, American Educational Research Association, and National Council of Measurement, *Technical Recommendations for Psychological Tests and Diagnostic Techniques.* Supplement to *Psychological Bulletin,* (1954), 21-38.

17. A. J. Jones and L. M. Miller, "The National Picture of Pupil Personnel and Guidance Services," *National Association of Secondary School Principals Bulletin,* 38 (1954), 105-6.

18. D. W. Louisell, "The Psychologist in Today's Legal World," *Minnesota Law Review,* 41 (1957), 731-50.

19. C. H. McCully, "The School Counselor: Strategy for Professionalization," *Personnel and Guidance Journal,* 40 (1962), 681-89.

20. J. F. McGowan and L. D. Schmidt, *Counseling: Readings in Theory and Practice.* New York: Holt, Rinehart & Winston, 1962.

21. M. M. Ohlsen, *Guidance Services in the Modern School.* New York: Harcourt, Grace & World, 1964.

22. C. H. Patterson, *Counseling and Psychotherapy: Theory and Practice.* New York: Harper and Brothers, 1959.

23. C. H. Patterson, "The Place of Values in Counseling and Psychotherapy," *Journal of Counseling Psychology,* 5 (1958), 216-23.

24. L. D. Schmidt, "Some Ethical, Professional, and Legal Considerations for School Counselors," *Personnel and Guidance Journal,* 44 (1965), 376-82.

25. M. Schwebel, "Why? Unethical Practice," *Counseling Psychology,* 2 (1955), 122-28.

26. T. B. Shrewsbury, "Legal Implications for Student Personnel Workers," in E. Lloyd-Jones and M. Smith, eds., *Student Personnel Work as Deeper Teaching,* New York: Harper & Row, 1954.

27. C. E. Smith, *Development of Ethical Standards in the Secondary School Counseling Relationship for the Use of Counseling Information.* Unpublished Doctoral Dissertation, University of Southern California, 1956.

28. L. H. Stewart and C. F. Warnath, *The Counselor and Society.* Boston: Houghton Mifflin Co., 1965.

29. M. Ware, *Law of Guidance and Counseling.* Cincinnati, Ohio: W. H. Anderson Co., 1964.

30. R. Warner, *Commitment to Youth.* Washington, D.C.: U.S. Office of Education, 1964.

31. E. G. Williamson, "Value Orientation in Counseling," *Personnel and Guidance Journal,* 36 (1958), 520-28.

32. M. Wiskoff, "Ethical Standards and Divided Loyalties," *American Psychologist,* 15 (1960), 656-60.

33. C. G. Wrenn, "The Ethics of Counseling," *Educational and Psychological Measurement,* 12 (1952), 161-77.

34. C. G. Wrenn, "The Fault, Dear Brutus—," *Educational and Psychological Measurement,* 9 (1949), 360-78.

35. C. Zilboorg, "Clinical Variants of Moral Values," *American Journal of Psychiatry,* 106 (1950), 744-47.

chapter 15

Issues and Problems in the Field of Guidance

American education has grown up to the accompaniment of criticism—continual, biting criticism—from many individuals and groups who want education to be still better. It is very probable that this constant criticism has contributed positively to the prodigious strength that education in this country has developed. Educators themselves have increasingly applied to their own efforts more systematic, more critical, more constructive evaluation. Leaders in education are imbued with the conviction that education can be still better.

As education has grown in a society of increasing complexity, it has felt the need for and fostered the development of guidance and student personnel work to help it accomplish some of its most important purposes. Social and education forces have impinged on guidance-personnel work so strongly that it has developed an exaggerated illusion of traveling under its own steam, establishing its own directions, and knowing where it is going. It is interesting to realize that guidance-personnel work has not yet had much criticism. Most of those outside this field who write about it advocate more of it and set up more things for it to do. Those inside have been so busy advocating partial views and jockeying for position that they have neglected to get on with the business of criticizing and evaluating what they have done and are doing.*

Implicit in most discussions of issues and problems is the notion that the existence of disagreements which have not yet been resolved weakens the field of guidance—that unresolved matters have a generally detrimental effect. While it is obvious that unresolved problems can be harmful, it does not follow that the mere presence of problems or issues per se is harmful to the well-being of the field. The critical factor, it would seem, is not the presence of issues but rather what the field is doing to resolve them. Contemporary guidance is operating within an educational content that is rapidly evolving in part from innovations within the field of guidance and in part from community, governmental, societal, and even international forces. Education's response to external demands may

*From Ruth Barry and Beverly Wolf, *Modern Issues in Guidance-Personnel Work* (New York: Teachers College Press, 1957), p. ix. Copyright © by Teachers College, Columbia University. Reprinted by permission of the publisher.

be in the form of providing more services, altering contemporary practices to meet the needs of a certain segment of the population, or choosing not to meet the felt need of some sector of society. In a broad and complex endeavor such as contemporary education in America, there are bound to be differences of opinion with respect to what constitutes an appropriate educational response to these internal and external demands. Thus, issues and problems arise.

Progress results, however, when new and better ways of serving the individual and society are adopted. The raising of issues may indeed be a healthy sign that guidance is considering new and more adequate solutions to old issues or focusing on ways of meeting current problems. The field of guidance has received relatively little criticism from education and society. As noted in Chapter 10, it was the felt need of education in an increasingly complex society that fostered the growth of the guidance movement. In general, most of the writers outside the field of guidance have advocated the provision of both *more guidance personnel* in schools and a *broader range of guidance services.* Most of the issues have been raised by members of the guidance profession, either collectively as members of special groups or as individuals.

Virtually all aspects of the guidance process have occasioned the raising of issues. Often, the issues have been raised implicitly, as in the case of guidance textbooks which have espoused differing points of view regarding the nature and scope of guidance. To date, however, the journals, professional conventions, professional organization committees, and several monographs have constituted the major media for the presentation and discussion of issues.

Journal articles tend to focus on a single issue or a group of related issues. Shertzer and Stone discuss nineteen basic issues facing the field of guidance by grouping them into three major categories (85): the role and function of guidance, the preparation and certification of guidance workers, and guidance practices and program policies. Barry and Wolf consider guidance issues from a historical perspective, identifying three general types of issues (5): (*a*) issues that have persistently troubled guidance workers since the inception of the guidance movement (recurrent issues), (*b*) issues that have appeared before, were temporarily resolved, and have recently appeared in somewhat changed form (renascent issues), and (*c*) issues that are new and possibly unrecognized, undiscussed, or ignored (incipient issues). Thus, issues have been considered singly, in groups relating to certain general problem areas, or against a historical backdrop.

One of the major themes of this book has been that guidance practice should be derived at least in part from theory. A paradigm or model was presented in Chapter 1 in which a theorĕtical orientation to guidance was developed from philosophy, which provides the goals or ends (objectives) of the guidance process, and from knowledge in source fields which provide operational concepts and techniques for implementing guidance. The process of guidance, in turn, is derived from theory as theory leads to policy, planning, program structure, general procedures (functions), personnel, and facilities.

ISSUES RELATING TO PHILOSOPHY

The major issues which relate to philosophy center upon the following questions:

1. What philosophy of education should the school adopt?
2. What should be the guidance worker's philosophy of guidance?
3. What influence should philosophy have upon guidance theory?
4. What influence should philosophy have upon guidance practice?

Fundamental to any philosophy of guidance is the more general philosophy of education. Although some writers in guidance have tacitly suggested that the guidance program function relatively independently from the rest of the school system and its philosophy of education, most feel that the guidance program should operate closely within the basic philosophy that comes from the school system. The philosophy of the guidance program should in turn (most writers feel) then articulate with the more general philosophy of the school system. With the passage of time, the guidance program and its philosophy may influence to a greater or lesser extent the philosophy of the school system.

While there are continua of thought regarding the degree to which the philosophies of the educational system and the guidance program should influence each other, the extreme views are (a) two relatively independent philosophies and (b) either the school system's or the guidance program's philosophy prevailing over the other. Twelve basic philosophies of education are summarized as follows:

1. *Experimentalism*:   belief in an active school; emphasis on guided experience; learning solves present problems; knowledge and truth change; knowledge should not be revered just because it comes from the past; knowledge is derived from social experience.

2. *Classical realism*:   stems from Plato and Aristotle; emphasis on the form of things; emphasis on general education and general laws; "theoretical"; stress on "big ideas."

3. *Education for life adjustment*:   purpose of education is to give youth attitudes and skills to cope with situations (problems) of everyday life.

4. *Education for intellectual discipline*:   emphasis on the "generative" subjects, training the mind, and basic learnings.

5. *Education for psychological maturity*:   goal is to help develop attitudes of self-understanding and self-acceptance.

6. *Education for moral character*:   function of education is to teach individuals the right thing to do; emphasis upon honesty; truthfulness, and industry.

7. *Protestant view of education*:   religion and education should not be separated; emphasis upon uniting protestant ideas and the goal of education.

8. *Roman Catholic view of education*: general curriculum of the school is either (*a*) viewed from a Catholic point of view or (*b*) supplemented by religious instruction.

9. *Jewish view of education*: education is a continuing task which begins in the family and then goes out to the community; an ignorant individual cannot be truly free; education is the "bread of life"; emphasis on intellectualism and tradition.

10. *Conservative view of education*: goal of education is to transmit well-tested ideas and worthy traditions of the past; emphasis on traditionalism and the cultural heritage.

11. *Reconstructionist view of education*: society- and culture-oriented; curriculum of education centers on the problems of politics, religion, aesthetics, etc.

12. *Education for national survival*: education is an instrument of power; national survival depends upon proper uses of educational resources; emphasis upon proper allocation of human resources and talent.

Beck reviews the guidance literature regarding philosophy and identifies elements of realism, neo-realism, theism, idealism, *Daseinanalyse*, determinism, existentialism, positivism, and instrumentalism in contemporary guidance thought (6).

In addition to the foregoing issues have been questions such as (*a*) What should be the relationship of the counselors' personal (informal) philosophy of life to his practice? and (*b*) What should be the nature, extent, and timing of courses in philosophy in the formal academic preparation of school counselors?

Until quite recently the major focus of guidance has remained on the practitioner and his work in the school. It has become increasingly evident, however, that many of the pragmatic problems and related issues can be traced back to unresolved philosophical questions. Thus, there has been a growing interest in grappling with the basic philosophical issues underlying the entire guidance process. If the guidance counselor derives his practice from a systematic theoretical frame of reference, and if philosophy and a philosophical stance are a part of that framework, then the resolution of the philosophical questions in the thinking of the guidance practitioner becomes even more crucial.

ISSUES RELATING TO THE BEHAVIORAL SCIENCES

Although the broadening of the basis of guidance theory and practice by means of an interdisciplinary perspective has remained an issue for many years, it has in recent years assumed major importance. As noted in Chapter 10, there has been a trend for guidance to express an increasing interest in the utilization of knowledge from the behavioral sciences. There is also some evidence that individual writers have begun to explore concepts and principles in the behavioral

sciences as they relate to guidance. The major issues pertaining to the relationship of the behavioral sciences to guidance are summarized in Table 15-1.

TABLE 15-1

Issues: The Behavioral Sciences and Guidance

Issue	Patterns or Points of View
1. To what extent should various source fields be utilized for (*a*) counselor preparation and (*b*) guidance theory?	1. Wide range: from very little utilization of other source fields to a heavy emphasis on utilizing them.
2. What shall constitute source fields for guidance?	2. Various combinations of the following: *a.* Behavioral sciences: psychology, social psychology, sociology, anthropology, etc. *b.* Social sciences: economics, political science, law, government, history, etc. *c.* Humanities: philosophy
3. When shall the behavioral sciences and other source fields be offered in the counselor education curriculum?	3. Wide range: most heavily at beginning; most heavily at end; throughout *a.* Bachelors degree level *b.* Master's degree level *c.* 6th year level *d.* Doctoral level *e.* Postdoctoral level
4. Who shall teach courses in the behavioral sciences and other source fields?	4. Following points of view: *a.* Professors in counselor education *b.* Professors in source fields *c.* Combination of above (1) each teaching some courses (2) joint teaching assignments (3) combination of 1 and 2

Despite the increasing interest in the behavioral sciences by guidance writers,
a study by Riccio found that while a surprising number of counselor educators
were interested primarily in personality theory, not a single one of the 746 counselor educators responding to the questionnaire expressed a primary interest in
any one of the behavioral sciences (78). As a result of his findings, Riccio raises
the provocative question of whether or not counselor educators are paying lip
service to the concept of an interdisciplinary approach to guidance.

The relatively strong interest in personality theory suggests that counselor
educators may be more interested in clinical approaches to counseling. There
can be no question that while there appears to increasing interest in the behavioral sciences, the interest is a peripheral one for most writers. While psychological frames of reference and psychological constructs tend to dominate contemporary theory-building efforts in guidance, the unresolved issue of the place
of the other behavioral sciences in relation to theory and practice continues to
plague the field.

ISSUES RELATING TO GUIDANCE THEORY

The general trend in guidance has been to develop a more adequate theoretical basis for practice. As noted above, most guidance theory has stemmed from psychology. Yet, there remains the basic issue of the extent to which guidance practice should be derived from a systematic theoretical base as opposed to the derivation of practice from the general model of an art. Those who favor basing guidance practice upon a better theoretical foundation tend to envision the evolution of guidance in the general model of a science. The most ardent group of theorists favoring the science model are the behaviorists, who might define the guidance worker as an applied learning theorist who utilizes the principles of reinforcement and extinction to achieve his objectives. Although the general movement of the field of guidance is toward more elaborate approaches to guidance in the scientific tradition, there is an underlying current of discontent—a point of view which might possibly reverse the contemporary trend.

ISSUES RELATING TO GUIDANCE POLICY

There is general agreement that the board of education has the function of determining basic educational policies, which should in turn be implemented via the administrative hierarchy within the local school system. Because there has been no constant source of policy at a broader level, there has been no control guiding policy for the entire field of guidance. To date, governmental action (national, state, and local), professional associations, individual members, and outside forces have exerted varying amounts of leadership and policy-making functions for guidance. In recent years, federal governmental influence has been very great through the government-sponsored research bureaus, the U.S. Office of Education, and the various types of federal aid to education which determine the segment of the student population receiving assistance supported by governmental funds. The federal government has also influenced guidance through the establishment of the special guidance-personnel section of the U.S. Office of Education, which affects the training of school counselors via the NDEA guidance institutes. Various publications of the Office of Education have also been interpreted as policy statements.

The entire system of state-defined certification standards constitutes another governmental policy influence. If the work of the guidance counselor is influenced by his education, and the education is in turn influenced by state certification requirements, then the state policy regarding certification indirectly influences guidance practice. Thus state certification requirements are, in effect, policy statements for guidance.

Barry and Wolf note that the influence of city systems has been considerable and of a much more specific nature than the influence of national and state governments because various city school systems have typically offered explicit and direct policy statements which have in turn been adopted by other school systems (5). Often, for example, the guidance programs in large cities have been utilized as demonstration programs for guidance. Of historical interest is the strong influence of the original program of vocational guidance of the Boston school system. More recently, the guidance programs of New York City (Higher Horizons) and White Plains, N.Y. (teacher-counselors), and the more generalized programs of guidance in Providence and Chicago have served to influence guidance program policies in other cities. Time and again, individual programs have served as prototypes of practices, organizational patterns, architectural designs, techniques, etc. Publications of various school systems have also served to influence guidance policy. Handbooks, various types of guides for guidance counselors, and descriptions of programs have served as blueprints for other programs of guidance.

Professional associations have also provided varying amounts and qualities of leadership and policy-making throughout the history of the guidance movement. The National Vocational Guidance Association, the National Association of Women Deans and Counselors, the American College Personnel Association, the American School Counselor Association, the Association of Counselor Education and Supervision, and, more recently, the American Personnel and Guidance Association have each provided leadership through policy statements proposed by various committees. These statements concern a wide range of policies, such as standards for counselor preparation (17, 18), counselor role (1, 2, 49), code of ethics (19), roles of subprofessionals in guidance (76), etc. Although association leadership has been widespread, the influence has been varied and sometimes counterbalancing because of interassociational competition for dominance in regard to the policy-making function.

The influence of individuals on policy has continuously diminished since the early years of the guidance movement. Although the individual is always a possible source for policy-making, since the 1930's the focus has shifted from individual practitioners to counselor educators with the following results (5, p. 204):

1. An emphasis upon dividing theory and practice.
2. Frequent advances in theory.
3. Relatively fewer advances in practical aspects of guidance.
4. Less direct "reporting from the field."
5. More attempts to bridge the widening gap between theory and practice.

Another major influence on guidance policies has come from outside the field of guidance: both individuals and outside organizations (e.g., American Psychological Association, American Council on Education) have had indirect influences on the field.

Thus, the issue emerges into the most concise form: Who should be responsible for developing guidance policy? As noted above, there has been no single source for guidance policy, nor has there been any single combination of sources that has consistently provided leadership and policy-making for the field of guidance. Both the advantages and disadvantages of this situation have been described (5, 63). The advantages include flexibility, adaptability, and the ability to be sensitive to societal demands, while the disadvantages are the inhibition of the development of free experimentation, the reinforcement of traditional patterns, and some loss of continuity and coordination.

At the local school system level there is the parallel issue of who should determine local policies affecting the guidance worker and his practice. The various points of view include (*a*) all policy-making as administrative function, (*b*) policy-making as a guidance function (when it relates directly to the guidance process), and (*c*) policy-making as joint administration-guidance function. A corollary issue is whether guidance policies should be explicit or implied.

ISSUES RELATED TO PLANNING

The importance of adequate planning for guidance has been stressed by virtually all writers who have discussed the implementation of guidance. The basic issues revolve about the following points:

1. Who should be responsible for planning concerning guidance matters?
2. What should be the relative influence of administrators, guidance personnel, teachers, students, parents, and others on guidance planning?
3. Through what process should the planning occur:
   a. Administrative fiat
   b. Committee
   c. Combination of the above
4. To what extent should the planning focus on maintaining traditional practices as opposed to planning for innovation in guidance?

While there is a wide spectrum of thought in regard to these issues, the fundamental issue in planning concerns the relative authority of administration and guidance and primary responsible for making plans for the guidance process. Virtually all possible points of view have been held.

ISSUES RELATING TO PROGRAM STRUCTURE

Throughout Part I of the book, the description of each of the seven major orientations to guidance included some typical organizational patterns. The program structure in guidance is organized according to two basic patterns: staff-and-line pattern and the organic or circular pattern. The nature, advantages, and disadvantages of these organizational patterns were discussed in Chapter 8. As noted earlier, virtually all schools have the line-and-staff type of program structure. The basic problem emerges in the form of the question: How should the guidance program be organized?

More specifically, the basic question in terms of the school counselors is: To whom should the guidance counselor be administratively responsible? Each of the basic patterns shown in Figure 15-1 is utilized in contemporary programs of guidance. Each pattern has its advantages and disadvantages. In Patterns A and B the teacher is the guidance functionary and is in a line relationship with the

FIGURE 15-1
Some Organizational Patterns in Contemporary Education

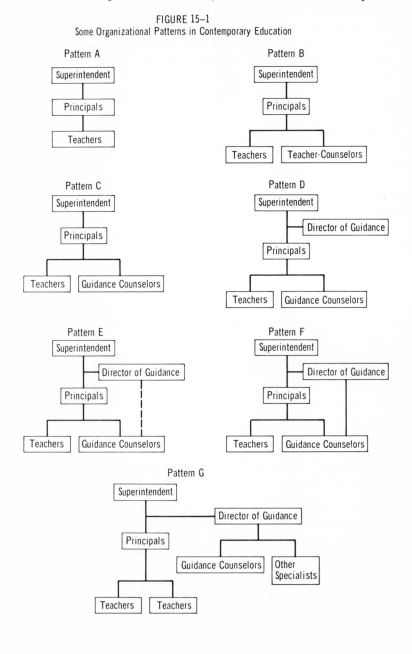

principal. Patterns C and D provide program structures that are basically similar to A and B. The guidance counselor is in a line relationship with the principal and there may or may not be a guidance administrator. In Pattern E the guidance counselor is in a line relationship with the principal and in an advisory relationship with the guidance administrator. Pattern F has the guidance counselor responsible to both the principal and the guidance administrator. In Pattern G the program structure of guidance is organized around the concept of supplementary services with the guidance counselor functioning in a line relationship with the guidance administrator.

ISSUES RELATING TO PROGRAM ACTIVITIES AND PROCEDURES

In the broadest sense, the issues relating to program activities and procedures involve the role and function of the guidance worker. There have been numerous studies of what the guidance counselor actually does in both elementary- and secondary-school settings. (3, 13, 26, 31, 38, 40, 52, 62, 66, 68, 69, 72, 77, 82, 89). While earlier studies were limited inquiries regarding specific activities, some recent studies have sought to describe the guidance worker's role and function within the broader context of general approaches or strategies of guidance. Thus, the issue regarding the guidance counselor's role and function has emerged in the form of the generalist-specialist debate.

The traditional arguments for and against each of these roles have been summarized by numerous writers (7, 8, 37, 42, 43, 53, 83). It has been argued, on the other hand, that the traditional generalist-specialist issue beclouds the more fundamental problems of role and function by couching the problem in terms that are broad, vague, and ill-defined(9). There are many varieties of generalists and specialists. This point of view holds that the issue can be resolved only through the consideration of the subissues of guidance objectives, focus, context, and continuity.

The model proposed in Chapter 9 represents this writer's attempt to sharpen and point up the issue in order that its most pertinent dimensions might be identified and considered. The model has four basic dimensions: (*a*) theoretical orientation, (*b*) goal orientation, (*c*) focal orientation, and (*d*) process orientation. Thus, when the various subdimensions are plotted, the resulting profile describes the guidance worker's role and function.

MISCELLANEOUS ISSUES

Terminology

The terminology issue has become a serious one in recent years. In attempting to clarify the problems in this area writers have referred to "serious errors in nomenclature" (46), "terminology tangles" (5) and the guidance "tower of

Babel" (23). The most troublesome terms have continued to be (*a*) guidance, (*b*) counseling (*c*) psychotherapy, and to a lesser degree (*d*) guidance services, (*e*) pupil personnel work (services), (*f*) student personnel work (services) and (*g*) guidance-personnel work. The terms have been used as synonyms for each other. Almost all writers agree that the terms are quite similar, and yet most agree that there are also differences between them. The problems arise when there is an attempt to communicate similarities and differences. For example, there are over 150 different definitions of the word guidance and probably as many definitions of related terms such as counseling and psychotherapy.

Several strategies have been utilized to resolve the terminology problem. Gustad, for example, has surveyed definitions of counseling and has noted three common characteristics (32):

1. *Participants*: usually two; one person with a problem and the second person with specific role of helper.
2. *Goals*: wide range; most often including better adjustment, higher level of functioning, or greater happiness.
3. *Learning*: typically emphasized throughout the counseling relationship.

Other writers (4, 9, 12, 14, 54, 61), on the other hand, have attempted to make detailed distinctions between various terms. In general, efforts to differentiate among the terms have not met with any degree of success. Some attempts to smooth over the differences and contradictions in terms emphasize that the differences are only in degree and not in kind. Also, continua of thought have been suggested. The field of guidance is caught in a semantic wasteland of confusion and conflict over terminology. Unfortunately, more important than the controversy of the use of terms per se is the correlative confusion over meanings.

Evaluation of Guidance

The issue of how guidance should be evaluated is a perplexing one. While there is general agreement with respect to the nature of the global process of evaluation, there is widespread disagreement regarding criteria and general methodology. Listed below are 22 criteria that have been utilized to evaluate guidance:

1. Proportion of students with educational plans.
2. Degree of harmony between educational and vocational plans and capacity.
3. Extent of failure in courses.
4. Harmony between vocational choices and educational plans.
5. Agreement between subjects taken or planned and the entrance requirements of the college at which attendance is planned.
6. Success in passing college entrance examinations.
7. Success in the work of the chosen college.
8. Participation in extracurricular activities.

9. Proportion of students with vocational choices and preferences.
10. Extent and nature of shifts in vocational choices.
11. Extent to which students enter and remain in the occupation chosen when in high school.
12. Success in work after school.
13. Amount of maladjustment.
14. Number of personal conflicts.

TABLE 15-2

Basic Approaches for Evaluating Guidance

Method	Theme	Description and Underlying Assumptions
External criteria	"Do you do this?"	The program is evaluated in terms of the general practices of the program. It is assumed that if a program has adequate practices it is a good program.
Follow-up	"What happened then?"	Students are evaluated in terms of various criteria after they have left the school. It is assumed that a good guidance program will have beneficial results in students in terms of success, satisfaction, adjustment, etc.
Client opinion	"What do you think?"	Students are asked to evaluate the services provided by the guidance program. It is assumed that effective guidance will be reflected in client satisfaction with the help received.
Expert opinion	"Information please?"	Experts evaluate the guidance program in terms of survey of the facilities of the program. It is assumed that a good program must have good facilities.
Specific techniques	"Little by little"	The guidance program is evaluated in terms of the effectiveness of specific techniques. It is assumed that the program can best be evaluated by focusing upon practices and results.
Within-the-group-changes	"Before and after"	Clients are evaluated before and after having received guidance. It is assumed that changes in clients result from the guidance they receive.
Between-the-group-changes	"What's the difference?"	This is the traditional experimental approach in which one of two matched groups of students receives guidance and the other group serves as a control. Both groups are then evaluated. It is assumed that if the experimental group improves more than the control group, the improvement is due to the guidance received.

15. Accuracy of students' self-ratings.
16. Recognition of false guidance.
17. Information about school subjects.
18. Reasons for choosing a curriculum or subject or occupation.
19. Reasons for choosing a college or university.
20. Amount of occupational information.
21. Extent to which students are aware of the types of information to be considered in making an occupational choice.
22. Nature of reasons for drop-out.

In his classical review of 177 research studies of the evaluation of guidance, Froehlich identifies seven basic approaches to evaluation (29). These approaches and their underlying assumptions are summarized in Table 15-2. An annotated bibliography of representative studies over the last three decades attempting to evaluate school guidance is presented in Appendices A and B. Both institutional research and evaluation tend to be de-emphasized by practitioners in the school setting.

Teaching Experience

Numerous writers have directed their attention to the issue of whether or not teaching experience is a necessary prerequisite for becoming a guidance counselor (16, 28, 44, 45, 80). Those favoring the continuance of the teaching experience requirement offer the following points: (a) teaching gives the guidance counselor insight into the nature of the school as a social system; (b) teaching provides the guidance counselor with an understanding of teachers' problems and perspectives; (c) administrators will not employ guidance counselors without teaching experience; and (d) if the teaching requirement is not maintained, then the field of guidance might become a dumping ground for marginal candidates not committed to education.

The counterproposal of eliminating the teaching requirement has been supported by the following arguments: (a) since teaching and counseling are inherently different, teaching experience may be a hindrance to the potential counselor; (b) the compulsory teaching requirement may eliminate many good counselor condidates; (c) some other types of background and experience might be just as good as teaching experience; (d) it is impossible to fill the need for additional guidance counselors from the teaching ranks alone; (e) research findings do not indicate that teaching experience contributed to the role and function of the guidance counselor; and (f) taking teachers out of the classroom to become guidance counselors aggravates critical shortages in teaching.

Counselor Preparation

There are many subissues relating to the fundamental question of what should be the nature, scope, and sequence of counselor education. In addition to the question concerning the place of the behavioral sciences in counselor education discussed above, there are the following issues:

1. Should the guidance counselor be educated as a professional or trained as a technician? (26, 30, 58, 59, 60, 87, 88, 90)
2. Are there more scientific or adequate methods for the selection and retention of students in counselor education? (15, 41, 47, 50, 57, 75)
3. To what extent should counselor education emphasize theory vs. practice? (5)
4. What should be the nature, timing, and scope of the counseling practicum? (10, 14, 20, 21, 33, 55, 74, 79)
5. To what extent should regular programs of counselor education be supplemented by guidance institutes, fellowships, or scholarship support? (22, 25, 27, 51, 70)
6. How should didactic instruction and practicum be articulated and integrated? (11, 20, 21, 24, 34, 35, 36, 39, 48, 56, 64, 71, 81, 86)

One of the basic and critical issues is the question of whether it is necessary to spend two years of full-time study as the minimum preparation for guidance counselors. Arguments for requiring two years of full-time study include: (*a*) while states generally define one year of graduate education as the minimum, the guidance field should keep its standards above the minimum; (*b*) a longer period of education is necessary because of the increasingly complex role and function of guidance; (*c*) the goals of guidance cannot be achieved without more adequate education; (*d*) part-time study results in a fragmentary experience and a failure to develop a professional identity; (*e*) in general, a longer period of education tends to lead to higher professional status, and (*f*) a longer period of education results in higher salaries, which in turn attracts better personnel to the field.

The four major reasons for not extending the minimum period of counselor education are: (*a*) requiring a longer period of education would aggravate the current nationwide shortage of counselors; (*b*) the additional education might tend to isolate the guidance counselor from teachers and administrators who have only one year of graduate education; (*c*) the guidance counselor's role and function does not require a second year of graduate study; and (*d*) many potential guidance counselors might not enter the field because of the extended length of education and the financial burden.

SUMMARY

This chapter has considered some of the major issues and problems confronting the field of guidance. While some individuals have taken a pessimistic view of the contemporary status of guidance because of the presence of unresolved issues, this writer feels that issues reflect a healthy state of affairs in a dynamic and evolving educational venture. If the past is really a prologue to the future, then we have every reason to believe that contemporary coping with issues will eventually resolve them.

Underlying current attempts to cope with the dilemmas described above are a number of untested assumptions (5). Since these assumptions are widely accepted, they are rarely examined, tested, or questioned. It is generally held, for example, that most, if not all, of the present procedures and practices of guidance should be retained. A closely related assumption holds that the majority of current guidance processes are worthy of continuing refinement. Another implicit assumption is that most, if not all, current guidance procedures should be incorporated into any guidance program that purposes to be adequate and complete. Too, it is very widely held that today's procedures and practices can be utilized to meet the objectives of contemporary guidance even though all of the general practices were developed twenty or thirty years ago.

Barry and Wolf note that while societal needs, mores, and values have undergone substantial change in recent decades, guidance has responded to these needs in terms of refinements in old practices rather than the development of new ones (5). While they neither advocate nor condemn innovation per se, Barry and Wolf question both the refinement of old constructs and procedures and any change merely for the sake of change. Indeed, they raise a number of valid criticisms of each of the untested assumptions.

And so the issues stand. Some individuals prefer to view them as a conglomerate aggregation of pending problems. On the other hand, they may be in reality an indication of the vital conflict occurring within a young, vigorous profession attempting to consolidate a professional self-concept, trying to find a way of serving society more adequately, and searching for its place among the other traditional professions. There are a number of possible solutions to each issue. There are a number of ways of resolving each problem. There are protagonists and critics of each point of view, each stance, and each strategy. Only the future can evaluate the adequacy of contemporary efforts to resolve these problems and issues.

REFERENCES

1. American School Counselors Association, *Policy for Secondary School Counselors.* Washington, D.C.: American Personnel and Guidance Association, 1964.

2. American School Counselors Association, *Statement of Policy for Implementation of the ASCA Statement of Policy for Secondary School Counselors.* Washington, D.C.: American Personnel and Guidance Association, 1964.

3. D. S. Arbuckle, "The Conflicting Functions of the School Counselor," *Counselor Education and Supervision,* 1 (1961), 54–59.

4. D. S. Arbuckle, *Counseling: Philosophy, Theory and Practice.* Boston: Allyn & Bacon, 1965.

5. R. Barry and B. Wolf, *Modern Issues in Guidance-Personnel Work.* New York: Teachers College Press, Columbia University, 1957.

6. C. E. Beck, *Philosophical Foundations of Guidance.* Englewood Cliffs, N.J.: Prentice-Hall, 1963.

7. L. Beymer, "The Procrustean Counselor: Myth or Reality?" *Vocational Guidance Quarterly,* 1 (1961), 19–23.

8. D. H. Blocher, W. W. Tennyson, and R. H. Johnson, "The Dilemma of Counselor Identity," *Journal of Counseling Psychology,* 10 (1963), 344–49.

9. E. S. Bordin, *Psychological Counseling.* New York: Appleton-Century-Crofts, 1955.

10. A. V. Boy and G. J. Pine, "A Recommendation to Counselor Educators," *The School Counselor,* 12 (1964), 80–84.

11. A. V. Boy and G. J. Pine, "Strengthening the Off-Campus Practicum," *Counselor Education and Supervision,* 6 (1966), 40–43.

12. L. M. Brammer and E. L. Shostram, *Therapeutic Psychology.* Englewood Cliffs, N.J.: Prentice-Hall, 1960.

13. J. R. Brough, "Sources of Student Perceptions of the Role of the Counselor," *Personnel and Guidance Journal,* 40 (1965), 597–99.

14. A. Buchheimer and S. C. Balogh, *The Counseling Relationship.* Chicago: Science Research Associates, 1961.

15. J. Chenault, "Professional Standards and Philosophical Freedom: A Peaceful Coexistence," *Counselor Education and Supervision,* 10 (1963), 344–49.

16. N. C. Cohen, "Must Teaching Be a Prerequisite for Guidance?" *Counselor Education and Supervision,* 1 (1961), 69–71.

17. Committee on Counselor Education Standards in the Preparation of Secondary School Counselors of the Association for Counselor Education and Supervision, *Standards for Counselor Education in the Preparation of Secondary School Counselors.* Washington, D.C.: American Personnel and Guidance Association, 1964.

18. Committee on Counselor Education Standards in the Preparation of Secondary School Counselors of the Association for Counselor Education and Supervision, *Standards for the Preparation of Secondary School Counselors.* Washington, D.C.: American Personnel and Guidance Association, 1967.

19. Committee on Ethics of the American Personnel and Guidance Association, "Code of Ethics," *Personnel and Guidance Journal,* 40 (1961), 206–09.

20. T. N. Davidson and E. T. Emmer, "Immediate Effect of Supportive and Nonsupportive Supervisory Behavior on Counselor Candidate's Focus of Concern," *Counselor Education and Supervision,* 6 (1966), 27–31.

21. D. J. Delaney and J. C. Moore, "Student Expectations of the Role of Practicum Supervisor," *Counselor Education and Supervision,* 6 (1966), 11—17.

22. E. G. Dettloff, "Attitudes Toward Guidance Institutes," *Counselor Education and Supervision,* 4 (1964), 32-36.

23. J. W. Dietz, "Critical Issues in Guidance and Personnel," *Occupations,* 15 (1937), 690-94.

24. R. Dreikurs and M. Sonstegard, "A Specific Approach to Practicum Supervision," *Counselor Education and Supervision,* 6 (1966), 18-25.

25. W. E. Dugan, "Guidance in the 1970's," *The School Counselor,* 10 (1963), 96-100.

26. C. C. Dunsmoor, "Counselor—Or What?" *Personnel and Guidance Journal,* 43 (1964), 135-38.

27. W. J. Foley and F. C. Proff, "NDEA Institute Trainees and Vocational Rehabilitation Counselors: A Comparison of Characteristics," *Counselor Education and Supervision,* 4 (1965), 154-59.

28. R. H. Fredrickson and R. R. Pippert, "Teaching Experience in the Employment of School Counselors," *Counselor Education and Supervision,* 4 (1964), 24-27.

29. C. P. Froehlich, *Evaluating Guidance Procedures.* Washington, D.C.: Office of Education, 1949.

30. N. S. Gilbert, "When the School Counselor is a Disciplinarian," *Personnel and Guidance Journal,* 43 (1965), 485-91.

31. C. W. Grant, "The Counselor's Role," *Personnel and Guidance Journal,* 33 (1954), 74-77.

32. J. W. Gustad, "The Definition of Counseling," in R. R. Berdie, ed., *Roles and Relationships in Counseling.* Minneapolis: University of Minnesota, 1953.

33. N. C. Gysbers and J. A. Johnston, "Expectations of a Practicum Supervisor's Role," *Counselor Education and Supervision,* 4 (1965), 68-74.

34. J. C. Hansen, "Trainee's Expectations of Supervision in the Counseling Practicum," *Counselor Education and Supervision,* 4 (1965), 75-80.

35. J. C. Hansen and G. C. Moore, "The Off-Campus Practicum," *Counselor Education and Supervision,* 6 (1966), 32-39.

36. L. L. Haseley and H. J. Peters, "Practicum: On Campus and Off-Campus," *Counselor Education and Supervision,* 5 (1966), 141-47.

37. M. Heilfron, "Changing Students' Perceptions of the Counselor's Role," *The School Counselor,* 11 (1964), 221-25.

38. M. Heilfron, "The Function of Counseling as Perceived by High School Students," *Personnel and Guidance Journal,* 39 (1960), 133-36.

39. R. A. Heimann and R. G. Whittemore, Jr., "Electronic Aids to Practicum Supervision," *Counselor Education and Supervision,* 3 (1964), 104-7.

40. G. E. Hill, "How to Define the Functions of the School Counselor," *Counselor Education and Supervision,* 3 (1964), 56-61.

41. G. E. Hill, "The Selection of School Counselors," *Personnel and Guidance Journal,* 39 (1961), 355-60.

42. K. Hoyt, "Guidance: A Constellation of Services," *Personnel and Guidance Journal,* 40 (1961), 690–97.

43. K. Hoyt, "What the School Has a Right to Expect of Its Counselor," *Personnel and Guidance Journal,* 40 (1961), 129–33.

44. G. R. Hudson, "Counselors Need Teaching Experience," *Counselor Education and Supervision,* 0 (1961), 24–27.

45. P. W. Hutson, "Another 'Position' Paper," *Counselor Education and Supervision,* 2 (1962), 40–44.

46. B. G. Johnson, "Guidance and Counseling: A Serious Error in Nomenclature," *Counselor Education and Supervision,* 5 (1966), 198–204.

47. R. H. Johnson, "Selection of School Counselors: An Example," *Counselor Education and Supervision,* 2 (1963), 66–68.

48. J. A. Johnston and N. C. Gysbers, "Practicum Supervisory Relationships: A Majority Report," *Counselor Education and Supervision,* 6 (1966), 3–10.

49. Joint ACES-ASCA Committee on the Elementary School Counselor, "Preliminary Statement," *Personnel and Guidance Journal,* 44 (1966), 658–61.

50. G. L. Keppers, "Selection (If Any) of Graduate Students in Guidance and Counseling," *Vocational Guidance Quarterly,* 9 (1960–61), 90–94.

51. G. Klopf and N. Cohen, "The Impact of the NDEA Counseling and Guidance Institutes on the Professional Education of School Counselors," *Counselor Education and Supervision,* 3 (1964), 151–61.

52. R. P. Koeppe, "The Elementary School Counselor—What is He?" *The School Counselor,* 12 (1964), 11–13.

53. J. D. Krumboltz, "Parable of the Good Counselor," *Personnel and Guidance Journal,* 43 (1964), 118–24.

54. G. F. J. Lehner, "Defining Psychotherapy," *American Psychologist,* 7 (1952), 452–59.

55. J. L. Lister, "Supervised Counseling Experiences: Some Comments," *Counselor Education and Supervision,* 6 (1966), 69–72.

56. E. Lloyd-Jones, "Implications of the Wrenn Report for Counselor Education," *Counselor Education and Supervision,* 2 (1962), 17–25.

57. J. W. Loughary, *et al.,* eds., *Counseling, A Growing Profession.* Washington, D.C.: American Personnel and Guidance Association, 1965.

58. C. H. McCully, "The Counselor—Instrument of Change," *Teachers College Record,* 65 (1965), 405–12.

59. C. H. McCully, "Professionalization: Symbol or Substance?" *Counselor Education and Supervision,* 2 (1963), 106–11.

60. C. H. McCully, "The School Counselor: Strategy for Professionalization," *Personnel and Guidance Journal,* 40 (1962), 681–89.

61. J. F. McGowan and L. D. Schmidt, *Counseling: Readings in Theory and Practice.* New York: Holt, Rinehart & Winston, 1962.

62. K. A. Martyn, "We are Wasting the Counselor's Time," *California Journal of Secondary Education*, 32 (1957), 439-41.

63. R. H. Mathewson, *Guidance Policy and Practice.* New York: Harper & Row, 1962.

64. C. R. Meek and A. W. Parker, "Introductory Counseling Course: Use of Practicum Students," *Counselor Education and Supervision*, 5 (1966), 154-58.

65. A. R. Meeks, "Elementary School Counseling," *The School Counselor*, 10 (1963), 108-11.

66. G. D. Moore and E. L. Gaier, "Social Forces and Counselor Role," *Counselor Education and Supervision*, 3 (1963), 29-36.

67. F. C. Noble, "The Two-Year Graduate Program in Counselor Education: A Reexamination," *Counselor Education and Supervision*, 4 (1965), 160-62.

68. C. O'Brien, R. E. Bailey, and P. W. Fitzgerald, "School Counseling Internship: An Examination," *Counselor Education and Supervision*, 6 (1966), 44-49.

69. B. Oldridge, "Two Roles for Elementary School Guidance Personnel," *Personnel and Guidance Journal*, 43 (1964), 367-70.

70. C. H. Patterson, "The NDEA and Counselor Education," *Counselor Education and Supervision*, 3 (1963), 4-7.

71. C. H. Patterson, "An Off-Campus Practicum," *Counselor Education and Supervision*, 5 (1966), 166-68.

72. J. W. Payne, "Impact of the ASCA Statement of Counselor Role," *The School Counselor*, 12 (1965), 136-39.

73. P. A. Perrone and D. L. Evans, "The Elementary School Counselor: Coordinator? Or What?" *Counselor Education and Supervision*, 4 (1964), 28-31.

74. P. A. Perrone and M. P. Sanbor, "Early Observation: An Apprenticeship Approach to Counselor Education," *Counselor Education and Supervision*, 6 (1966), 63-68.

75. G. A. Pierson, *An Evaluation: Counselor Education in Regular Session Institutes.* Washington, D.C.: U.S. Department of Health, Education, and Welfare, Office of Education, 1965.

76. Professional Preparation and Standards Committee, *Support Personnel for the Counselor: Their Technical and Non-Technical Roles and Preparation, A Statement of Policy.* Mimeographed. Washington, D.C.: American Personnel and Guidance Association, 1966.

77. F. Purcell, "Counselor Duties—A Survey," *School Counselor*, 4 (1957), 35-38.

78. A. C. Riccio, "The Expressed Interests of ACES," *Counselor Education and Supervision*, 4 (1965), 61-63.

79. B. D. Rippee, W. E. Hanvey, and C. Parker, "The Influence of Counseling on the Perception of Counselor Role," *Personnel and Guidance Journal*, 43 (1965), 696-701.

80. R. Rossberg, "To Teach or Not To Teach: Is That The Question?" *Counselor Education and Supervision,* 2 (1963), 121-25.

81. M. Salim, "A Basic Practicum and Stall Area for Counselor Education," *Counselor Education and Supervision,* 3 (1964), 98-103.

82. E. W. Schock, "Practicum Counselor's Behavioral Changes," *Counselor Education and Supervision,* 6 (1966), 57-62.

83. R. Sherman, "The School Counselor: Generalist or Specialist," *Counselor Education and Supervision,* 1 (1962), 203-11.

84. B. Shertzer and C. T. Lundy, "Administrators' Image of an Elementary School Counselor," *The School Counselor,* 11 (1964), 211-14.

85. B. Shertzer and S. Stone, *Fundamentals of Guidance.* Boston: Houghton Mifflin Co., 1966.

86. G. Sorenson, "Laboratory Experiences: Counseling Classes," *Counselor Education and Supervision,* 5 (1966), 148-53.

87. B. Stefflre, "What Price Professionalization?" *Personnel and Guidance Journal,* 42 (1964), 654-59.

88. D. V. Tiedeman and F. L. Field, "Guidance: The Science of Purposeful Action Through Education," *Harvard Educational Review,* 32 (1962), 481–501.

89. E. A. Wicas and T. W. Mahan, Jr., "Characteristics of Counselors Rated Effective by Supervisors and Peers," *Counselor Education and Supervision,* 6 (1966), 50-56.

90. C. G. Wrenn, *The Counselor in a Changing World.* Washington, D.C.: American Personnel and Guidance Association, 1962.

chapter 16

Trends in the Field of Guidance

Recommendation 1 (in part): The Counseling System. In a satisfactory school system the counseling should start in the elementary school, and there should be good articulation between counseling in the junior and senior high schools if the pattern is 6–3–3 or between the counseling in the elementary school and the high school if the system is organized on an 8–4 basis. (4, p. 44)

Recommendation 15 (in part): The school can provide and maintain a curriculum appropriately balanced for each student by offering a comprehensive program of studies, making early and continuous assessment of individual potentialities and achievements, and providing individualized programs based on careful counseling. (12, p. 47)

The two quotations cited above are recommendations of two prominent committees which have made intensive studies of contemporary public education, suggesting some proposals and guidelines for future growth. In the five years since the above reports were published, education has moved toward implementing these proposals. Indeed, if the recommendations were stated somewhat differently, they would encapsulate the essence of the major trends in guidance. While the most pervasive trends can be summarized in terms of such words as expansion, growth, and professionalization, perhaps a brief review of the more general developments in contemporary education would be helpful in illuminating the backdrop against which the current trends in guidance must be viewed.

Contemporary guidance is functioning within the context of a rapidly changing educational system. The impetus for change in education comes from many quarters and the recent innovative trends in education have taken many forms. Some of the major changes are summarized below:

1. *Consolidation of school districts*: The number of school districts is changing from about 42,000 in 1959 to an anticipated 10,000 in 1970.

2. *More functional design of school buildings*: Classrooms are becoming more varied in size and shape to fit the unique needs of the curriculum; larger libraries are being built in schools; there is a greatly increased utilization of centers—i.e., instructional, audiovideo, etc.

3. *Increased use of educational television and instructional television* (ETV and ITV): New approaches to teaching and learning have resulted from the use of television as an educational medium.

4. *More adequate use of the school plant*: A variety of current operational plans are being expanded, e.g., voluntary summer school programs, lengthening of the school year, trimester schedules, staggered quarter plans (a fourth of the students are on vacation and three quarters of the students are in school during each of the four quarters of the academic school year).

5. *Extensive use of self-instructional approaches*: The traditional approaches to didactic instruction will be increasingly complemented by programmed instruction, teaching machines, computerized instruction, etc.

6. *Greater automation in the educational setting*: Electronic data processing is being used more frequently for a variety of tasks such as preparing student report cards, storing and retrieving cumulative data about each student, selecting classes and class hours for students on the basis of master class lists, making master schedules for an entire school, correcting tests, analyzing test results, preparing test information for teachers and counselors, gathering and disseminating statistics about the school.

7. *Increasingly wide acceptance of the concept of continuing education*: A variety of programs are being implemented for the purpose of continuing the development of the individual because of upgrading required in the work setting or for general personal enhancement.

8. *Utilization of unique plans for better implementation of learning process*: A variety of innovations in this area include new kinds of grouping based on intellectual and nonintellectual factors, team teaching, variable-sized learning groups, a greatly modified curriculum, etc.

A recent report of the National Education Project on Instruction makes recommendations for contemporary education and projects future trends in terms of the following (12): (*a*) clarification of the objectives of education, (*b*) an educational focus on intellectual competence, (*c*) an educational focus on vocational competence, (*d*) development of the potential of the individual, (*e*) more functional school and classroom organization, (*f*) more effective use of time, space, and instructional resources, (*g*) greater emphases on research, innovation, and experimentation, and (*h*) increasing self-study by the school. Another review of contemporary education summarized the following trends (7):

From	To
1. Emphasis on groups of students	Emphasis on the individual student
2. Memory-type learning	Scientific inquiry
3. Spiritless climate in the classroom and school	Zest for learning
4. The traditionally graded school	The ungraded school
5. Self-contained classroom	Self-contained school
6. Classes scheduled inflexibly	Appointments and independent learning
7. The teacher functioning as a general practitioner	The teacher as a clinical specialist and member of a team

From	To
8. Use of school building based on:	School use reflecting:
a. Agrarian society	*a.* Urban society
b. Nine-month year	*b.* Twelve-month year
c. Exclusive use by children	*c.* Available to all age groups
9. Classrooms that are similar to kitchens	Classrooms that are like libraries and living rooms
10. Schools designed like boxes and egg crates	Schools designed in terms of clusters and zones of space
11. Teaching as telling	Teaching as guiding
12. A teaching schedule composed of 30 contact hours with students and 15 hours for planning and correcting papers	A teaching schedule composed of 15 contact-hours with students and 30 hours for research, planning, and development

There is relative agreement among educators in terms of the general trends in the total educational system. At last it appears that the previously empty educational platitudes of "global education," "the whole child," "realizing full potential," etc. can begin to take on a realistic meaning. Probably the most significant general trend in education has been the appearance of innovations described above, which taken cumulatively now enable education to realize its goals—goals which in prior decades rang with overtones of nostalgia, utopia or outright fantasy. There has been a traditional lag of several decades between theory and practice in education. The huge expenditure of money, time, and research effort, coupled with a new *Zeitgeist* in education, however, has begun to pay off. The lag between theory and practice has diminished significantly.

Indeed, the watchword in education today in innovation—change that hopefully is purposeful and meaningful, rather than innovation merely for the sake of innovation. Contemporary guidance is standing as the figure against the backdrop of a rapidly evolving educational system which is increasingly focusing on the learner as its base by recognizing and nurturing creativity, promoting the development of responsibility, promoting the development of positive self-attitudes, relating learning to the development of students, acknowledging inter-and intraindividual differences, and acknowledging social-group differences. The individual as a base for education is being supplemented and complemented by a correlative focus on the nature of our contemporary society and on organized knowledge—i.e., the "information revolution" (12, pp. 9-11).

The above points of emphasis have been continuing ones in guidance. As noted above, education has changed from teaching as telling to teaching as guiding. Paradoxically, however, education and guidance have become both more similar and more different. They are becoming more similar in their general theoretical orientation. They are becoming more similar in their goals. They are becoming more similar in their focus on the individual student. But education and guidance have tended to become more dissimilar in terms of their specialization of effort. Both teachers and guidance counselors have become specialists. Whereas teachers are increasingly becoming specialists in subject matter areas with a general mental hygiene or guidance perspective, school counselors have tended to become professional guidance specialists with a broad educational perspective.

Described below are a number of trends in the field of guidance. Many of these trends have been alluded to in prior chapters. Some of the trends are stated with relatively little elaboration either because they have been discussed in earlier chapters of this book or because they need no further elaboration. Other trends will be described in substantially greater detail. Although trends in guidance are obviously functionally related, for purposes of presentation they will be listed and described separately.

Trend I: The Field of Guidance Will Continue to Undergo a Period of Unprecedented Growth

It is hardly necessary to belabor the point that the growth and expansion of guidance services is probably the most pervasive of all of the trends in contemporary guidance. The growth is occurring both in terms of the numbers of guidance personnel functioning in the school setting and in terms of the guidance services offered to students. While guidance in the past tended to focus upon limited groups of students—e.g., the gifted, the college-bound, the underachievers, the disadvantaged (i.e., problem-centered guidance); as the counselor-to-student ratio continues to decrease, guidance services are being made available to larger segments of the student population. Concomitantly, the largely remedial focus of guidance is being complemented by a cumulative, long-term, developmental guidance effort directed toward the prevention of many problems.

Trend II: Counselor Education Programs Are Undergoing Many Changes

Coupled with a growing number of elementary school counselor preparation programs is a trend toward more programs for preparing counselors in a variety of student personnel work settings in higher education, such as those in technical schools, community colleges, junior colleges, and the traditional student personnel programs for positions in four-year colleges and universities. Also, there are more and more two-year graduate programs in counselor education. It is becoming increasingly obvious that guidance workers cannot achieve their goals with their present one-year graduate preparation programs. Under the present system, practitioners lack both sufficient theory and supervised practical experience.

Although the federal government will probably continue to provide massive programs of financial support for guidance, there will probably be some changes in the types of support for counselor trainees. While the direction in which this support will go is still unclear, there appears to be growing dissatisfaction with the guidance institute model for supporting graduate students in guidance. Some people favor assistantships, some people favor more scholarships, and others advocate fellowships, loans, and/or various combinations of these types of financial assistance.

While there is general agreement with the trend toward longer and more adequate programs of preparation for guidance counselors, there has been considerable disagreement concerning the content of the second year of graduate education in guidance. There will be a great deal of effort directed toward adopting better criteria for admission and retention in guidance programs. It appears that the continuing emphasis upon academic performance criteria will be supplemented by a variety of other measures such as a constellation of personality factors needed for adequate performance as a guidance counselor in the school setting. The counselor education curriculum is also undergoing extensive revision. There appears to be a growing use of interdisciplinary integrative siminars. Preparation programs are also beginning to make use of gaming and simulation materials in order to provide more realism for counselor education. Another trend in this area includes more emphasis upon self-understanding and realization of the contribution of the counselor's personality to the dynamics of his role and function.

Trend III. Guidance Programs Will Make Increasing Use of Subprofessional Support Personnel to Supplement and Complement the Work of the Counselor Performing Professional Functions

This trend has just begun. In fact, the trend is still in the planning phase. Were it not for the fact that the utilization of subprofessional support personnel potentially could drastically change the role and function of guidance counselors, this "trend" would not be included herein. In effect, the future trend toward the use of support personnel in guidance parallels the team teaching concept in instruction. The following discussion is based upon the formal statement of the American Personnel and Guidance Association (11). Because the term "support personnel" is a somewhat confusing one, the APGA policy statement clearly differentiates the line relationship between the counselor and support personnel from reciprocal lateral (staff) relationships between the counselor and other collaborating staff members such as teachers, social workers, psychologists, and physicians. The APGA policy statement outlines the counselor's function in terms of *counseling* and *leadership.*

While the concept of support personnel is not new, systematic planning for the implementation of support personnel is a recent trend. The general rationale for support personnel is based on the premise that the support personnel will be able to perform functions under the direct supervision of the counselor and that their roles will mutually reinforce each other in such a way that the entire guidance program will be more effective. While the exact nature of the duties of support personnel have not been completely described, the APGA policy statement makes a clear distinction between the general roles of counselors and support personnel. First, the functions of the counselor are broad and the work of support personnel is limited. Second, while the work of the counselor is based upon theory, authoritative knowledge of effective procedures, and his evaluation of his work, the work of support personnel is characterized by "greater dependence upon intuitive judgment, little or no theoretical background, more limited preparation, and less comprehensive understanding of the total endeavor" (11, p.3).

Third, only the counselor performs counseling. Support personnel perform significant related activities which are necessary parts of the overall program. Fourth, the counselor should decide who will perform the various duties. Some guidance functions—e.g., counseling—will be performed only by the counselor and other duties may be shared or else performed solely by support personnel. Lastly, the support personnel job may be either terminal or may lead to the job of professional counselor. Support personnel can become counselors, however, only through professional education and training, graduating from an approved program of counseling and guidance from an accredited institution. The general activities of support personnel have been tentatively outlined as follows:

Direct Helping Relationships. A number of support personnel activities involve direct person-to-person relationships, but they are not identical or equivalent to counseling as conducted by the counselor. Prominent among these functions and activities would be the following (11, pp. 4-5):

1. Individual Interviewing Function:
   a. Secure information from an interviewee by means of a semi-structured or structured interview schedule. The information elicited would tend to be factual and limited in nature.
   b. Give information prepared in advance and approved by counselor for its appropriateness for the interviewee. Such information would usually be factual rather than interpretative.
   c. Explain the purposes and procedures of counseling in practical lay terms.
   d. Engage the counselee in informal, casual, colloquial discussion as a means of putting him at ease and establishing an openness to counseling. Such a dyadic activity may be especially important when performed by an interviewer who is making initial contact with potential counselees who are hostile toward or apprehensive of counseling.
   e. Provide informal follow-up support to a former counselee.
2. Small-Group Interviewing or Discussion Function:
   a. In structured groups with a largely preplanned program, guide discussions as a discussion leader.
   b. Describe staff and material available to the group, as an information resource person, or tell the group how and where to acquire needed resources.
   c. Act as recorder in a variety of small-group discussion or counseling situations, under the supervision of the counselor.
   d. Observe verbal and non-verbal interaction in groups, following predetermined cues and procedures for making observations.
   e. Participate in informal superficial social conversation in a small group of counselees to help put them at ease and to establish the beginning of help relationships that may be provided by forthcoming counseling.
   f. Informally provide information and support to former counselees.
   g. Circulate among people who may be potential counselees and strive to develop attitudes of group cohesion and good orientation for educational and/or recreational ends.

Indirect Helping Relationships. Most of the activities of support personnel appear to involve providing help indirectly rather than directly to counselees, even though some of these activities do involve face-to-face relationships with counselees. Among the functions and activities may be these (11, pp. 5–8):

1. Information Gathering and Processing Function.
   a. Administer, score, and profile routine standardized tests and other appraisal instruments (nonclinical type).
   b. Obtain and maintain routine information on the scope and character of the world of work with current reference to employment trends, in accordance with instructions established by the counselor.
   c. Contact various sources for needed records and related information relevant to counseling.
   d. Search for new sources of information about counselees and/or the environment under direction of the counselor.
   e. Prepare educational, occupational, and personal-social information for visual-auditory verbal and graphic presentation or transmittal to others for use, in accordance with instructions established by the counselor.
   f. Under the counselor's supervision, search for new sources to which the counselee may be referred.
   g. Secure specific special information about former counselees upon request and under the supervision of the counselor.
   h. Operate technical communications media involving printed and electronic process of a visual-auditory nature for the counselee's benefit.
2. Referral Function:
   a. Initiate general contacts with specific referral agencies.
   b. Initiate contact for specific individuals with given referral agencies.
   c. Aid individuals in making proper contact with referral agencies.
3. Placement and Routine Follow-up Function:
   a. Through appropriate channels, establish and maintain working relationships with organized placement agencies in the community.
   b. Develop specific placement opportunities for individual cases not handled through cooperation with other placement agencies.
   c. Maintain continuous surveys of placement conditions and trends as requested by the counselor.
   d. Search for new placement resources that may be useful to counselees.
   e. Secure follow-up information of a routine nature according to a general follow-up plan.
4. Program Planning and Management Function:
   a. Perform routine collecting and analytical statistical operations as a research assistant.
   b. Procure and prepare supplies of materials of various sorts for the counselor.
   c. Prepare standardized reports of contact with counselees, potential counselees, referral, placement, and follow-up agencies and persons.
   d. Maintain appropriate personnel and information records for the counselor.
   e. Supervise and coordinate the activities of clerical or other skilled personnel under the general supervision of the counselor.

Trend IV: An Increasingly Adequate Theoretical Basis for Guidance Will Continue to Be Developed and Subsequently Implemented in the School Setting

Although how much influence the various behavioral sciences and other disciplines will have on future guidance theory is still unclear it does seem clear that there is a vital force attempting to build a better theoretical foundation for guidance practice. As noted throughout this book, contemporary formulations in the field of guidance are somewhat limited. This writer has characterized them as "approaches" or "orientations" to guidance. Nevertheless, the relatively young field of guidance has made many significant advances in this area in recent years. Current efforts at theory building will develop formulations that will increasingly provide the practitioner with a better basis for guidance practice.

Trend V: There Will Be Substantially Increased Use of Automated Equipment in Guidance

As noted in Chapter 12, automated equipment in guidance has the most significant applications for conducting a school census, setting up student programs and schedules, reporting students' grades, evaluating students, identifying and placing students, pupil accounting, and recording and reporting kinds of information. "The school system of the near future will have information centers where three kinds of information are electronically collated, analyzed, and transmitted for use by various members of the staff—centers for educational information, for vocational information, and for information about student characteristics" (16, p. 145).

A number of new computer programs are now under development. The purpose of these programs is develop computerized systems of material that will provide students with complete up-to-date information on many occupations and then relate this information to their abilities and interests. Although computers and other types of automated equipment will be increasingly used in schools, they will never replace the face-to-face contact of the counselor and student. Rather, these new innovations are intended to save time and effort, thereby enabling the guidance worker of the near future to perform his role and function more efficiently and adequately.

Trend VI: The Field of Guidance Will Focus More Attention on Girls and Their Developmental Problems

The general concern for the contemporary woman and her special problems stems from many quarters and has been described in such terms as the home-making career dilemma, the talent loss, the female identity crisis, and the feminine mystique. In the past, both the theoretical and operational aspects of guidance have tended to be male-centered, particularly in the area of vocational guidance. With the emergence of modern woman, however, guidance is beginning to provide more help for girls.

In a recent speech Fullmer highlights the situation as follows (6, p. 16):

> It is reasonable for us to expect all of the very desirable female images to be achieved by most girls when everything in the culture that is supposed to make its influence felt upon the girl's development actually works. But when these molders of our culture—the inculcators and the educators and the counselors—fail, we all

lose. Counseling girls in the 1960's will be considered successful only if it preserves what is now necessary and desirable in the image of American womanhood, that is, the mother and the home. Beyond that, counseling must provide the Nation with access to the potential womanpower that would be made available through career development. It is not an easy task. However, we now possess the knowledge and the skills and the financial basis for doing it.

Few counselors in the schools are capable of doing the job we need to do. Precedents are laughed at by today's young people. Therefore, most of our traditional models of womanhood are unacceptable to today's youth. Youth have better models in their peer groups than adults provide in women counselors as role models in the schools. Counselors of girls must supply what the social system omits in the socialization of the female. Almost all socialization takes place within groups—family or peer groups, work groups, or other reference groups. Therefore group counseling, or counseling by the use of groups, is a solid and basic way to proceed.

Because girls are usually taught and counseled separately from boys, in keeping with the culture's socialization procedures, it becomes imperative for the counselor to reach girls and boys together in groups. We do not want to stop teaching girls to be competitive with boys in those areas where equality is an essential, such as in school subjects. We do want to teach girls how to complement boys in areas where girls want to be feminine. Groups provide the only approach through which boys and girls can *learn together* the skills and attitudes of complementary behavior.

Trend VII: The Profession-Technician Dichotomy That Exists Today Is Being Resolved in Favor of Increasing Professionalization of Guidance Personnel

A corollary issue to the generalist-specialist debate discussed in Chapter 15 is the question of whether guidance personnel should identify themselves and function primarily as professionals or as technicians. Arguments have been proposed both in favor of the guidance worker as a professional and the guidance worker as a technician (3, 4, 15, 16). Although the issue has not yet been completely resolved, it appears quite clear that the field of guidance is working toward the resolution of the problem in favor of increased professionalism. That this is the case is evident from the following subtrends:

1. Increasingly important role of professional organizations.
2. Increasing emphasis of professional organizations on professionalization.
   a. Publications (16).
   b. APGA code of ethics (3).
   c. Standards for the education of school counselors (2).
   d. ASCA-ACES Policy Statements (8, 9, 10, 11).
   e. Guidelines for implementing the ASCA policy statement (1).
3. Trend toward life-long career commitment to guidance, rather than using guidance as an escape from the classroom or a steppingstone to an administrative position.
4. Trend toward more adequate theoretical basis for guidance practice.

5. Trend toward longer programs of counselor "education" rather than "training."

In what is in effect a status report, Stoughton notes (14, p. 17):

> Thus is illustrated the fact that our present policies and standards represent only one step in the long journey toward sound professional standards . . . Only through planned evaluation and a willingness to make revisions—to seek continuous professional growth—can we hope that our policies and standards will be adequate for a rapidly growing profession whose responsibilities are constantly becoming greater and more complex."

Miscellaneous Trends

The following trends are miscellaneous only in the sense that they have been described in previous chapters and are merely listed below without further elaboration.

1. There is an increasing specialization in the role and function of school counselors.
2. Elementary school guidance is growing at a rapid rate.
3. There tends to be an increasing agreement in terms of the general role and function of guidance personnel in both elementary and secondary school settings functioning as (*a*) counselor to students (*b*) consultant to teachers, parents and administrators.
4. A number of governmental accrediting and professional organizations will increasingly influence counselor preparation and certification.
5. A growing body of research suggests that group work is a useful and effective approach for helping youth. Work with individual students will increasingly be supplemented and complemented by group work. Both counselor preparation programs and actual practice in the school settings will make increasing use of group guidance, group counseling, sensitivity training (T-group), group dynamics, etc.

SUMMARY AND PROSPECTUS

The trends noted above suggest a bright and promising future for the field of guidance. It is anticipated that guidance will continue to grow as an integral aspect of contemporary education and that it will also achieve increasing recognition as a profession. The various growing edges of the field—theory building, counselor preparation programs, and research—are all healthy and vigorous. Public and professional opinion are favorable. More and more school systems are either initiating new guidance programs or expanding existing ones.

Accompanying the expected growth and professionalization of the field, however, will be new opportunities, new issues, and new challenges. Dugan has summarized perhaps the dominant striving of the field of guidance as follows (5, p. iii):

> The single most important objective for the counseling profession in this decade is the achievement of quality: quality in counselor preparation, standards of state certification, and the guarantee of competence for school counselors in the profession roles they must fill. . . . This commitment of where we stand and for what we stand professionally is positive evidence of our desire to aspire to excellence. The children and youth of this nation deserve no less from each of us in our endeavor to assist them in fulfilling their highest potentials.

REFERENCES

1. American School Counselor Association, "Guidelines for Implementation of the ASCA Statement of Policy for Secondary School Counselors," in J. W. Loughary, ed., *Counseling, a Growing Profession.* Washington, D.C.: American Personnel and Guidance Association, 1965.

2. Committee on Counselor Education Standards in the Preparation of Secondary School Counselors of the Association for Counselor Education and Supervision, *Standards for Counselor Education in the Preparation of Secondary School Counselors.* Washington, D.C.: American Personnel and Guidance Association, 1964.

3. Committee on Ethics of the American Personnel and Guidance Association, "Code of Ethics," *Personnel and Guidance Journal*, 40 (1961), 206–09.

4. J. B. Conant, *The American High School Today.* New York: McGraw-Hill, 1959.

5. W. E. Dugan, "Preface," in Loughary, J. W., ed., *Counseling, a Growing Profession.* Washington, D.C.: American Personnel and Guidance Association, 1965.

6. D. W. Fullmer, "Male-Order Female–The Symbol and the Substance" in *Counseling Girls toward New Perspectives.* Washington, D.C.: U.S. Office of Education, 1966.

7. H. B. Gores, "The Big Change." An address delivered to the 43rd annual convention of the New York State School Boards Association, December 1962.

8. Joint ACES–ASCA Committee on the Elementary School Counselor, "Preliminary Statement," *Personnel and Guidance Journal*, 44 (1966), 658–61.

9. National Planning Committee, *American School Counselor Association Statement of Policy for Secondary School Counselors.* Washington, D.C.: American Personnel and Guidance Association, 1964.

10. Professional Preparation and Standards Committee, *The Counselor: Professional Preparation and Role, A Statement Policy.* Washington, D.C.: American Personnel and Guidance Association, 1964.

11. Professional Preparation and Standards Committee, *Support Personnel*

for the Counselor: Their Technical and Non-Technical Roles and Preparation, A Statement of Policy. Mimeographed. Washington, D.C.: American Personnel and Guidance Association, 1966.

12. Project on Instruction of the National Education Association, *Schools for the Sixties.* New York: McGraw-Hill, 1963.

13. B. Shertzer and S. C. Stone, *Fundamentals of Guidance.* Boston: Houghton Mifflin Co., 1966.

14. R. W. Stoughton, "APGA and Counselor Professionalization," in J. W. Loughary, ed., *Counseling, a Growing Profession.* Washington, D.C.: American Personnel and Guidance Association, 1965.

15. D. V. Tiedeman, and F. L. Field, "Guidance: The Science of Purposeful Action Applied Through Education," *Harvard Educational Review,* 32 (1962), 483-501.

16. C. G. Wrenn, *The Counselor in a Changing World.* Washington, D.C.: American Personnel and Guidance Association, 1962.

A Selected Annotated Bibliography

Three Decades of Evaluating Guidance Programs, 1930-1959

Barber, J. E. *Evaluating School Guidance.* New York: Foster and Stewart, 1946.
A monograph giving brief review of earlier attempts to evaluate guidance, a description of the East Aurora High School, and a description of the evaluation of the East Aurora High School guidance system.

Cantini, L. J. "Reunion Party," *Clearing House,* 29 (1955), 466-69.
A "reunion party" is used to followup a group of students who had earlier been subjects of an evaluation study.

Cartwright, R. S. "Business Education Day Extended for Seniors," *National Association of Secondary School Principals Bulletin,* 34 (1951), 123-26.
The entire senior class of a high school spends a day visiting business and industry. Evaluation of the project is made by a student questionnaire.

Coleman, W. "The Role of Evaluation in Improving Guidance and Counseling Services," *Personnel and Guidance Journal,* 34 (1957), 441-44.
An essay discussing some possible reasons for the lack of comprehensive research and a review of what the author believes to be "better studies."

Cottle, W. C., "The Evaluation of Guidance Services," *Review of Educational Research,* 27 (1957), 229-34.
A survey of recent approaches to evaluation giving designs and general findings of many studies.

Eells, W. C. "Judgments of Parents Concerning American Secondary Schools," *School and Society,* 46 (1937), 409-16.
Two hundred schools in various parts of the U.S. are evaluated by the opinions of parents as expressed in a questionnaire.

Froehlich, C. P. *Evaluating Guidance Procedures.* Washington, D.C.: Office of Education, 1949.
This monograph classifies approaches to evaluation and reviews 177 evaluation studies, surveys and commentaries.

Hatch, R. N., and Stefflre, B. "Evaluation of Guidance Services," Chapter VII, *Administration of Guidance Services.* Englewood Cliffs, N.J.: Prentice-Hall, 1958.
This chapter of a general text gives an overall view of evaluation of guidance programs.

Hedge, J. W., and Hutson, P. W. "A Technique for Evaluating Guidance Activities," *School Review,* 12 (1931), 508-12.
A guidance program is evaluated on the basis of the appropriateness of student decisions.

Hill, G. E., and Morrow, R. O. "Guidance and the Drop-Out Rate," *Vocational Guidance Quarterly,* 5 (1957), 153-55.
This article is a report of an experiment to determine if the quality of a guidance program has any effect on the drop-out rate.

Hutson, P. W., and Webster, A. D. "An Experiment in the Educational and Vocational Guidance of Tenth Grade Pupils," *Educational and Psychological Measurement,* 3 (1943), 3-21.
Appropriateness of educational and vocational choices of students who had guidance services are compared with choices of uncounseled students.

Kefauver, G. N., and Hand, H. C. "An Appraisal of Guidance Occupations," *Occupations,* 11 (1933), 53-58.
Nine guidance programs having been evaluated, the best and worst of these are compared in terms of the presence of several criteria in the students served by these two programs.

Kefauver, G. N., and Hand, H. C. "Measurement of Outcomes of Guidance in Secondary Schools," *Teachers College Record,* 33 (1946), 314-34.
An essay discussing the new role of the high school, a plea of evaluating guidance, and a comprehensive list of suggested criteria.

Lowenstein, N., and Hoppock, R. "High School Occupations Course Helps Students Adjust in College," *Personnel and Guidance Journal,* 34 (1955), 21-23.
This article is a description of an experiment in which students are given an occupations course in high school and then followed up in college.

Moser, W. E. "Evaluation of a Guidance Program by Means of a Student's Checklist," *Journal of Educational Research,* 42 (1949), 609-17.
This article describes the use of a student checklist as a basis for evaluating a guidance program.

Rankin, P. T. "The Place of Research in a Guidance Program" *Vocational Guidance Magazine,* 9 (1931), 380-84.
An essay (reading) of the types of research and their places in guidance programs.

Rothney, W. M. "Counseling Does Help," *Vocational Guidance Quarterly,* 6 (1957), 15-18.
Two large groups of students (counseled and uncounseled) are compared in terms of various criteria.

Strang, R. "Major Limitations of Current Evaluation Studies," *Educational and Psychological Measurement* 10 (1950), 531-36.
This survey discusses the shortcomings of current evaluations and points out some possibilities for future evaluative studies.

Tyler, L. E. "Significance of Evaluation Studies," Chapter XII, *The Work of the Counselor*. New York: Appleton-Century-Crofts, 1953.

This chapter of the well-known text describes the types of research and summarizes a number of evaluation studies.

appendix **B**

The Evaluation of Guidance Services

A Selected Bibliography of Studies for the Years 1960-1966

Ashcraft, K. B., and Doi, E. "Promoting Guidance Evaluation in Colorado," *Counselor Education and Supervision*, 4 (1965), 198-201.

Bergstein, H. B., and Grant, C. W. "Who Helps Children? Parents' Conceptions," *The School Counselor*, 12 (1964), 67-72.

Gibson, R. L. "Pupil Opinions of High School Guidance Programs," *Personnel and Guidance Journal*, 40 (1962), 453-57.

Gribbons, W. D. "Evaluation of an Eighth Grade Group Guidance Program," *Personnel and Guidance Journal*, 38 (1960), 740-45.

Hill, G. E. "Elementary School Guidance: Criteria for Approval by State Departments of Education," *Counselor Education and Supervision*, 2 (1963), 137-43.

Hill, G. E., and Nitszchke, D. *Students and Parents Evaluate the School's Guidance Program*. Athens, Ohio: Ohio University, Center for Educational Service, Pupil Services Series (No. 2), 1960.

Herr, E. L. "Basic Issues in Research and Evaluation of Guidance Services," *Counselor Education and Supervision*, 4 (1964), 9-16.

Kasper, E. C., *et al*. "Student Perceptions of the Environment in Guidance and Non-Guidance Schools," *Personnel and Guidance Journal*, 42 (1965), 674-77.

Metzler, J. H. "Evaluating Counseling and Guidance Programs: A Review of the Literature," *Vocational Guidance Quarterly*, 12 (1964), 285-89.

Morehead, C. G. "An Experimental Evaluation of a Small High School Counseling Program," *The School Counselor* 7 (1960), 71-77.

Patterson, C. H. "Methodological Problems in Evaluation," *Personnel and Guidance Journal* 39 (1960), 270-74.

Program for Evaluation of Guidance (PEA). Columbus: State of Ohio, Dept. of Education, Division of Guidance and Testing, 1962.

Report of the Ohio Program for the Evaluation of Guidance. Columbus: State of Ohio, Dept. of Education, Division of Guidance and Testing, 1963.

Rosengarten, W. "Another Job Course Pays Off," *Personnel and Guidance Journal*, 41 (1963), 531-34.

Rothney, J. W. "What Are High School Graduates Doing Ten Years after Graduation," *Vocational Guidance Quarterly*, 13 (1965), 134–36.

Russel, J. C., and Willis, A. R. "A Survey of Teachers' Opinions of Guidance Services," *Personnel and Guidance Journal*, 42 (1964), 707–9.

Wighl, J., *et al.* "Parental Attitudes Toward Specific Guidance Services," *The School Counselor*, 14 (1966), 33–35.

Wellman, F. E., and Twiford, D. D. *Guidance, Counseling and Testing Program Evaluation.*(No. -25020). Washington, D.C.: U.S. Dept. of Health, Education, and Welfare, 1961.

Ethical Standards

American Personnel and Guidance Association

PREAMBLE

The American Personnel and Guidance Association is an educational, scientific, and professional organization dedicated to service to society. This service is committed to profound faith in the worth, dignity, and great potentiality of the individual human being.

The marks of a profession, and therefore of a professional organization, can be stated as follows:

1. Possession of a body of specialized knowledge, skills, and attitudes known and practiced by its members.

2. This body of specialized knowledge, skills, and attitudes is derived through scientific inquiry and scholarly learning.

3. This body of specialized knowledge, skills, and attitudes is acquired through professional preparation, preferably on the graduate level, in a college or university as well as through continuous in-service training and personal growth after completion of formal education.

4. This body of specialized knowledge, skills, and attitudes, is constantly tested and extended through research and scholarly inquiry.

5. A profession has a literature of its own, even though it may, and indeed must, draw portions of its content from other areas of knowledge.

6. A profession exalts service to the individual and society above personal gain. It possesses a philosophy and a code of ethics.

7. A profession through the voluntary association of its members constantly examines and improves the quality of its professional preparation and services to the individual and society.

8. Membership in the professional organization and the practice of the profession must be limited to persons meeting stated standards of preparation and competencies.

9. The profession affords a life career and permanent membership as long as services meet professional standards.

10. The public recognizes, has confidence in, and is willing to compensate the members of the profession for their services.

The Association recognizes that the vocational roles and settings of its members are identified with a wide variety of academic disciplines and levels of academic preparation. This diversity reflects the pervasiveness of the Association's interest and influence. It also poses challenging complexities in efforts to conceptualize:

    a. the characteristics of members;

    b. desired or requisite preparation or practice; and

    c. supporting social, legal and/or ethical controls.

The specification of ethical standards enables the Association to clarify to members, future members, and to those served by members the nature of ethical responsibilities held in common by its members.

The introduction of such standards will inevitably stimulate greater concern by members for practice and preparation for practice. It will also stimulate a general growth and identification with and appreciation for both the common and diverse characteristics of the definable roles within the world of work of Association members.

There are six major areas of professional activity which encompass the work of members of APGA. For each of these areas certain general principles are listed below to serve as guide lines for ethical practice. These are preceded by a general section which includes certain principles germane to the six areas and common to the entire work of the Association members.

Section A

GENERAL

1. The member exerts what influence he can to foster the development and improvement of the profession and continues his professional growth throughout his career.

2. The member has a responsibility to the institution within which he serves. His acceptance of employment by the institution implies that he is in substantial agreement with the general policies and principles of the institution. Therefore, his professional activities are also in accord with the objectives of the institution. Within the member's own work setting, if, despite his efforts, he cannot reach agreement as to acceptable ethical standards of conduct with his superiors, he should end his affiliation with them.

3. The member must expect ethical behavior among his professional associates in APGA at all times. He is obligated, in situations where he possesses information raising serious doubt as to the ethical behavior of other members, to attempt to rectify such conditions.

4. The member is obligated to concern himself with the degree to which the personnel functions of non-members with whose work he is acquainted

represent competent and ethical performance. Where his information raises serious doubt as to the ethical behavior of such persons, it is his responsibility to attempt to rectify such conditions.

5. The member must not seek self-enhancement through expressing evaluations or comparisons damaging to other ethical professional workers.

6. The member should not claim or imply professional qualifications exceeding those possessed and is responsible for correcting any misrepresentations of his qualifications by others.

7. The member providing services for personal remuneration shall, in establishing fees for such services, take careful account of the charges made for comparable services by other professional persons.

8. The member who provides information to the public or to his subordinates, peers, or superiors has a clear responsibility to see that both the content and the manner of presentation are accurate and appropriate to the situation.

9. The member has an obligation to ensure that evaluative information about such persons as clients, students, and applicants shall be shared only with those persons who will use such information for professional purposes.

10. The member shall offer professional services only, through the context of a professional relationship. Thus testing, counseling, and other services are not to be provided through the mail by means of newspaper or magazine articles, radio or television programs, or public performances.

Section B

COUNSELING

This section refers to practices involving a counseling relationship with a counselee or client and is not intended to be applicable to practices involving administrative relationships with the persons being helped. A counseling relationship denotes that the person seeking help retain full freedom of choice and decision and that the helping person has no authority or responsibility to approve or disapprove of the choices or decisions of the counselee or client. "Counselee" or "client" is used here to indicate the person (or persons) for whom the member has assumed a professional responsibility. Typically the counselee or client is the individual with whom the member has direct and primary contact. However, at times, "client" may include another person(s) when the other person(s) exercise significant control and direction over the individual being helped in connection with the decisions and plans being considered in counseling.

1. The member's *primary* obligation is to respect the integrity and promote the welfare of the counselee or client with whom he is working.

2. The counseling relationship and information resulting therefrom must be kept confidential consistent with the obligations of the member as a professional person.

3. Records of the counseling relationship including interview notes, test

data, correspondence, tape recordings and other documents are to be considered professional information for use in counseling, research, and teaching of counselors but always with full protection of the identity of the client and with precaution so that no harm will come to him.

4. The counselee or client should be informed of the conditions under which he may receive counseling assistance at or before the time he enters the counseling relationship. This is particularly true in the event that there exist conditions of which the counselee or client would not likely be aware.

5. The member reserves the right to consult with any other professionally competent person about his counselee client. In choosing his professional consultant the member must avoid placing the consultant in a conflict of interest situation, i.e., the consultant must be free of any other obligatory relation to the member's client that would preclude the consultant being a proper party to the member's efforts to help the counselee or client.

6. The member shall decline to initiate or shall terminate a counseling relationship when he cannot be of professional assistance to the counselee or client either because of lack of competence or personal limitation. In such instances the member shall refer his counselee or client to an appropriate specialist. In the event the counselee or client declines the suggested referral, the member is not obligated to continue the counseling relationship.

7. When the member learns from counseling relationships of conditions which are likely to harm others over whom his institution or agency has responsibility, he is expected to report *the condition* to the appropriate responsible authority, but in such a manner as not to reveal the identity of his counselee or clients.

8. In the event that the counselee or client's condition is such as to require others to assume responsibility for him, or when there is clean and imminent danger to the counselee or client or to others, the member is expected to report this fact to an appropriate responsible authority, and/or take such other emergency measures as the situation demands.

9. Should the member be engaged in a work setting which calls for any variation from the above statements, the member is obligated to ascertain that such variations are justifiable under the conditions and that such variations are clearly specified and made known to all concerned with such counseling services.

Section C

TESTING

1. The primary purpose of psychological testing is to provide objective and comparative measures for use in self-evaluation or evaluation by others of general or specific attributes.

2. Generally, test results constitute only one of a variety or pertinent data

for personnel and guidance decisions. It is the member's responsibility to provide adequate orientation or information to the examinee(s) so that the results of testing may be placed in proper perspective with other relevant factors.

3. When making any statements to the public about tests and testing care must be taken to give accurate information and to avoid any false claims or misconceptions.

4. Different tests demand different levels of competence for administration, scoring, and interpretation. It is therefore the responsibility of the member to recognize the limits of his competence and to perform only those functions which fall within his preparation and competence.

5. In selecting tests for use in a given situation or with a particular client the member must consider not only general but also specific validity, reliability, and appropriateness of the test(s).

6. Tests should be administered under the same conditions which were established in their standardization. Except for research purposes explicitly stated, any departures from these conditions, as well as unusual behavior or irregularities during the testing-session which may affect the interpretation of the test results, must be fully noted and reported. In this connection, unsupervised test-taking or the use of tests through the mails are of questionable value.

7. The value of psychological tests depends in part on the novelty to persons taking them. Any prior information, coaching, or reproduction of test materials tends to invalidate test results. Therefore, test security is one of the professional obligations to the member.

8. The member has the responsibility to inform the examinee(s) as to the purpose of testing. The criteria of examinee's welfare and/or explicit prior understanding with him should determine who the recipients of the test results may be.

9. The member should guard against the appropriation, reproduction, or modifications of published tests or parts thereof without express permission and adequate recognition of the original author or publisher.

Regarding the preparation, publication, and distribution of tests reference should be made to:

"Tests and Diagnostic Techniques"—Report of the Joint Committee of the American Psychological Association, American Educational Research Association, and National Council of Measurements used in Education. Supplement to *Psychological Bulletin*, 1954, 2, 1–38.

Section D

RESEARCH AND PUBLICATION

1. In the performance of any research on human subjects, the member must avoid causing any injurious effects or after-effects of the experiment upon his subjects.

2. The member may withhold information or provide misinformation to subjects only when it is essential to the investigation and where he assumes responsibility for corrective action following the investigation.

3. In reporting research results, explicit mention must be made of all variables and conditions known to the investigator which might affect interpretation of the data.

4. The member is responsible for conducting and reporting his investigations so as to minimize the possibility that his findings will be misleading.

5. The member has an obligation to make available original research data to qualified others who may wish to replicate or verify the study.

6. In reporting research results or in making original data available, due care must be taken to disguise the identity of the subjects, in the absence of specific permission from such subjects to do otherwise.

7. In conducting and reporting research, the member should be familiar with, and give recognition to, previous work on the topic.

8. The member has the obligation to give due credit to those who have contributed significantly to his research, in accordance with their contributions.

9. The member has the obligation to honor commitments made to subjects of research in return for their cooperation.

10. The member is expected to communicate to other members the results of any research he judges to be of professional or scientific value.

Section E

CONSULTING AND PRIVATE PRACTICE

Consulting refers to a voluntary relationship between a professional helper and help-needing social unit (industry, business, school, college, etc.) in which the consultant is attempting to give help to the client in the solving of some current or potential problem.

1. The member acting as a consultant must have a high degree of self-awareness of his own values and needs in entering a helping relationship which involves change in a social unit.

2. There should be understanding and agreement between consultant and client as to directions or goals of the attempted change.

3. The consultant must be reasonably certain that he or his organization have the necessary skills and resources for giving the kind of help which is needed now or that may develop later.

4. The consulting relationship must be one in which client adaptability and growth toward self-direction are encouraged and cultivated. The consultant must consistently maintain his role as a consultant and not become a decision maker for the client.

5. The consultant in announcing his availability for service as a consultant follows professional rather than commercial standards in describing his services with accuracy, dignity, and caution.

6. For private practice in testing, counseling, or consulting the ethical principles stated in all previous sections of this document are pertinent. In addition, any individual, agency, or institution offering educational and vocational counseling to the public should meet the standards of the American Board on Professional Standards in Vocational Counseling, Inc.

Section F

PERSONNEL ADMINISTRATION

1. The member is responsible for establishing working agreements with supervisors and with subordinates especially regarding counseling or clinical relationships, confidentiality, distinction between public and private material, and a mutual respect for the positions of parties involved in such issues.

2. Such working agreements may vary from one institutional setting to another. What should be the case in each instance, however, is that agreements have been specified, made known to those concerned, and whenever possible the agreements reflect institutional policy rather than personal judgment.

3. The member's responsibility to his superiors requires that he keep them aware of conditions affecting the institution, particularly those which may be potentially disrupting or damaging to the institution.

4. The member has a responsibility to select competent persons for assigned responsibilities and to see that his personnel are used maximally for the skills and experience they possess.

5. The member has responsibility for constantly stimulating his staff for their and his own continued growth and improvement. He must see that staff members are adequately supervised as to the quality of their functioning and for purposes of professional development.

6. The member is responsible for seeing that his staff is informed of policies, goals, and programs toward which the department's operations are oriented.

Section G

PREPARATION FOR PERSONNEL WORK

1. The member in charge of training sets up a strong program of academic study and supervised practice in order to prepare the trainees for their future responsibilities.

2. The training program should aim to develop in the trainee not only skills and knowledge, but also self-understanding.

3. The member should be aware of any manifestations of personal limitations in a student trainee which may influence the latter's provision of competent services and has an obligation to offer assistance to the trainee in securing professional remedial help.

4. The training program should include preparation in research and stimulation for the future personnel worker to do research and add to the knowledge in his field.

5. The training program should make the trainee aware of the ethical responsibilities and standards of the profession he is entering.

6. The program of preparation should aim at inculcating among the trainees, who will later become the practitioners of our profession, the ideal of service to individual and society above personal gain.

Index

American College Personnel Association, 225

American Personnel and Guidance Association, 224–227

American Rehabilitation Counseling Association, 226

American School Counselor Association, 226

Annotated bibliography, evaluation of guidance, 1930–1959, 262–264

Appraisal service, 82–84

Architectural aspects of guidance, 171–176

Association for Counselor Education and Supervision, 225

Association for Measurement and Evaluation in Guidance, 226–227

Assumptions
  counseling approach, 43
  developmental approach, 105
  educational vocational approach, 27
  educative approach, 20–21
  integrative approach, 122
  problem centered/adjustment approach, 66–67
  services approach, 92–93

Attendance service, 88

Automation
  in business and industry, 182–186
  defined, 181–182
  in educational settings, 187–193
  uses of in education, 187–193

Automation and guidance, 193–197

Behavioral sciences and guidance, 233–234

Broad fields curriculum and guidance, 14

Cardinal Principles of Education, 20

Child labor laws, 213

Classical realism, 232

Code of ethics (APGA), 267–274

Codes
  purposes of, 219
  types of, 219–230

Confidentiality, 205–207

Conservative view of education, 233

Consulting vs. counseling, 161–163

Core curriculum and guidance, 15

Counseling
  client-centered, 45–50
  definition, 42
  for girls, 257–258
  service, 84–85

Counseling vs. consulting, 161–163

Counselor responsibility, 204–205, 222–223

Counselor role, 47–50, 53

Culturally deprived and guidance, 70–71

Cumulative folder, 82–84

Cumulative record, 82–84

Defamation, 207–208

Developmental tasks, 107–110

Divisive factors in education, 115

Doolittle Project, 71

Dropout and guidance, 67–70

Education
  for intellectual discipline, 232
  for moral character, 232
  for national survival, 233
  for psychological maturity, 232

Educative approach, 12–26

Elementary school, 149–151

Elementary school guidance techniques
  child appraisal, 155–156
  classroom methods, 156–157
  group methods, 156
  individual counseling, 156
  vocational guidance, 157–159

Ethical responsibilities, 220–223

Evaluation service, 86–87

Experimentalism, 232

Financial aspects of guidance, 176–177

Future of guidance, 259–260

Gifted students and guidance, 72–73
Goals of education, 70
Goals of guidance, 7
Great Cities Grey Areas Project, 71
Growth of guidance, 223
Guidance
climate, 22
functions, 160
for girls, 257–258
policy issues, 235–237
services, 80–87

Handicapped students and guidance, 71–72
Health services, 88–89
Higher Horizons Project, 71
Homeroom guidance, 15–17

Information service, 80–82
Inventory service, 82–84

Jewish view of education, 233

Libel, 207–208
Life adjustment education, 232
Life pattern theory, 30–31
Line and staff theory, 118–120

Marking system and guidance, 23
Mental health
personal, 61–62
theory, 63
Miscellaneous issues
counselor preparation, 242–243
evaluation of guidance, 240–241
teaching experience, 242
terminology, 239–240
Models, types of, 139–143

National Defense Education Act, 72
National Education Project, 251
National Employment Counselors Association, 227
National Vocational Guidance Association, 225

Operational aspects of guidance
counseling approach, 51–53
developmental approach, 110–113
educational-vocational approach, 36–38
educative approach, 21–24
integrative approach, 122–129
problem centered/adjustment approach, 67
services approach, 93–99
Organic administration, 120–121
Orientation service, 85–86

Philosophical issues, 232–233
Philosophy
counseling approach, 44
developmental approach, 106–107
of education, 232–233
educational vocational approach, 35–36
educative approach, 19–20
integrative approach, 121–122
problem centered/adjustment approach, 91–92
services approach, 91–92
Planning, 237
Practice, bases for, 1–10
authority, 5–6
commonsense, 4
intuition, 3–4
philosophy, 6
theory, 8
tradition, 4–5
unified theory, 8–10
Problems of adolescence, 65
Problems of gifted students, 73
Professional responsibilities, 220–233
Professionalization of guidance, 258–259
Program activities issues, 239
Program structure issues, 237
Project Head Start, 71
Protestant view of education, 232
Psychological services, 89–90
Psychology of adjustment, 63–65
Psychometrist, 90
Psychotherapy
research, 45
theory, 45
Pupil accounting service, 88
Pupil personnel services, 87–90

Reconstructionist view of education, 233
Relationship
with parents, 56
with students, 55
Relationships
with administrators, 56
with teachers, 55–56
Release of records, 208–211
Remedial reading and guidance, 90
Research service, 86–87
Roman Catholic view of education, 233

School psychologist, 89–90
Search of students, 211–213
Slander, 207–208
Special education and guidance, 90
Speech correction and guidance, 90
Stages of vocational development, 30–31
Student activities and guidance, 90

Student Personnel Association for
      Teacher Education, 225–226
Subprofessional personnel in guidance,
      254–256
Supplementary guidance specialist
      approach, 17

Teacher counselor approach, 17–18
Testing, 53, 54–55
Theoretical basis
   counseling approach, 43–44
   developmental approach, 110–113
   educational-vocational approach, 28–34
   educative approach, 18–19
   integrative approach, 116–118
   problem centered/adjustment approach,
      63–67
   services approach, 91
Theory
   of freedom, 217–218
   function of, 132–133
   guidance theory, 134–135
   nature of, 132

Theory (*continued*)
   of restraint, 218
   theory building, 133–134
Trait and factor theory, 29–30
Trends
   automation, 257
   counselor education programs, 253–254
   in educational system, 250–253
   elementary education, 152–154
   generalist vs. specialist, 258
   growth of guidance, 253
   miscellaneous, 259
   use of subprofessionals

Vocational development stages, 30–31
Vocational development theories
   life pattern, 30–31
   needs, 32–33
   psychoanalytic, 32
   sociological, 31
   trait and factor, 29–30
Vocational guidance
   history of, 27–28
   theory, 34